A Town without Pity

UNIVERSITY PRESS OF FLORIDA

Florida A&M University, Tallahassee
Florida Atlantic University, Boca Raton
Florida Gulf Coast University, Ft. Myers
Florida International University, Miami
Florida State University, Tallahassee
New College of Florida, Sarasota
University of Central Florida, Orlando
University of Florida, Gainesville
University of North Florida, Jacksonville
University of South Florida, Tampa
University of West Florida, Pensacola

ALSO BY JASON VUIC

The Swamp Peddlers: How Lot Sellers, Land Scammers, and Retirees Built Modern Florida and Transformed the American Dream

The Yucks: Two Years in Tampa with the Losingest Team in NFL History

The Sarajevo Olympics: A History of the 1984 Winter Games

The Yugo: The Rise and Fall of the Worst Car in History

Jason Vuic

A TOWN WITHOUT PITY

AIDS, RACE, AND RESISTANCE IN FLORIDA'S DEEP SOUTH

UNIVERSITY PRESS OF FLORIDA
Gainesville / Tallahassee / Tampa
Boca Raton / Pensacola / Orlando / Miami / Jacksonville / Ft. Myers / Sarasota

Cover: Downtown Arcadia. Courtesy of Manatee County Public Library Historical Digital Collections.

Copyright 2025 by Jason Vuic

All rights reserved

Published in the United States of America

30 29 28 27 26 25   6 5 4 3 2 1

LIBRARY OF CONGRESS CATALOGING-IN-PUBLICATION DATA

Names: Vuic, Jason, 1972– author.
Title: A town without pity : AIDS, race, and resistance in Florida's deep South / Jason Vuic.
Description: 1. | Gainesville : University Press of Florida, [2025] | Includes bibliographical references and index.
Identifiers: LCCN 2025013278 (print) | LCCN 2025013279 (ebook) | ISBN 9780813081175 (paperback) | ISBN 9780813073972 (ebook)
Subjects: LCSH: AIDS (Disease) in children—Patients—Education—Florida—Arcadia. | Chronically ill children—Education—Florida—Arcadia. | AIDS (Disease)—Social aspects—Florida—Arcadia. | Sick children—Education—Florida—Arcadia. | BISAC: HISTORY / United States / State & Local / South (AL, AR, FL, GA, KY, LA, MS, NC, SC, TN, VA, WV) | TRUE CRIME / Historical
Classification: LCC LC4562.F6 V85 2025 (print) | LCC LC4562.F6 (ebook) | DDC 371.7/1/0975959—dc23/eng/20250515
LC record available at https://lccn.loc.gov/2025013278
LC ebook record available at https://lccn.loc.gov/2025013279

The University Press of Florida is the scholarly publishing agency for the State University System of Florida, comprising Florida A&M University, Florida Atlantic University, Florida Gulf Coast University, Florida International University, Florida State University, New College of Florida, University of Central Florida, University of Florida, University of North Florida, University of South Florida, and University of West Florida.

University Press of Florida
2046 NE Waldo Road
Suite 2100
Gainesville, FL 32609
http://upress.ufl.edu

GPSR EU Authorized Representative: Mare Nostrum Group B.V., Mauritskade 21D, 1091 GC Amsterdam, The Netherlands, gpsr@mare-nostrum.co.uk

TO KELLY

"You've been more places than me,
  Frog, what with all them trips after drives
  and when we don't have much to do. What's the rough-
  est town there is, with the meanest men
  you can find anywhere?"

> "There ain't no doubt about
> that one," Frog mumbled,
> his mouth full of roast beef.
> "It's Arcadia."

PATRICK D. SMITH,
A Land Remembered

CONTENTS

INTRODUCTION / In This Cow Town Heaven / *1*

ONE / Upstream in the River of Time / *12*

TWO / Old Habits Die Hard / *23*

THREE / Ever Put a Penny in Your Mouth? / *35*

FOUR / A Stubborn and Purposeful Man / *49*

FIVE / No Workinghard Man / *60*

SIX / Quid Pro Quo / *71*

SEVEN / The Lawyer-Turned-Pamphleteer / *81*

EIGHT / A Florida Enigma / *92*

NINE / Factor VIII / *106*

TEN / The Coward's Way Out / *116*

ELEVEN / We Treated Them Young 'Uns Wrong / *124*

TWELVE / Hatesville, USA / *135*

THIRTEEN / The Ne'er-Do-Well / *152*

FOURTEEN / Anatomy of a Frame-Up / *161*

FIFTEEN / But They're Gone Home / *171*

SIXTEEN / I Didn't Lose My Battle / *179*

SEVENTEEN / An Isolated Island of a Place / *189*

EPILOGUE / Things That Weren't So Good / *201*

ACKNOWLEDGMENTS / *207*

NOTES / *209*

INDEX / *241*

INTRODUCTION

IN THIS COW TOWN HEAVEN

They called themselves Citizens Against AIDS in Schools, the thousand-or-so-member parental rights group formed in August 1987 in the Southwest Florida cattle-and-orange community of Arcadia. Its members, all white, were salt-of-the-earth ranch hands and farmers, prison guards, and state mental institution workers who bonded together in a panic after a judge in Tampa ruled that three HIV-positive brothers—white boys named Ricky, Robert, and Randy Ray—had been deprived of a fair education when put into separate-but-equal classrooms by the DeSoto County School Board.

The boys had hemophilia, which meant their blood didn't clot, so after bumping their heads or skinning their knees on the playground, they injected themselves with a protein called factor VIII. Factor VIII stopped the bleeds as if by a miracle, but since the medicine had been manufactured from pools of donated blood during the pre-HIV-test 1980s, thousands of hemophilia patients got sick.

Crushed spiritually and in need of support, parents Clifford and Louise Ray turned to their pastor, who took up a collection for the family but, the Rays alleged, asked them not to come back. Then, when the Rays told the boys' elementary school staff about their affliction, the district's superintendent and school board banned their sons from class. They could learn at home with a tutor or at school in a portable classroom quarantined from other kids.

The court said that was illegal; a judge had ruled (and doctors had affirmed) that HIV couldn't be spread through casual contact, only through sex and needles. Sneezing, hugging, kissing, coughing—nothing that kids would do in school at that age would transmit AIDS. But this was the 1980s, when many Americans viewed AIDS as a plague, in some quarters a second

Armageddon, in which infected salad bars, dirty toilet seats, and even mosquitos could spread the disease. They didn't, of course, and public health officials had said so repeatedly, but few people in Arcadia listened.

A tough agricultural town some fifty miles inland from Sarasota, Arcadia had a reputation as one of the meanest places in the state. It had rough honky-tonks, off-grid migrant encampments, and an African American section still known as "the Quarters." As late as the 1960s, its high school marching band wore Confederate officers' uniforms and had a policy, backed by the school board, of refusing to march behind Black high school bands in local parades.[1]

Integration moved slowly there, in stages, and it wasn't until 1965 that Arcadia's DeSoto High School saw its first African American students enroll, more than a decade after *Brown v. Board of Education*. The school integrated because it had to; courts forced it to, though a majority of white Arcadians and even the school superintendent were opposed. So in 1987, when a federal judge ordered the Ray brothers back into regular school, many whites in Arcadia likened the decision to forced integration, something Yankees and outsiders and coastal Florida liberals required them to do.

Thus, the community's response to AIDS was especially shrill, a mixture of antigovernment and antigay messaging, plus anger at civil rights legislation and anger at the Rays. An August 1987 Citizens Against AIDS in Schools rally was a case in point. Held at Arcadia's ancient rodeo arena, it featured Rebel flags, an antigay evangelical invocation, and several antigovernment screeds, including one by the president of the group, who exclaimed, "The courts are shoving this down our throats like they did with civil rights!"[2]

Author and journalist Steven Petrow, who at the time was researching a book on America's AIDS epidemic, was there to see it. Petrow observed, "From portal to portal, the rodeo stands were crowded with white faces, some young, many older. A seething anger permeated the night air, but few knew where to direct it. A sense of humiliation was evident on many faces, but rather than admit it, the people raised their voices and arms in defiance."[3]

They were angry at how they'd been treated after ABC's *World News Tonight* had dubbed the community a "town without pity," a reference to a well-known Gene Pitney song and 1961 Kirk Douglas film about a town in Germany that ostracized a girl after she'd been raped. "This isn't a town without pity," an Arcadia resident told a reporter in 1987. "The situation was

Brothers Ricky, Randy, and Robert Ray (*left to right*), 1987. The boys contracted HIV from hemophilia treatments and became victims of anti-AIDS hysteria. The Ray family was ostracized in Arcadia and thrust into the national spotlight. Courtesy *Orlando Sentinel*/TCA.

being handled quietly in school. . . . Things were going along real good until the press got hold of it. The feeling in the community . . . [is that people are being] selfish for their own."[4]

Maybe so, but local protestations were off the hook, crazed even, with one Citizens Against AIDS in Schools leader comparing the disease to leprosy and arguing that its victims should be put into camps. Others claimed that AIDS was like citrus canker, a common crop disease in Florida that growers would cure by burning it out. The rhetoric was frightening, not to mention dehumanizing, but the Rays and their attorney fired back, testifying before Congress, filing a civil suit, and appearing on TV talk shows with hosts Phil Donahue, Geraldo Rivera, and Larry King, among others.[5]

The boys reentered regular school in August 1987, but fearful parents staged a boycott, the school received bomb threats, and callers left messages with the Rays that warned, "Your children will die."[6] It was a crazy first week of classes, in which undercover sheriff's deputies patrolled school hallways and the boys' father, Clifford Ray, slept with a gun beside him. Then, that Friday, the Ray home burned in a fire. It started *inside* the house, while an uncle was there sleeping, but when the Rays fled to Sarasota, many in the media blamed the town.

In TV and newspaper reports nationwide, the family had been "burned out," even "chased out," and soon tiny Arcadia was the most hated municipality in the United States. At one point, residents 2,600 miles away in Arcadia, California, petitioned Arcadia, Florida, to change its name.[7] The writer of an opinion piece in the Portland, Maine, *Evening Express* called Arcadia "a pitiless place, a barbaric place," and wrote, "In Arcadia, three brothers with the AIDS virus . . . were burned out of their home and forced to leave town. What appalling cruelty. What sick ignorance. What lack of mercy. . . . In Arcadia, a rock was turned over and evil ran out."[8]

However, Arcadia wasn't an island, and it wasn't the only place to have acted irrationally toward children with AIDS. In Russiaville, Indiana, a local school board ignored medical evidence and denied admittance to an HIV-positive thirteen-year-old with hemophilia named Ryan White. The boy and his mother sued, but locals made life miserable for them by calling them names in public, by refusing to touch money that they had touched at grocery stores, and by shooting a bullet into their home. In August 1987, the same month as the Ray house fire, parents boycotted schools and staged protests in Lake City, Tennessee; Kunkletown, Pennsylvania; Roseburg, Oregon; Glendale, Arizona; and Belleville, Illinois.

What set Arcadia apart was its churlishness, its overtly hostile, us-versus-them mentality when called out as a community for its treatment of the Rays. Arcadia is a town "united," wrote *Washington Post* reporter Myra McPherson, and "everyone from the superintendent of schools to the town barber voices the same sentiments: No one ran the Rays out of town; the Ray children were offered a separate but equal education, and instead the parents exposed their children to publicity for personal gain."[9]

When the "Heartland" section of the *Tampa Tribune*—covering Hardee, Highlands, Okeechobee, and DeSoto Counties—asked for comments regarding the Rays, an Arcadian named Dorothy Garza submitted a poem. She called it her "Redneck Rhyme." In it, she argued the town's case like no one had before:

In the middle of the year in '87,
Hell broke loose in this cow town heaven.
The school board spoke and the sky turned gray,

The problem was AIDS, the family was Ray.
The board stood fast to wait on the judge,
Facing the Rays, they refused to budge.
The court came to order, the judge she ruled.
The three Ray boys would have to be schooled.
Media mania struck our town,
TV and paper, they all put us down.
A phrase was coined about our city,
Arcadia is a "Town without Pity."
You may judge and cuss and label us "Bud,"
But the lives we protect are our own flesh and blood.
AIDS and the antibody, its cause has been pled,
With care and caution, it cannot be spread.
Your child or mine, it's all the same,
Those three boys are not to blame.
God will judge surely one day,
How a mother and father let three boys pay.
Their aim is clouded by the words they spout,
By greed and gain, there's not much doubt.
The house was burned, suspicions were raised,
Who burned the house of those poor, poor Rays?
The battle is won, the family left town,
Gossip and rumors and opinions abound.
The fact remains, our city was raped,
By TV and paper, nothing escaped.
But listen world, and you will hear,
Of a small town of rednecks who spoke this year.
Country bumpkin, cowboy, and hick,
Call us the worst, but together we stick.[10]

Although cheeky and simple, Garza's poem summarized in only a few stanzas how many people in Arcadia felt, that the school board was right, the Rays were wrong, and the media had insulted the town. It didn't matter that what the school board had done was illegal; Arcadians blamed others for the circus-like media attention they themselves had caused.

They'd done it before, in the late 1960s, with the arrest and conviction of an African American migrant worker named James Richardson. Then in his thirties, Richardson received the death penalty (later commuted to life) from an all-white jury in Fort Myers for poisoning his seven children. He had been living in a duplex in Arcadia's racially segregated Quarters, where one night in October 1967, wife Annie Mae cooked beans and rice and a dish called hogshead for the children's lunch.

A babysitter was to feed it to them while Richardson and Annie Mae were in the fields, but when the children ate the food, each convulsed violently and died. Lab tests confirmed they'd consumed parathion, an exceptionally deadly orange-grove insecticide, but no bag, box, or source of the poison was found. Therefore, the chief suspects should have been the parents and the babysitter. After all, the parents had left the children the food and the babysitter had fed it to them, but DeSoto County Sheriff Frank Cline jumped ahead of the investigation to arrest Richardson.

Cline had no evidence, only a business card from a white insurance salesman named Gerald Purvis who drummed up business door to door in Black communities and who'd met Richardson, by chance, the evening before the children died. But Richardson didn't buy a policy. He didn't have any money, and Purvis didn't give him a receipt. However, Cline continued to insist that insurance was the motive. He actually told that to a grand jury, under oath, while implying falsely that Richardson had killed three other kids from a previous relationship, when in fact he hadn't.

Why Cline targeted the man is unknown, especially when the babysitter, Betsy Reese, had served time in prison for murdering her husband. Rumors swirled. One held that Reese ran a gambling racket in the Quarters and that Cline took a cut; another that Cline, a white man, had been sleeping with Reese's daughter and arrested Richardson to keep his secret from coming out. None of this would be proven. But as the press descended upon Arcadia, a portrait emerged of a corrupt sheriff's office in a deeply segregated town.

Was Richardson guilty? Most likely not. Almost definitely not. But no matter what the case, he shouldn't have gone to trial, as prosecuting attorney Frank Schaub had no murder weapon and no motive, and his only evidence against Richardson was the testimony of three jailhouse snitches whom Cline himself had found. Schaub also withheld evidence from the defense—namely

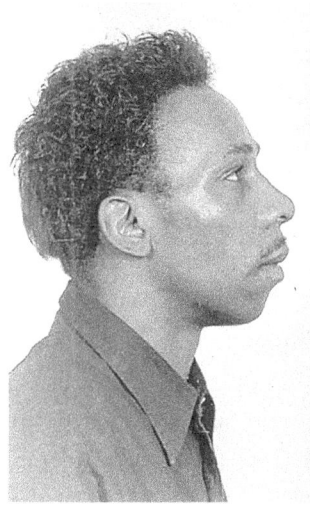

James Richardson at Florida State Prison, 1968. Richardson was convicted of poisoning his seven children in Arcadia and received the death penalty. The prosecution won a conviction by withholding exculpatory evidence. Courtesy Florida Department of Corrections.

Purvis's statements—and allowed Cline to perjure himself on the stand when Cline called Purvis's business card a "receipt." So Richardson went to prison, a victim of an overly zealous sheriff and prosecutor and his own weak defense.

The press, however, knew something was wrong. Why hadn't the babysitter testified? And what about those rumors involving Cline? They rankled more than one observer, including the author, lawyer, and conspiracy theorist Mark Lane. A former New York state assemblyman from Harlem, Lane had popularized the famed "grassy knoll" Kennedy assassination theory with his bestselling 1966 work *Rush to Judgment* and in 1970 penned a book on the Richardson case titled *Arcadia*. "Black poverty in Arcadia is like an iceberg," Lane declared. "It is massive, awesome. Yet not until it is examined more closely can its depths be comprehended. The shacks that line the roads appear to rival those anywhere for degeneracy."[11]

That may have been true, but Lane's *Arcadia* did nothing for Richardson. In fact, the book flopped, and Richardson spent most of the next twenty years at the Florida State Prison at Raiford. He'd been forgotten by the 1980s, but as Arcadia struggled with the Ray case, a rumor spread through the Quarters that an ailing Betsy Reese at a nursing home in Wauchula had said more than a hundred times, "I killed those children."

Therefore, in August 1988, just twelve months after the Rays' house had burned, Arcadia witnessed yet another media circus. Observers wondered first if Richardson was innocent and second, what on Earth was wrong with this town. To answer the first question, Lane returned to Arcadia and hosted a meeting in the Quarters to drum up support for Richardson. There he found new evidence in the form of stolen files that proved unequivocally that Schaub had denied Richardson a fair trial.

Then Lane teamed with grandstanding Miami attorney Ellis Rubin to represent the imprisoned man and pressure Florida Governor Bob Martinez to review the case. Meanwhile, investigative reporting by the *Miami Herald*, the *Seminole Tribune*, and the *Sarasota Herald-Tribune*, among others, brought widespread attention to Richardson, who in January 1989 appeared in the first-ever episode of the tabloid TV news program *Inside Edition*.

For a time, Arcadia was everywhere, though now, instead of the "AIDS boys," viewers saw Richardson. "Richardson's case is compelling," wrote a *Bradenton Herald* reporter, and has "all the makings of a blockbuster made-for-television movie. The setting: Arcadia . . . a small Florida town where racial tensions and fears about lynch-mob justice smolder beneath the surface."[12]

To be sure, the town had matured some since the children's deaths; its schools had integrated, and owing to a selection process in which city council members rotated into the mayor's seat, it'd even had a Black mayor, the first in Southwest Florida. Yet problems would persist. Well into the 1970s, Arcadia discriminated against Black residents in how it apportioned public services, leading famed civil rights leader Julian Bond to describe it as a place "virtually untouched by the civil rights movement."[13]

At the time Lane visited in 1988, no African American had ever held or even run for a countywide office in DeSoto because voting there wasn't done by district but at large, an illegal, intentionally segregationist tactic used in the South to enable white residents to win every seat. When local Black leaders including DeSoto County National Association for the Advancement of Colored People (NAACP) president Helen Washington threatened to sue, Washington received an anonymous phone call. "You know what happened to the Ray family?" a man asked. "The same thing's going to happen to you."[14]

In the end, Washington prevailed; DeSoto County changed how its citizens voted. And in February 1989 Governor Martinez asked Dade County State Attorney Janet Reno to review the Richardson case. It took Reno just two months to uncover what officials called "serious problems in the handling of the prosecution," and in a dramatic hearing at a packed Arcadia courthouse that April, Richardson was released.[15]

Bowed and gray, the freed man didn't know the Rays. However, their terrible pasts, not to mention much of the suffering they'd experienced, had been indelibly linked to Arcadia. It's an ironic name, Arcadia, one that refers to a place in Greece once mythologized for its rustic innocence, as a kind of Garden of Eden, but Florida's Arcadia was anything but innocent. Named by a Confederate veteran who during the Seminole Wars had fought to displace Native Americans, it was a tough Southern town, a frontier town, to many a town stuck in the past.

"We're fifty miles and fifty years from Sarasota!" locals quipped, which was Arcadia in a nutshell: an insular, conservative burg a stone's throw from modern Florida that seemed to resist modern Florida entirely. It was what natives called "Old Florida," a place of powerful landed families, including some who'd run the town for a hundred years or more, as well as poor white farmers and cattlemen and even poorer Blacks. This was a town without pity, a town that during a two-year period at the end of the Reagan era was forced to confront not only the AIDS virus but also the remnants of a racist past.

The following work is a history of Arcadia, Florida, through two momentous events: the arrest and conviction in the 1960s and exoneration in the 1980s of African American migrant laborer James Richardson, and the 1987 firestorm surrounding the AIDS-in-schools debate and the treatment by the community of the white working-class family the Rays. Were these two events connected? No, not directly. But what binds them together is the town. Left behind as Florida grew and prospered during the post–World War II period, Arcadia was an anachronism, a rural holdout, a town fearful of change and outside influences, and a town willing to resist.

In 2004, *Tampa Tribune* reporter John W. Allman wrote,

Some cities, but not all, exude a sense of place. Florida, with its sun-drenched beaches, snowbird-packed coastal communities and transient population, has a history of forever changing. For every Punta Gorda

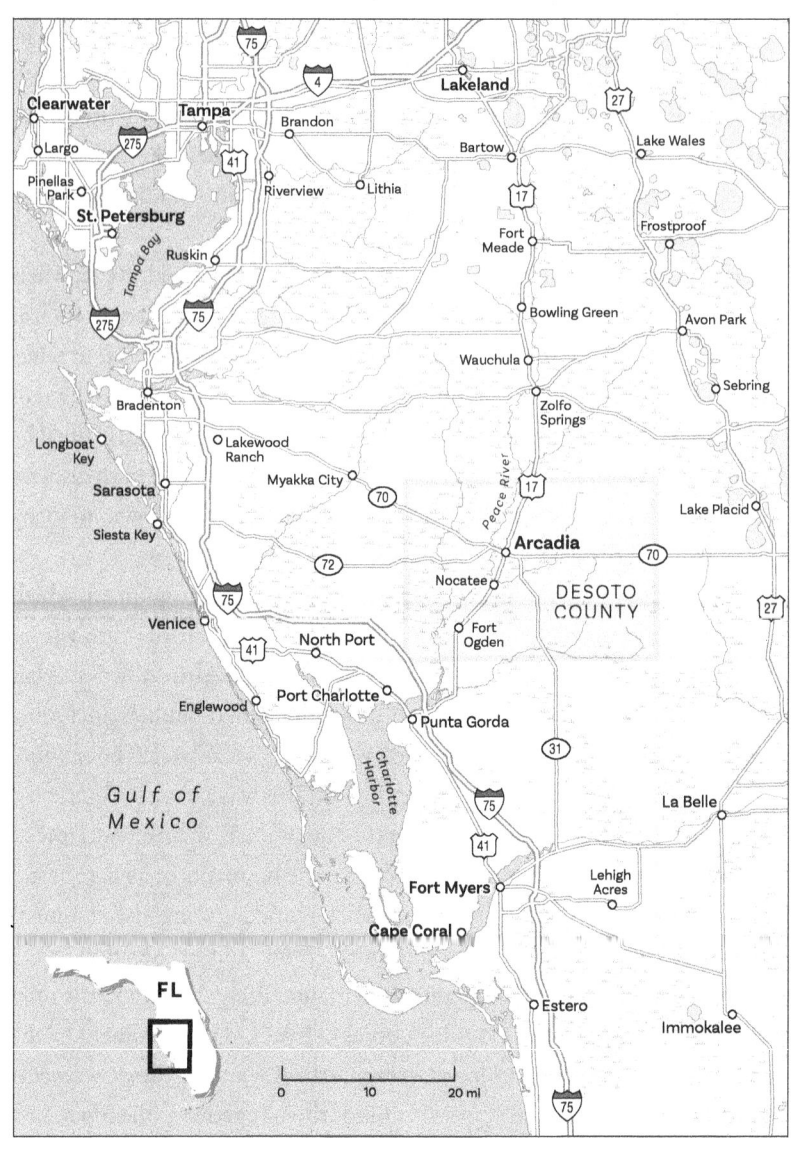

DeSoto County, Florida. Courtesy Erin Greb Cartography.

there is a Weston—a planned community near Fort Lauderdale with no downtown, only subdivisions, golf courses, and strip malls. For every Miami, there is an Arcadia, where the outside world may try to intrude, but its people push back.[16]

That pushback is what Arcadia was known for, as an entrenched, sometimes angry conservatism that said, "No one's gonna tell us what to do!" Be it resistance to integration or the inhumane treatment of innocent Black residents such as James Richardson or unfortunate whites like the Rays, a majority of Arcadians fought doggedly to preserve the status quo. In a state where just 35 percent of residents are born there, Arcadia's state senator in 2025, representing Charlotte, DeSoto, Hardee, and parts of Polk and Lee Counties, is Ben Albritton, a fifth-generation Floridian and citrus grower whose distant relative is Arcadia Albritton, a settler girl from the 1880s for whom Arcadia is named.

Look up property today in Arcadia's old, majestic courthouse, and the names repeat themselves: Albritton, Parker, Brewer, Whidden, Turner, Cline, Langford, Hendry, and Mizell. These are descendants of frontier families who settled an unforgiving prairie and never left. Small towns and old families go hand in hand, especially in the South. But in Florida's South, in Southwest Florida in particular, 150-year-old families are unheard of because few are from there and even fewer stay there—except maybe in Arcadia.

ONE

UPSTREAM IN THE RIVER OF TIME

Located in the interior of Southwest Florida, Arcadia was the administrative seat of rural DeSoto County, whose cowboy roots, low-wage agricultural industries, and violent frontier history made it perhaps the most out-of-place place in Florida. For DeSoto was a curious mix of the desolate ranchlands of West Texas and the stately homes and bitter race relations of the South—the Deep (Deep) South.

Traveling from Sarasota to Arcadia, wrote journalist Craig Pittman in 1992, "is like swimming upstream in the river of time. You leave behind the modern-day Florida of beachfront condominiums and cookie-cutter subdivisions" to encounter a town whose neighborhoods "look much as they did in the 1920s." But if you "stray across the railroad tracks from the white-columned homes of the historic district, [you'll] see some other ancient dwellings: the tumbledown shacks of the poorer Black residents, who have repeatedly sued the city contending Arcadia is just a few steps away from apartheid."[1]

The town was founded in 1886 by the Reverend James M. "Boss" Hendry, a veteran of both the Third Seminole War and the Civil War who built a sawmill on a bluff overlooking the Peace River. Legend has it that when Hendry arrived in the area, he stayed with a family of settlers whose daughter Arcadia baked him a birthday cake, so he named the new town in her honor.[2]

It wasn't much, this new Arcadia—a sawmill, a general store, and a post office—but unbeknown to Hendry, in 1881 Captain Francis LeBaron of the US Army Corps of Engineers had been surveying the area in hopes of building a canal from the St. Johns River in eastern Florida to the Peace River and the Gulf. Although LeBaron decided that a canal wasn't practical, while surveying the Peace River near what became Arcadia, he found nine barrels of prehistoric fossils protruding from a sandbar.[3]

However, the sandbar, LeBaron discovered, wasn't sand. It was phosphate, in small pebbles of rock containing a valuable mineral called phosphorus, used in fertilizer. LeBaron collected samples, then returned to the area in 1886 to dig test pits before telling people what he had found. The result was a mad rush to Arcadia that a visiting geologist described in 1890.

> [It] reminds one of the early days of the oil fever in Pennsylvania, or the boom of a new Western mining camp.... Wealthy men from Boston, Philadelphia, and New York are in camp and shifting from day to day... and the Crackers—the poor white who lives on gophers all summer and Yankees all winter—is nearly stirred up to animation and nearly as excited as he can well be.[4]

By 1889 there were twelve companies mining the Peace River. They used barges equipped with steam dredgers to suck up the phosphate for transport to Arcadia, where, day and night, workers dried the mineral in kilns before sending it to ports on the Gulf.[5] Soon, Arcadia had more than eight hundred residents, a bank, two hotels, some dry goods stores, several fruit distributors, and even a train station to hasten its exports to the north.[6]

Yet, Arcadia wasn't just a phosphate boomtown; it was a shoot-'em-up, saloon-and-brothel frontier town, the Deadwood of Florida, which famed sculptor and illustrator Frederic Remington visited in 1895. By then, Remington was done with the West. The frontier had closed, he lamented, and the cowboys he so idealized in his art were now little more than "tame hired men."[7] He therefore stayed east, drawing western scenes from memory until asked to report on Florida's Cracker cowboys who roamed what was still an open prairie between the Kissimmee River to the east and ports on the Peace and Caloosahatchee Rivers to the west, essentially the open range from Orlando to Fort Myers.

Widely seen as pejorative today, the term "Cracker" stems from a sixteenth-century English word meaning braggart or bloviator, as in a person who "cracked" jokes. In early America it referred to poor white settlers in the South, particularly in Florida, where families of older lineage still consider

Fighting over a Stolen Herd, Frederic Remington, 1895. In the late 1800s Arcadia was a frontier settlement on the edge of Florida's "Ninety-Mile Prairie." In 1895 famed illustrator Frederic Remington visited the area to cover a range war there. Courtesy State Archives of Florida.

the word "Cracker" to be one of distinction.[8] In fact, they embrace it, with zero sense of irony or need to reappropriate the word linguistically.

A *Tampa Magazine* writer explained in 2017, "To a Florida native, being called a 'Cracker' is a compliment. It recalls the grit and tenacity of laboring cowboys" and their descendants.[9] Today, there are Cracker festivals all over Florida, including one in Jacksonville that's been held for more than sixty years; the state maintains a permanent Cracker Country Rural Museum in Tampa, and Arcadia has a bookstore called Cracker House Books.

Yet the Cracker cowboys Remington discovered had a "bedraggled appearance." They wore tattered clothes and farmers' shoes instead of boots, and they used dogs instead of lariats to force cattle from the bush.[10] Remington wasn't impressed, but Florida's cowboys were an incredibly tough breed whose job it was to wander a barren outback herding wild cows, the descendants of Andalusian cows set free by the Spanish when they abandoned Florida in the eighteenth and nineteenth centuries.

Hardened by years in the muck and willing to kill each other indiscriminately, they fought a series of range wars, including one near Arcadia in the 1890s. "I can tell you, there were some savage years here," an eighty-one-year-old DeSoto County resident and cattleman recalled in 1959. "Place had a lot of saloons, lot of men that went to them. Had some men here who were as wild as anyone you ever heard of in Texas or those places. Would shoot you down as soon as not."[11] One resident recalled fifty fights a day; another, women hiding indoors at night; and still another, men shooting guns into the air and racing down Main Street as if "hell-bent for election."[12]

As an elderly rancher in neighboring Highlands County recounted in 1965,

> People came in and settled this area in the 1860s and 1870s—muscle-hard, tough-minded people like Granddaddy. By the middle of the 1880s, there wasn't much room for newcomers.... They'd get into arguments over little things—like the ownership of a pig. And then there were more serious things, like a cattleman seeing a yearling of his with another man's brand on it.[13]

That was the origin of the Florida range wars of the 1890s, men stealing cattle and rebranding them, leading other men to retaliate. "A Murderer Murdered," read a headline from a newspaper in nearby Polk County in 1897.

> John Lucas, who is well known to this county, and who it will be remembered, shot and killed Dempsey Crews, of DeSoto County, about a year ago, and afterwards killed Jim North, who was an outlaw, charged with having murdered Bud Sauls, was, according to reports, himself cut literally to pieces by one Dennis Sheridan, on last Saturday afternoon at Langford's ranch.[14]

Exacerbating matters was that Florida's great prairie, known to locals as the Ninety-Mile Prairie or simply the Big Ninety, wasn't fenced in. Regardless of who owned the land—mainly the state or timber companies—cattlemen in the area used it as open range, with cattle belonging to one rancher roaming freely and breeding with cattle of another. Rustling was common; one cattleman lost a reported 3,000 head in a year. Also common was the illicit branding of unmarked calves, called "heretics" (or sometimes "hairy dicks"), that others owned.[15]

Then, there were rebrands, which Remington described in his 1895 *Harper's Magazine* article "Cracker Cowboys of Florida." "See yer; ye see that?" a drunken cowboy told him as he grabbed a pencil and some wrapping paper to demonstrate. He drew a circle, wrote Remington, then a ring around the circle and said, "[Now] that brand ain't no good." The cowboy then crossed out three additional brands, but Remington got the point: on Florida's Ninety-Mile Prairie, men had accustomed themselves to what he called "lawless rustling," to a world where "might makes right" and "low-browed cow-folks" were killing each other for a skin-and-bones bovine "no bigger than a donkey."[16]

Known as the Florida scrub cow, that bovine was a wiry animal that Florida chronicler Stetson Kennedy described in 1942 as foraging "on a range so sparse that heavier-blooded stock" introduced there would "literally walk themselves to death trying to find something to eat."[17] Small in stature, less beef cattle than raw-boned survivors, the Florida scrub cow wasn't a valuable breed. The only market for it outside of Florida was Cuba, so cowboys drove herds past Arcadia to the Gulf, to barges at a port called Punta Rassa near Fort Myers.

There, much of the Florida-to-Cuba trade went through a middleman dry goods grocer named Ziba King, a 6-foot-6, 225-pound former Confederate soldier from Georgia who went AWOL during the war and fled to Florida.[18] Like many refugees, King struggled at first, striking out with a store in Tampa before moving in 1868 to a hamlet south of Arcadia called Fort Ogden. Down to just three sacks of corn, his partner having left the area before committing suicide, King heard that due to an insurrection in the Cuban hinterland, Spanish traders were badly in need of beef.

So beginning in 1872, for a $1 commission on each $20 cow, King took herds from ranchers and drove them to port. As a Georgia newspaper article put it in 1898, "He returned to his people with more money than they had ever seen before," and his "stock went up like a pennant on a flagstaff."[19] Soon King purchased his own herds, chartered his own ships, and by 1900 owned some 50,000 head, one out of every nine cows in Florida.[20]

In the 1890s King moved his operations to Arcadia, where as a judge and state representative, he owned a bank and several citrus groves and ruled with an iron fist. King "had hundreds of men in his employ," explained one observer, "and they obeyed him unquestioningly as a retainer of the Middle

Ages obeyed his liege."[21] They rustled cows for him, thousands of them, and during the range wars killed anyone who had rustled cows from him.

One widely told story involved the longtime King ranch hand Morgan Bonaparte "Bone" Mizell, a wily, folkloric character revered in Florida as a kind of Cracker Paul Bunyon. Bone, the story goes, had stolen some of King's cows, and King, a judge, had brought Bone into his court. "'Now see here, [King],' said Bone. 'What do you want for to go and git me arrested for? I have stole thousands of cattle and put your mark and brand on 'em, and jes because I have stole a couple of hundred from you, you go and get me indicted. You jes better go and get that whole deal nol prossed.'"[22]

A frequent gambler who wore starched shirts with diamond studs and carried $1,000 bills in his pocket, King stood up at the 1894 Jim Corbett–Charley Mitchell prize fight in Jacksonville and yelled, "I'll bet 1,000 yearlings to a $1,000 on Corbett!" Wisely, no one accepted King's offer, though the audience roared with laughter when someone said, "Bring in your cattle!"[23] Once, King paid a hotel bill in Tampa with an uncut sheet of $5 bills "to amaze his country cowboys"; in another instance he was accused of offering $6,000 to the mother of a young Florida woman to have sex with the daughter.[24]

King survived several assassination attempts, but he escalated the range war by hiring men like Jim North.[25] A gunslinger from Texas, North died in an ambush, but not before killing who knows how many men by the time the war ended in 1896. By then, the Florida-to-Cuba cattle trade had started to dry up. Ranching persisted, as did phosphate drying, but as mines moved to open pits in neighboring Polk and Manatee Counties, Arcadia expanded its businesses to include commercial crop farming and orange groves.

When King died in 1901, an obituary praised his "rugged force of character," while the *Tampa Weekly Tribune* reveled in a story of how King, in his younger days, had donned head feathers and attempted to fool legislators in Tallahassee by appearing as a "delegate for the Seminoles" and doing a "Green Corn" dance on the statehouse floor.[26] But no one mentioned the range wars, or the killings, or that King, in cornering the market in scrub cows, had brought to Arcadia some of the worst elements of the frontier.

Only the *St. Petersburg Times* would criticize King at all, describing him as a "potentate of the lower coast" who had "fattened" himself on Florida's open prairie at little expense to himself.[27] That system was changing as bigger and more valuable cattle required better grasses, not to mention dipping for ticks, neither of which cattlemen could introduce unless they divided the prairie into privately owned ranches with fences.

The process of fencing ranchlands took years, decades even, and it wasn't until 1949 that the state introduced a law on fencing that effectively ended the open range. However, in DeSoto County, where Ziba King's six sons inherited his business empire and his eldest son, T. B. "Buck" King, ran its cattle, the enclosing of ranchland began much earlier, in 1901, when Buck bought a 65,000-acre spread shortly after his father died.[28] In time, he and other ranchers bought or leased additional spreads, where they improved the pastures with imported Guinea and Para grasses and introduced a much bigger, more heat-tolerant breed of cattle from India called the Brahman.[29]

Meanwhile, Arcadia modernized as well, forced in part by disaster. In 1905 its wooden sidewalks and clapboard storefronts burned in a massive fire that claimed almost all of its downtown. No one died, but since Arcadia lacked water lines or even basic fire-fighting equipment, the town's harried residents used dynamite in a vain and counterproductive attempt to blow the fire out. After an hourslong conflagration, only three of its reported forty-six buildings survived, and all that was left, said one witness, were piles of soot and ash and mangled pieces of tin.[30]

Yet somehow—due in part, probably, to profits from its now booming citrus industry—within two years Arcadia was completely rebuilt, with brick and cement edifices legally required by code, and electric, water, sewer, and telephone lines stretching from the downtown area to a white residential district. By then Arcadia had about 2,000 residents and was the central business hub of the third-largest county in Florida, a truly massive, 2.4 million-acre, pine, prairie, and scrub brush wilderness bigger than Delaware and Rhode Island combined. "DeSoto County is an empire within itself," the *Punta Gorda Herald* declared in 1908. "The population is very small," and "one may travel in the county east from Arcadia for a distance of forty miles and see just a single habitation."[31]

DeSoto County had at least 250,000 head of cattle that in the early 1900s outnumbered the county's 12,000 or so residents at least 20 to 1. The cattle were worth an estimated $3.75 million in 1909 (about $130 million in 2025), but its field and fruit crops, then valued at $2.45 million, were starting to catch up. In 1906, DeSoto produced nearly 600,000 crates of oranges, more than any other Florida county, while fully 10 percent of Florida's orange crop moved through Arcadia every year.

There, eight packing houses employed 500 workers who loaded thirty railcars a day.[32] The owners were white, the managers were white, but those who picked the fruit and loaded the trains were Black, members of a grindingly poor and semipermanent underclass who came to Arcadia during its phosphate days and stayed. In time, a community developed, with an African Methodist Episcopal church and a Baptist church and the segregated neighborhood called the Quarters, a reference to workers' quarters, that whites also called N****rtown.[33]

Like other communities in the South, Arcadia oppressed its African Americans, who at best were treated as second-class citizens and at worst, in the eyes of many whites, were brutes. Blacks could vote, at least in theory, but faced a poll tax in Florida beginning in 1889, a dollar a year, with receipts required showing payments of two consecutive years. Thus, an African American man making a dollar a day mining phosphate, the going rate in the 1890s, had to spend two days' wages to vote, so he wasn't likely to vote.

Under Florida law, Blacks couldn't go to school with whites or be taught by white teachers (1895); they couldn't marry whites if they had even one Black great-grandparent (1903); they couldn't sit with whites on trains or streetcars or be shackled to whites on the way to prison (1905).[34] There were separate schools, separate churches, separate drinking fountains, and separate beaches because whites in Florida and elsewhere in the South implemented Jim Crow laws to keep the races separate.[35]

An editor at the *Arcadia News* declared in 1911,

> [We have] no remedy for the solution of the race problem. We are no statesman. Yet we have some notion about the Negroes. Social equality between the white and Negro will never be practiced in the South. Any effort looking in that direction, like mixed schools, mixed churches, and mixed lodges, is a step backward and downward ... [and will result in] the natural outcome of this social mixing. It means intermarriage and a mongrel degenerated race.[36]

In 1896 the famed *Plessy v. Ferguson* Supreme Court case had upheld the constitutionality of segregation so long as the facilities that were segregated were equal. But they weren't equal, not in Florida, and not anywhere in Arcadia. In 1925, when the town's white students attended classes over an eight-month school year, its Black students attended for six. That year, a group of African American leaders approached the county school board with a deal: if the board would pay for seven months of instruction, Arcadia's Black community would host ice cream suppers and other events to pay for the eighth. The board agreed.[37]

Black teachers made less than white teachers, on average half, a disparity seen throughout Florida but one ruled legal by the courts in 1939.[38] Facilities-wise, whites in Arcadia had a $65,000 high school, built in 1914, while Blacks attended class at a church, a lodge hall, and an old derelict hotel. "It has been said that the school facilities of Arcadia's colored quarters are the worst of any town of its size in the state," read an editorial in the *Arcadian* newspaper in 1941. "We are not in a position to know, as to comparative conditions, but we do know from personal observation that if those of any other community are worse they would have to be unbelievably bad."[39] In 1946 the county finally opened a new African American school, the Smith-Brown School, but only after Black residents had agreed to provide, through their own labor, 8,000 cement blocks.

Labor, that's what Blacks were in Arcadia, where, prior to the civil rights movement, virtually every job above the level of janitor was reserved for a white. The police were white and the judges were white, as were mailmen, city councilmen, county commissioners, tax accessors, school board members, lawyers, store clerks, bank tellers, and farm managers—anyone of social and economic standing anywhere in Arcadia was white.[40] Perhaps the most telling statistic regarding the town's racial disparities appeared in *The Floridian* magazine in 1968: "Many of the Negroes [here] work in the outlying citrus groves, or on farms which produce watermelons, tomatoes, and other crops from DeSoto's rich, sandy soil." However, "none of Arcadia's seven physicians and four dentists is a Negro, . . . [and] there are no professional people in its Negro population."[41]

With some notable exceptions, cattle hunting was a white men's endeavor, for even Remington noted that DeSoto County's cowboys were distinctly "ante bellum" in their views. So Blacks were day-wage farmers, fruit pickers, porters, stevedores, cooks, butlers, nannies, and maids, while Black convicts did the most odious job of all, harvesting pine sap for turpentine.[42]

They didn't have a choice, because local officials leased Black prisoners to so-called naval stores companies that set up makeshift distillation camps in the rugged pine forests of southern DeSoto County near Punta Gorda and Englewood. Working from "can't to can't," read one local history, from "can't see in the morning until can't see at night," convict turpentiners performed truly dangerous work, as pine resin was highly flammable, and mounted overseers, called "tally whackers," whipped those who didn't work.[43]

A Punta Gorda attorney remembered visiting a camp near the present-day Cecil Webb Wildlife Refuge as a boy. The camp had a still "and a whipping post with a ring attached," he said. "Prisoners who did not work hard enough were tied by their hands to the ring, stripped to the waist and beat with a strap until they collapsed."[44] Fights between prisoners were common, as were killings, and given the opportunity, men would run.

A June 1915 article in the *DeSoto County News* reported,

> Three negro convicts have escaped from Boyd's turpentine camp at Murdock. Two oozed out yesterday and one this morning. There is a reward of $100 for the capture of each.... They are: Charlie Jones, escaped today. A light ginger bread looking n****r, about 5 feet and 8 inches in height; wears No. 9 shoes; good teeth; femenie voice; weighs 150 pounds; stated that when last seen he was coming toward Arcadia. William Graham, a yellow fella, 5 feet, 10 inches in height; slender build; 150 pounds; thick shoulders. Will Lewis, a dark ginger break kinky head; turning grey slightly, weighs 175 pounds. Catch 'em and get the $300.[45]

Although Blacks in Arcadia were considered docile by some, they were kept in line by a racist police force, a citizenry willing to lynch on occasion, and the Ku Klux Klan, which established a klavern in Arcadia in 1924.[46] That year, after a man named Grady Herndon, a white Baptist minister and assistant principal at DeSoto High School, passed out a pamphlet in church denouncing the Klan, he was confronted by two local ministers and a railroad official who asked him to reconsider. When Herndon refused, county superintendent C. H. Smith met with the school board, and Herndon was fired. "You, by your own admission," wrote Smith in Herndon's termination letter, "have perpetrated an attack on the Americanism and Christianity of an organization which includes in its membership a large number of patrons and taxpayers of the public schools of this county."[47]

Herndon found a new town, and a Klan-supporting Arcadia saw rallies and cross burnings throughout the twentieth century, when the town gained a reputation in Florida for rare yet spectacular instances of white-on-Black violence. In 1906 the *Ocala Evening Star* reported that an African American man named Drummond attempted to assault a white woman in town. The police arrested Drummond, but fearing a mob of angry whites would kill the man—or so they said—they took him into the woods and chained him to a tree. However, that night, residents learned of Drummond's location, and "about 100 masked men" overpowered the guards and castrated the man, who, bleeding and in agony, was made to drive a wagon back into Arcadia himself. The newspaper's headline read, "Preventive Punishment."[48]

In 1909 the *Tampa Tribune* reported a similar supposed crime, of a Black man named Smith allegedly attempting to assault a white woman somewhere in rural DeSoto County. Before a sheriff's deputy could arrest Smith, a posse strung up the man and reportedly riddled the body with bullets.[49] When the news broke, an indignant *Arcadia Champion* editor wrote, "Nothing could have been further from the truth." The body was *not* riddled with bullets. And "the people who punished the Negro considered that they were doing their duty to their community and went about the business . . . [with] no unseemly passion or excitement . . . whatsoever. All who participated went home and slept as if nothing unusual occurred."[50] Actually, nothing unusual had occurred, for this was Arcadia's second reported lynching in two months.[51]

In 1917 another African American man, George Mitchell, reportedly broke into a post office in Palmdale, a lonely hamlet in far eastern DeSoto County near Lake Okeechobee. Mitchell stole $10 worth of coins, but when he used the coins to pay for boat passage on the Caloosahatchee River from LaBelle to Fort Myers, the boat's engineer figured him out. Mitchell ran, dislocating his shoulder after jumping from a fifteen-foot river bank onto a mud flat, where he was captured. From there, the crew took Mitchell to jail in Fort Myers, in neighboring Lee County, where he reportedly begged deputies in a panic, "Please don't take me to Arcadia! The Crackers there are bad on bad n****rs."[52]

TWO

OLD HABITS DIE HARD

In the fall of 1971 Arcadia held its biennial city council elections, with eight candidates vying for five seats. The voting was at large, meaning there were no precincts, so the five contenders with the highest number of votes were the winners. That year, five incumbents ran, all reputable white men: a supermarket owner, an insurance agent, a telephone company manager, a motel owner, and a seventy-nine-year-old segregationist and longtime politician named Paul P. Speer.

Speer had been in office in one form or another since 1927, as mayor, municipal judge, city treasurer, and city council chairman, and had seen, in his forty-plus years of service, some truly fundamental changes. Originally from Jasper, Georgia, Speer had come to Arcadia in 1925 as a commercial agent for a railroad, just a few years after the Florida legislature divided DeSoto into five smaller counties—Charlotte, Hardee, DeSoto, Highlands, and Glades—to cut the once massive administrative district down to size.[1]

The new DeSoto County was landlocked. It still had access to the Peace River, but the port at Punta Gorda and all of its former Gulf coastline and beach were transferred to Charlotte County. At the same time, development in Southwest Florida began to reorient itself along the Tamiami Trail, a soon-to-be-completed highway connecting Tampa, Bradenton, Sarasota, Punta Gorda, Fort Myers, and Naples with Miami.

These were the area's emerging population centers; thus while Arcadia remained the conservative seat of an insular agricultural county whose biggest event was a rodeo, the towns on the coast attracted move-ins and tourists. When Speer entered office in DeSoto County in 1927, for example, the area north of Punta Gorda in Charlotte County was a 78,000-acre cattle ranch

Barrel racer at the Arcadia rodeo, 1979. During the booming post–World War II period, when the rest of Southwest Florida grew exponentially, Arcadia remained a rural holdout where the All-Florida Rodeo was the town's biggest annual event. Courtesy Manatee County Public Library Historical Digital Collections.

connected to DeSoto by a dirt road. (That road, interestingly enough, was called King's Highway because Ziba King once ran herds there.) By 1971, however, when Speer ran for office for the fifteenth time, the ranch had been bought up and subdivided into 200,000 residential lots for a planned community called Port Charlotte.

They were the old Florida and the new, Arcadia and Port Charlotte, a town in the heartland of farm and cattle country and a retiree exurb on the coast. Although just twenty-five miles apart, the two were worlds apart. While Port Charlotte hosted bingo nights and contract bridge tournaments and ballroom dancing courses at a retiree cultural center called Port Charlotte U, Arcadia hosted the All-Florida Rodeo, a twice-yearly celebration of calf roping and bull riding that began in 1929.

The rodeo was initially a fundraising effort. The Arcadia American Legion needed a meeting hall, so it staged a competition of South Florida cowboys at the City Athletic Park to raise money. The rodeo was supposed to be a local affair. But the Arcadians who organized it reached out to Florida newspapers and the Ringling Brothers and Barnum & Bailey Circus in Sarasota, who transformed the event into a major affair, with concerts, parades, airshows, mock bank robberies and shootouts (including one in 1967 that featured a hanging), and an all-female honor guard called the DeSoto County Possettes.[2]

Clearly, Arcadia was a cow town, but the All-Florida Rodeo made it the most famous cow town in the state, a summer tourist destination on July things-to-do lists along with NASCAR's Firecracker 400 races at Daytona and the Miss Universe beauty pageant at Miami Beach.[3] The rodeo drew thousands, bringing life and tourist dollars to what even by Florida's low standards was an incredibly poor county, where in 1960, 40 percent of families had yearly incomes of less than $3,000, which put them below the poverty line.[4] Jobwise, DeSoto County had 11,683 residents in 1960 and Arcadia 5,889, who found almost equal employment in cattle-rearing and farming as they did in other nonagricultural industries. Cattle was a mainstay, but many of the old settler families who'd built fortunes in scrub cows had either died out or moved on, leaving a new generation of owners, sometimes corporations, in their place.

In 1963 the heirs of Captain John Parker, an early South Florida settler whose sons had been close business partners of Ziba King and his family, sold the 80,000-acre Parker Brothers Ranch in western DeSoto County to Tennessee gas station magnate Calvin Houghland for $6 million. The ranch had been in the Parker family for more than a century. At 125 square miles, it covered one-fifth of the county, had 23 miles of frontage, more than 100 miles of fencing, 50 windmills, two runways, and a hangar.[5]

To manage its tens of thousands of cows, the Parker Brothers Ranch employed a mix of laborers, some full-timers who lived and worked on the property and functioned, essentially, as modern-day Bone Mizells, the last of the cow hunters. Then there were the day riders, men who lived off-property and commuted to work in pickup trucks pulling horses and trailers. These men would often split time between ranches, following the work, and some drove to and from the truly massive 331,000-acre Lykes Brothers Ranch in neighboring Highlands, Glades, and Hendry Counties or the 91,000-acre Babcock Ranch in Charlotte and Lee Counties.

It was a tough life for tough men who came to Arcadia for the state livestock market or hospital trips or groceries or sometimes to drink. Thus, the bars in the area were legendary, rough honky-tonks with names like the Corral, the Oasis, and the Reef & Beef. "These boys work hard and play hard," explained a Florida Department of Law Enforcement official in 1989.

> They're not afraid to walk up into somebody's face. Hell, they all got guns and knives. You take a place like Fort Lauderdale or Miami. There's a certain anonymity to living there. You can walk away from things. But in a place like Arcadia, if you're challenged and you choose to back down, you'll hear about it for the rest of your life.[6]

Locals often joked that the Oasis should have been called the Arcadia Knife and Gun Club, and more than one person remembered drunken cowboys riding horses into bars following rodeo parades and lassoing Black residents for fun.

"Back before we had all these racial problems," explained a white Arcadia resident and real estate agent named Eugene Turner Jr., "it was a tradition of the Fourth of July parade that the cowboys would give (black people) a hard time. They would ride their horses into bars and drink, and then they might rope one or two people and drag them around."[7] Of course, Arcadia's

African American residents didn't like being lassoed like cows, but no one in authority would speak for them.

The city didn't have an NAACP chapter until the mid-1960s. In 1968, DeSoto County Sheriff Frank Cline told a reporter he had "a theory that Negro intelligence is limited because their skulls are too small."[8] Both the town and the county were tough on unions as well, especially fruit pickers unions. For most of the 1960s, DeSoto County refused to take part in a federal surplus food program; a local employer explained the fear that if an "unemployed lazy worker" in the area's citrus industry received free food, the worker would "think twice before accepting a job."[9]

That job, presumably, involved long hours at little pay in one of the area's orange groves, where many of Arcadia's Blacks, a few whites, and increasing numbers of Hispanic migrants filled on average six 1,000-pound field tubs a day and received in the early to mid-1960s about $2.50 per tub. In 1965 *St. Petersburg Times* reporter Peter Kramer wrote a series of articles on his weeklong experiences working undercover as a fruit picker in Eloise, Florida, a town about sixty miles north of Arcadia. Kramer presented no identification, received no paperwork or training, but had to pay eight dollars in advance for a picking sack, essentially a big canvas bag with a shoulder strap that held ninety-five pounds of oranges when full. He wrote,

> Picking citrus is hard work. It entails knowing how to set and climb a heavy ladder that may be up to 20 feet long. The picker climbs to the ladder's top, balancing himself despite the bending and snapping of supporting branches and uses both hands to pick. He works his way down the ladder, filling a sack slung diagonally across his shoulders. . . . By midday the shoulders of even experienced pickers feel raw and their feet and legs ache.[10]

In the 1960s a large number of fruit pickers in Arcadia were migrant African Americans. Among them was the family of future DeSoto High School and New England Patriot football star Johnny Rembert. He and his eight brothers and sisters moved back and forth between crops in Florida and Mississippi. Other migrant workers followed the summer-to-fall, blueberry-to-apple, North Carolina-to-Maine route before returning to DeSoto County for the winter season and school. "We traveled a lot when I was a kid," Rembert

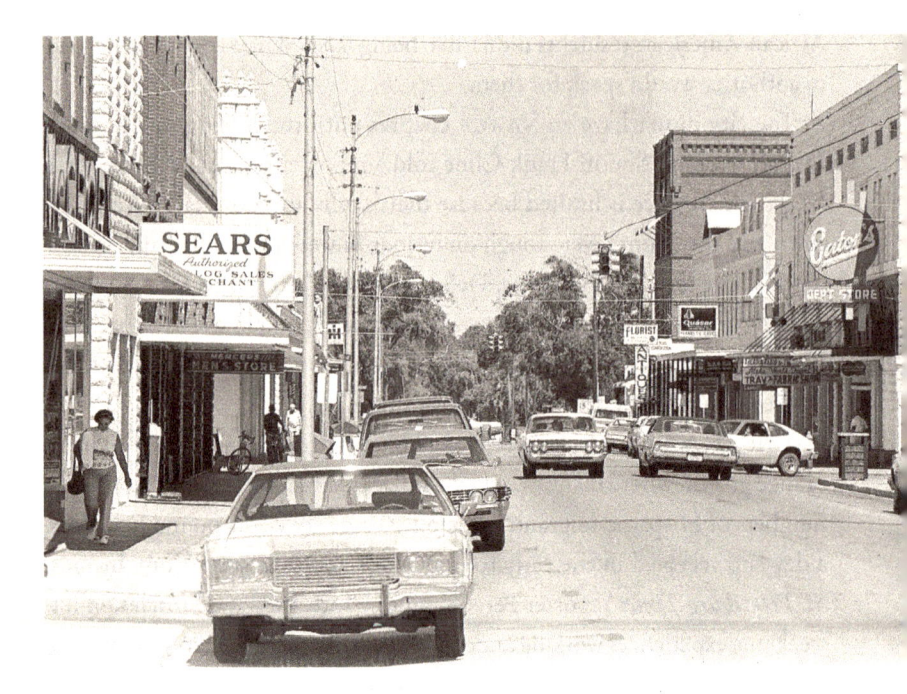

Downtown Arcadia, 1978. Known for its rough honky-tonks, sprawling agricultural industry, and racially segregated Quarters neighborhood, tiny Arcadia was and remains the administrative seat of rural DeSoto County. Courtesy Manatee County Public Library Historical Digital Collections.

recalled in a 1990 interview. "Back and forth, back and forth. I'd get out of school [in Arcadia], then reenroll back in."[11]

Through the early to mid-1960s, Hispanic migrants weren't yet a demographic factor in DeSoto County, where according to a 1962 estimate, there were just three hundred Spanish-speaking migrants in DeSoto and Hardee Counties in total, served by two Catholic priests.[12] That number would balloon through the 1970s to many thousands, single men and families who lived in Dust Bowl–like labor camps that lacked running water.

DeSoto County, which in 2024 had more citrus acreage under cultivation than any other county in Florida, first turned to Hispanic workers when local growers and outside companies like the American Agronomics Corporation added thousands of acres of groves just as Black migrant labor dried up. There were better jobs to be had, with better conditions and better pay, due to 1960s-era antidiscrimination hiring laws, while Hispanic migrants, many of whom had entered the United States without legal status, were willing to work for less.

Meanwhile, local African Americans and whites found jobs with a company called Gulf Naval Stores, a year-round outfit in Nocatee that made turpentine. A family-owned business from Alabama, Gulf built a factory in DeSoto County in 1958 and employed perhaps two hundred people. Among them were large work crews who scoured the county with bulldozers and backhoes, pulling up pine stumps that the factory then processed for their sap. The stumps, estimated at one million in number, were the turn-of-the-century by-product of exploitive lumber companies that had clear-cut the county's pine forests and left. Gulf had contracts for 310,000 acres' worth, enough for the next fifty years, a manager said.[13]

Pulling the stumps allowed area landowners to create even more pasturage and plant more groves, such as the Joshua Grove founded east of Arcadia by American Agronomics in 1970; at 42 square miles, the Joshua Grove was twice the size of Manhattan.[14]

Yet, American Agronomics wasn't the county's biggest employer. That was G. Pierce Wood, a two-site state mental hospital in southern and eastern DeSoto County established on the abandoned grounds of two former US Army Air Corps training facilities, Carlstrom Field and Dorr Field. Both had been temporary flight schools during World Wars I and II to train British and American pilots; the state took title to them in 1946.[15]

Initially Dorr housed women patients and Carlstrom men, but in 1968, the state incorporated the two groups at Carlstrom and turned Dorr into a residential facility for adults with mental disabilities and in 1970 converted it to a prison. State officials wanted G. Pierce Wood to be a spillover annex for its flagship mental hospital at Chattahoochee, in the Panhandle, but the decision to house patients on old Army bases in DeSoto County's barren outback turned out to be a mistake.

Because apart from its 1,000-employee support staff—mostly county residents who made between $200 and $260 a month in the early 1960s, more or less poverty wages—doctors, nurses, therapists, and other skilled caregivers just didn't want to work there. And besides, the Dorr and Carlstrom sites were overflowing with patients. There often were 2,000 of them crammed into small rooms in unsanitary conditions. "I could have taken you on a tour of this place [a decade or so ago]," said G. Pierce Wood's superintendent Dr. Clark Adair in 1976, "and you wouldn't have slept a wink that night. You would have vomited eight times before the tour was over."[16]

Dorr was the worst, a poor stepchild to a somewhat-modernized Carlstrom that in the 1950s was supposed to have been phased out but wasn't. Instead, Dorr lived on as an utterly neglected six hundred-patient hellhole with cubicles for rooms, cement floors, and wooden benches in empty living rooms called recreation areas, birds in the cafeteria rafters and droppings on the tables, a swarming mosquito problem, a feral cat problem, and just a single doctor. Dorr was so bad that workers at Carlstrom dubbed it Death Row, and once, when an out-of-state woman came for an interview, she left yelling, "My God! Let me out of here!"[17]

In 1968, things went from bad to worse when state officials turned Dorr into a home for mentally disabled adults. Called Sunland Center, this next-era Dorr facility received even less money than the old Dorr did, so residents continued to suffer. Newspapers did exposés, including one in 1968 by the *Orlando Sentinel* titled "Dorr Mental 'Hospital' Reeks of Misery" that convinced the state to act.[18]

The legislature held hearings, including one in which the director of Florida's mental disabilities services recommended closing Dorr and questioned the logic of segregating large groups of special-needs people in remote camps in rural Florida counties.[19] That was a criticism G. Pierce Wood had faced, and leaders in Arcadia feared that it could be closed, too—a catastrophic scenario for a town in which roughly one out of every seven to eight residents worked at G. Pierce Wood.

"We employ most of the employable people in the area," said a personnel director from the Florida Division of Mental Health. "Sometimes we employ whole families."[20] Luckily for Arcadia, though, at least employment-wise, the state converted Dorr to the DeSoto Correctional Institution, a medium-security prison that hired hundreds of area workers but soon gained a reputation for racial and sexual violence.[21]

Still, the DeSoto Correctional Institution meant jobs, and though locals were putting their proverbial employment eggs in a single governmental basket, Arcadia had grown, as one banker put it, "past the state where citrus and cattle [could] support it."[22] By the 1970s the town had grown in other ways as well. In 1971, in what was Paul P. Speer's fifteenth and final election, he finished sixth in Arcadia's five-seat city council race and lost to a Black man, a forty-one-year-old funeral home director and mortician named Eugene Hickson Sr.

Hickson was a 1948 graduate of the Smith-Brown School, Arcadia's African American high school, and became the first Black person ever elected to office in the ten-county region of Southwest Florida. His election shocked observers—a Black city councilman, in Arcadia?! Just a year earlier, there had been cross burnings in Arcadia, and for years, the DeSoto High School marching band carried a Stars-and-Bars Confederate battle flag that had been given to the school, in a kind of quasi-official ceremony, by the sheriff.[23]

"I was stunned," said Hickson, a soft-spoken father of three. "But it was the white vote that got me elected. I received 167 votes [out of 654] from the all-white youth center polling place." He said he hadn't done much reflecting. "I answered the phone until 1 a.m. last night. Folks kept calling me, black and white, to offer congratulations.... The next day, it started up again at 7 a.m. and when I went to town, people stopped me on the street to shake my hand, many saying it was time for a change."[24]

Born and raised in tiny Limestone, Florida, a timber and turpentine village in neighboring Hardee County, Hickson was the son of a sharecropper whose first experience with white students was at a Nashville embalming college where he was the only Black person. He bought his funeral home business in 1960 and handled only African Americans because, by custom, Blacks and whites in Arcadia had separate mortuaries and cemetery sections that divided the two races even in death.[25] That year, the town's schools, bars, buses, restaurants, some stores, its rodeo, and movie theater were segregated, all of its housing was segregated, and Arcadia General Hospital, the lone hospital in town, served only whites. Blacks went to the "Negro hospital" fifty miles away in Bradenton.

By 1971, though, due to a series of landmark civil rights acts and court rulings regarding schools, Arcadia would integrate. "I've seen a lot of changes for the black man's betterment," said Hickson after he won the election. "But ten years ago I would have laughed at you if you told me that I was going to be elected to the City Council or even run for it. Now here I am."[26]

Hickson surely realized that many white Arcadians would never accept him no matter what he did. One was the defeated candidate Speer, who told a *Fort Lauderdale News* reporter, "I reckon as long as they were determined to elect one [a Black man], I'm glad it was me who lost, 'cause I ain't servin' on the council with no n****r."[27] Speer then posed for a photographer under what a newspaper caption called a "hanging tree" and told a reporter his theory: sex and liquor were "goin' to ruin" America. He died a year later, a dinosaur, but the Arcadia city council (and Hickson) voted unanimously to name a recreation center after him.

Arcadia wouldn't miss Speer. Although a longtime community servant whose "accomplishments were exceeded by none," declared the city council, his racism was far too strident for younger white Arcadians to abide.[28] Indeed, by the 1970s, most were politely racist, admitting that Blacks and whites should go to school together or have equal access to jobs, but drew the line at close personal relationships and dating and rarely invited Black people into their homes.

As a white woman who worked at a downtown Arcadia drugstore put it, "It doesn't matter to me as long as they're a good person. That's the way I'm raising my kids. Course that's not to say I'd want them to marry one of them. But they should treat them like human beings."[29]

Yet old habits die hard. In the mid-1970s, Claudia Jones, the daughter of a prominent white Arcadia family worked at her father's real estate title office. It was downtown and employed an older African American man as a janitor who insisted on calling her "Miss Claudia." Jones recounted in a 2020 interview,

> I was maybe in high school then, and the janitor was a man named Ozell. He was in his late sixties, probably. He was a nice man and we all liked him, so I said: "Hey, Ozell, please call me Claudia. You don't have to call me *Miss* Claudia." But he went to my dad, and my dad came out and said, "Listen, he's got to call you Miss Claudia. He has to. He comes from a time when he had to speak to white people in a certain way or he would've been lynched. I don't like it, either. He calls me mister." So from then on, I was Miss Claudia.[30]

In 1976 DeSoto High School hired an African American man as head football coach, the first African American head coach at an integrated high school anywhere in Florida; but at home games, Blacks sat in one section of the bleachers, while whites sat in the other.[31] As late as 1979, it was alleged, Black police officers were permitted to patrol only the Quarters, and it wasn't until 1994 that Arcadia's two main white and Black Baptist churches, Calvary Baptist Church and St. John's Baptist Church, joined for a one-time service.[32] As St. John's pastor E. E. Cross said from the pulpit, "A few years ago, I couldn't be standing here in Calvary. Cross preaching at a white church? What? [But] I ask you to do something for me—forget about my color. Forget about me being black because, to tell you the truth, I had nothing to do with it."[33]

In terms of employment, African Americans made up a third of Arcadia's population in the 1970s but held just 17 percent of city jobs and less than 15 percent of county jobs at either the schools or the sheriff's office. Most were laborers.

An African American sergeant at the DeSoto Correctional Institution told a reporter in 1991,

> It's still white neighborhood, Black neighborhood even though the schools have been integrated. . . . Jobs play a big part of it—the salary range. They say it's OK for you to live in this neighborhood, but you don't make enough money. It's a disadvantage to both sides. White people don't get to know what black people are like. They just know what they heard or what they're told. And black people don't get to know what white people are like.[34]

Thankfully, the Klan had ceased functioning in Arcadia for some time. By the 1970s it was a fringe group in Florida that rallied occasionally in neighboring communities in Polk County, though a few older Arcadia residents still expressed sympathy for the organization and a handful probably still belonged. In 1977 a *Fort Myers News-Press* reporter visited Arcadia and spoke with a group of white patrons at the snack bar of the city's golf course, where Blacks "play nine holes," he wrote, but "don't use the facilities at the Arcadia Country Club next door."[35]

The snack bar patrons were older folks, among them the sixty-seven-year-old lifelong DeSoto County resident and farmer Burl Roberts, who admitted to being a former Klansman. "I'm not against n****rs," he explained. "I've worked with them all my life. I've employed them. I've even camped with them. I'm not prejudiced." But the problem with Arcadia, insisted Roberts, was that "there is no such thing as majority rule anymore," and if the Klan came back, he thought "everybody in town would support it."[36]

THREE

EVER PUT A PENNY IN YOUR MOUTH?

At 2 a.m. on the night of December 23, 1964, sleeping Arcadia residents woke with a start. Trucks with loudspeakers were driving up and down the streets blaring: "Do not drink the water! Do not drink any water from city taps! Parathion bags have been found in the river! Do not drink any water until further notice!"[1] The river was the Peace River, where the town got its drinking water; parathion was among the deadliest insecticides on Earth, one that migrant citrus workers diluted and sprayed to keep insects off of crops.

Parathion was so powerful that to cover an entire acre, workers mixed just a single pound of powder with a hundred gallons of water, then wore rubber suits and masks to shower it from crop dusters or shoot it from special rigs. After that, crews waited three full days to return to the fields. People's tolerance to parathion varied, but ingesting just a fortieth of a teaspoon could kill a person, and workers had died by simply touching the powder with their hands or breathing it in.

Light brown in color, smelling faintly of garlic, and bought over-the-counter at nurseries and farm stores throughout the state, parathion was a World War II-era Nazi invention that cost about forty cents a pound. In poor areas, peddlers sold it to people as a roach killer, and children and infants sometimes died violently in gagging fits as the lethal substance attacked their nervous systems and left them twitching on the floor.

"The firms which produce this stuff, the shippers and the storage warehouses and the farmers, all handle it with kid gloves," said an official in charge of insecticides at the state's agricultural department, so "it's the little people who somehow get their hands on it and cause the tragedies."[2] Just three months before the Arcadia incident, a three-year-old Miami boy died after eating a chicken wing dropped on the floor of an apartment dusted with parathion.³

A toddler succumbed in Pahokee, a two-year-old in Homestead, and a teenager and two young siblings in Tampa. However, the exact number of those killed by the insecticide is unknown, because parathion poisoning had often been misdiagnosed in Florida as encephalitis. Nevertheless, experts found in one two-year period eighty-nine confirmed parathion cases, including sixteen adult deaths and nine child deaths, in Dade County alone.⁴ And contrary to what the state Department of Agriculture claimed, farmers weren't careful when using or disposing of parathion at all.

"I've been in the fields," said a female laborer at the offices of a worker nonprofit in Fort Myers, "and they spray them while you're out there. Sometimes you have to run from the spray."⁵ Once, while driving through farms near Homestead, a local medical examiner spotted a pile of empty (but still incredibly dangerous) parathion cans tossed at the fence line. People would stop and pick them up, and several, he learned, ended up being used as mash pots at a moonshine still.⁶

The proper way to dispose of empty parathion containers, according to 1960s standards, was to bury them, a truly boneheaded idea, as even empty containers allowed trace elements to seep into the groundwater. But in Arcadia, orange grove owner John Parker, a descendant of the town's cattle-owning Parker family, hadn't even done that. According to press reports, Parker told a twenty-year-old grove hand named Jimmy Marriott to clean out a work shed and dump a reported fifty-four 4-pound bags of parathion "where they could [do] no harm to anyone."⁷ Parker claimed that he told Marriott to bury the bags, but Marriott told police that Parker had specifically said to throw the bags in the river, which is what he did. They were found by a fisherman on Wednesday afternoon, but fourteen bags, containing enough poison to kill every person in Arcadia, were missing.

Town officials panicked, shutting down the intake valves to its municipal water facility and switching its supply inland to a series of old sulfury wells. They also raced samples to MacDill Air Force Base in Tampa, where they were flown by jet to a lab in Tallahassee for testing. The lab found traces of parathion in the river, apparently not enough to hurt anyone, and the remnants, perhaps, of farm runoff from hundreds of agricultural concerns as far north as Auburndale.⁸

But who knew where it came from? In the 1960s, the Peace River was a cesspool, a 100-mile-long drainage ditch that citrus companies, phosphate companies, cattle ranches, slaughterhouses, tanneries, septic-tank owners, and even municipal sewer systems had been polluting for years. Just a few weeks prior to Arcadia's river poisoning, Mayor Paul P. Speer chaired an acrimonious meeting in Bartow between state and local officials, industry leaders, conservation groups, tourism officials, and residents on how to clean up the river.

There weren't any good answers, as even under the best circumstances citrus and phosphate companies were powerful polluters. Participants did discuss the water in and around Arcadia, where gobs of muck emitted a foul smell and anglers netted fish that were not only abnormally small but oddly "green around the mouth."[9] Now the Peace had been poisoned by parathion, and by only the dumbest of luck, Marriott had dumped the fifty-four bags across the river from Arcadia's intake pipes.

Had he dumped the bags directly in front of the pipes, hundreds or even thousands of people would have perished. That's what saved Arcadia, as one journalist put it, "from becoming a horror classic."[10] Sadly, the 1964 poisoning of the Peace River, for which Parker paid just $3,000 in cleanup costs, wouldn't be Arcadia's only brush with parathion.[11] Some three years later, someone put the deadly powder into a stove pot of beans and rice, evidently on purpose, and seven small children died.

Myrtice Jackson was a first-grade teacher at the Smith-Brown Elementary School in Arcadia. Smith-Brown had an open-lunch policy, so at 11 a.m. on Wednesday, October 25, 1967, Jackson sent her students home to eat. She did this every day, and students were back at their desks at 11:45 on the dot. But as class began after lunch, Jackson noticed seven-year-old Alice Richardson sitting rigidly at her desk. The small girl had grasped the tabletop in a death grip, her mouth was open, and she was trembling uncontrollably. "I thought she was having an epileptic fit," said Jackson. "She grabbed a hold of the table part ... [and] was retching and her head was going back and she was perspiring.... I didn't know what it was, so I sent for help."[12]

Jackson fetched a colleague named Ruby Faison, who pried Alice's hands from the desk and carried the now drooling girl to Principal Louis Anderson's office. Meanwhile, in neighboring classrooms, two other Richardson girls, six-year-old Susie and eight-year-old Betty Jean, had also gotten sick, though Betty Jean could still communicate. They'd eaten rice and beans for lunch, she told them, as Anderson, Faison, and a third teacher raced the girls to the recently integrated Arcadia General Hospital.

Suspecting poison, Anderson sent two other teachers to the Richardson home, and Faison, after a stop at the hospital, drove over to join them. Faison guessed correctly that the girls had ingested parathion. For one, Arcadia had a bad history with the insecticide; everyone knew its fields had once been bathed in it, and the girls' parents, James and Annie Mae Richardson, were fruit pickers. But Faison had also read in the newspaper that just a month earlier, seventeen children had died in Tijuana, Mexico, after eating sweet bread laced with parathion. The insecticide had gotten into the bread after workers had stored it in unsealed bags next to sugar and other foodstuffs in a warehouse.

That might have happened here, Faison surmised, as she drove up to an old dingy duplex, a former hotel converted to apartments at 131 Watson Avenue in the Quarters. She found two small children sprawled on the floor, a third standing with a broom and kind of hiding, and a fourth in the arms of a middle-age African American babysitter named Betsy Reese. "When I went to the house," explained Faison, "they were suffering from the same type thing, the same foaming." Their eyes "were tight and weren't focusing," she said, and "the one I took [to the hospital] was having diarrhea."[13]

As Faison parked and ran with the child into the emergency room, she felt the small body go limp. In all, two Richardson kids were dead on arrival, four succumbed that afternoon, and Betty Jean died the next morning. They'd all suffered from congestive heart failure brought on by a paralysis of the muscles, which parathion and other organophosphorus insecticides were known to cause.

The doctors had given the children the parathion antidotes atropine and protopine to block the insecticide's effect, but each had suffocated as their lungs filled with fluid: Diane (two years old), James Jr. (two), Vanesa (four), Doreen (five), Susie (six), Alice (seven), and Betty Jean (eight). It was a terrible way to die, and the question for DeSoto County Sheriff Frank Cline was whether the poisoning was an accident. The parents, James and Annie Mae, were fourteen miles away picking oranges when it happened. Someone called the grove owner, who radioed a manager to bring them to the hospital. There, a white Baptist minister, L. T. Fagan, took them to an on-site chapel and asked them to pray.

"What are we going to pray for?" asked James, who still didn't know what had happened.

"All your children are dead," replied Fagan.

"I looked around and saw my wife passed out on the floor," James remembered. "I said, 'Hell no! All my children ain't dead!' I couldn't believe it. I didn't believe it."[14]

Next to appear was Sheriff Cline, who brought longtime DeSoto County judge and coroner Gordon Hays with him. Cline was a big-boned, thirty-seven-year-old Arcadia native who'd only been sheriff since January 1967. While Cline was both liked and disliked among the citizenry, his predecessor, Lloyd Holton, had been wildly popular, a man who handled barbeque duties for Girl Scout troops and whose wife, Inez, cooked for prisoners at the jail.

The Holtons literally lived at the jail; they'd raised their children there, and when Lloyd died unexpectedly in 1965, DeSoto residents sent 1,500 telegrams to Florida Governor Haydon Burns's office demanding that Inez be appointed to finish her husband's term. Burns acquiesced, so from June 1965 until January 1966, DeSoto had what the *Tampa Tribune* called a "grandmother sheriff" who oversaw three full-time deputies, two special deputies in charge of radios and bloodhounds, two part-time African American deputies, and three jailers.[15]

Only one, Deputy Frank Cline, had any training whatsoever. In the early 1950s Cline served with the Florida Highway Patrol, then worked as an officer in Fort Myers and in the Lake Okeechobee town of South Bay. He was rumored to have had difficulties at work, particularly in South Bay, where in 1954, in an apparent fit of rage, he'd beaten an African American migrant worker who'd driven drunk through South Bay and on into Palm Beach County, where Cline caught up to him. The man was hospitalized from a beating so severe that even the FBI investigated, but the case went away when the charges of resisting arrest were dropped.[16] In 1957 Cline returned to

Arcadia, where, due to his experience as a patrolman and his skill at catching cattle rustlers, he emerged as Holton's top man. When Holton died, Cline ran the sheriff's office temporarily until Inez became sheriff.

It seems Inez didn't like Cline. In 1965 she reportedly refused to name him her chief deputy, though Florida sheriffs' offices typically had chief deputies and Cline had been acting sheriff. However, in 1966 Cline got his chance. Inez's term was expiring, and the fifty-three-year-old Arcadian told residents she wasn't going to run. People liked her and Lloyd, her husband, who had won three consecutive elections unopposed, but Cline, not so much.

In May 1966 a runoff election was held between Cline and Houston Hunter, a short-term Arcadia city policeman who'd been born in DeSoto County but spent much his life in Miami. Cline and Hunter tied, with 1,799 votes apiece. With his background in Arcadia and training in two police departments and the Highway Patrol, Cline should have won handily, but he only became sheriff through a 143-vote edge in absentee ballots.

Openly racist and an avid gun collector who was said to have shot his own finger off, Cline asserted that Blacks were less intelligent than whites and held the paternalistic view, as many Southerners did, that any racial discontent in Arcadia came from the outside. "The relationship between white and colored is far above average" in Arcadia, he told a reporter in 1968.[17] And Mark Lane, author of a 1970 book on Arcadia, quoted Cline as saying, "We don't have the problems here, I mean with the colored, that you have in those big cities.... What we do have is control. We just control the situation."[18]

In mid-1967, African Americans in Tampa and cities throughout the United States staged a series of riots in the so-called Summer of Rage. When two unidentified African Americans in Arcadia set fire to a wing of the Smith-Brown School, Cline ordered riot guns and brought in the all-white, forty-five-member DeSoto County Sheriff's Posse to help out.

Cline then formed a second auxiliary unit, an all-Black, thirty-two-member citizens' patrol in the Quarters, but while the white posse received combat firearms training and carried shotguns, the African American patrolmen did not.[19] The burning of Smith-Brown School left Arcadia nervous, as the 1967–1968 school year was DeSoto High School's first full year of integration. School officials had at first taken a gradual approach, accepting three African American girls in 1965, then a mixed group of thirty or so freshmen in 1966.

Things went well the first year, but when boys enrolled in the second year the situation did not go smoothly. James Faison, whose mother, Ruby Faison, taught one of the Richardson girls, attended DeSoto High in 1966. He explained in an interview,

> It wasn't like Little Rock or anything. There weren't any big crowds lining up to protest or rows of policemen or national guards. But we took a lot of harassment that year. You know, white kids saying "n****r this" and "n****r that." There were a lot of fights too. So we didn't spend much time studying or paying attention in class. We focused on surviving.[20]

Faison recalled that local African Americans despised Cline, who was widely rumored but not proven to have had clandestine sexual relations with women in the Quarters and to have fathered a child with one of them. He was also said to have skimmed money from illegal gambling in the Quarters and to have told deputies, without giving a reason, that "certain areas were off-limits to routine road patrols at certain times."[21] Why? Who knows, but Cline sometimes patrolled the Quarters at night by himself.

"It was just false accusations that I was a crook and a rogue," explained Cline in a 1980 interview. "I've been investigated by the masters of the art," including the FBI and the Florida Department of Law Enforcement, "and if anything had been wrong, they would have found out.... I feel anybody that's been chief law enforcement officer in this county will have jealousies, especially when they do the job thoroughly the way we have."[22]

"Thoroughly" was a stretch. Cline never did find the Smith-Brown arsonists, nor did he find or evidently even look for an unidentified white man who pointed a gun from his car at a group of Black students outside of DeSoto High School. The man was ready to shoot, James Faison recalled, when out of pure serendipity, an African American student named Lyle Lattimore was walking next to the car just as the man pointed the gun.

Lattimore, a gifted track athlete and one of the fastest sprinters in the state, lunged forward, snatching the gun from the man but did not get the license plate number as the car sped off. Shaken and angry, Lattimore gave the gun to the principal, who in turn gave it to Cline, but the sheriff failed to apprehend anyone or even alert the press. "It's crazy, I know," said Faison, who was a friend of Lattimore. "But we never found out why. I assume that with all the fights in the hallways and the fire over at Smith-Brown School, Cline wanted to keep things under wraps."[23]

That was just one event. A bad year in DeSoto County was about to get worse. It started with an explosion in January 1967 when a leak in a naphtha line ignited a 200-foot-high fireball over a turpentine extraction plant at the Gulf Naval Stores factory in Nocatee. Although the fire didn't kill anyone, it grew so hot that Gulf's aluminum outbuildings melted and fire trucks from five agencies, two tank wagons, and a bulldozer took more than two hours to put it out. The damage was in the millions of dollars.[24]

Then, in March, the *Orlando Sentinel* reported that "a great white mass of phosphate sludge, like a stream of flowing pancake batter," broke through the walls of a 180-acre settling pool at Fort Meade, to the north of Arcadia, where it flowed into the Peace River and south past the town, killing everything in its path.[25] In June the Gulf Naval Stores factory blew up again, then in August came the arson of Smith-Brown School. Now, in October, just ten months into office and facing reelection in May, Cline had a mystery to solve involving seven dead kids.

He felt enormous pressure and knew that if he botched the case, he and his wife, Donna Jo, whom Cline had hired as a clerk in the sheriff's office, would be out of work. Cline moved quickly, interrogating a stunned James Richardson in the hospital chapel. A resident described Cline in an interview in 2021.

> Cline was one of those old-timey sheriffs. He was a law-and-order guy who put a lot of emphasis on order. I remember he told my dad once that if you saw someone prowling in the yard, like a burglar, that you should shoot him, but before calling the police you should drag the body inside. That way you were clear legally because it was a home-invasion case. No kidding. That was his advice.[26]

Cline took an aggressive, damn-the-torpedoes approach to almost everything. He liked to capture suspects himself, often assisting in manhunts in other counties, and broke a bone in his foot jumping into a palmetto thicket while simulating a prison escape.[27] In September 1967, a month before the Richardson murders, Cline survived a gun battle with a fifty-year-old citrus worker named Frank Sloan. According to *St. Petersburg Times* reporter Ted Bryan,

Sloan, who lived in northeast Arcadia in a trailer owned by his ex-wife, had argued with her before fetching a gun. "I've been wanting to do this a long time," Sloan reportedly said before shooting her between the eyes. He then fired at his ex-wife's son and a second woman, who got away. Sloan stayed in the trailer, ranting to himself, until Cline and his deputies arrived. Cline thought the ex-wife was still alive, so as deputies shot tear gas into the trailer, Cline attacked, a one-man SWAT team, opening the door and crawling on his hands and knees to the center of the trailer as Sloan fired through the mist.

"I'm going to kill you, then I'll kill myself!" warned Sloan, who, though gagging on tear gas, still managed to shoot at Cline.[28] "I fired too when I saw the blue flame from his gun in the dark," explained the sheriff.[29] Cline's bullet hit Sloan in the head and would have killed him, but in one of those weird tales of law enforcement, a millisecond prior, Sloan had taken his own life by shooting himself in the head. As deputies stormed the trailer, Cline stumbled outside and fell, unconscious.[30]

Cline had suffered a small leg wound but recuperated by October, when he and Judge Hays spoke to Richardson in the chapel. The sheriff and judge had already been to the Richardson duplex, together, and both would testify that a strong metallic odor hung in the air. "It was so strong you could taste it," Cline said. "You ever put a penny in your mouth? Well, that's what it smelled like, like the taste of a penny in your mouth." He said the smell came "from the stove, from the pots and pans on the stove.... You could hardly breathe in there," so he and Hays covered their faces with handkerchiefs and opened the windows.[31]

Sixty-four-year-old Hays was not a medical examiner, but his job as coroner was to investigate causes of death; he knew immediately what it was: parathion. He and Cline spent maybe ten minutes in the apartment, being careful not to touch anything, then went to the hospital to tell doctors what they had found. They met the Richardsons in the chapel just as the couple had finished praying with Fagan.

Here's where the story is in dispute. Apparently, Fagan had asked the Richardsons if they had insurance; hospital staff had inquired and were worried about the expense. Fagan recounted, "Mr. Richardson said they didn't have any. They had had some but they had let it lapse because of unemployment" and "had taken out some more which would become effective on the following Friday. They had signed up for it the night before" the poisonings but didn't have the money to make the down payment. So as far as Richardson was concerned, observed Fagan, "he had no insurance"; the salesman was supposed to come back that Friday when Richardson got paid.[32]

However, Hays told a different story. After Fagan left, Hays asked Richardson if he was insured. "He said they were fully insured" and had double indemnity life insurance, Hays claimed. "I asked him when he got the insurance. He said, 'Just a couple nights ago.'"[33] Thus, Richardson's responses were contradictory. Or perhaps the men had misunderstood the grieving father, but Cline only believed Hays's version, and he and the judge went back to the duplex that day to find proof. They took a set of keys from Richardson at the chapel, including a house key and keys to two refrigerators: one containing food, the other, turned off and used as a closet, containing cleaning supplies.

When they asked Richardson what he thought had happened, he said he didn't know, explaining that he and Annie Mae had left the children with Betsy Reese, a friend and babysitter who lived next door to the Richardsons in the same building, and that Annie Mae had fixed grits for breakfast in one pot, and beans, rice, and a dish called hogshead for the children's lunch in the other. He knew nothing of any poison, had no idea how his kids had encountered such a poison, and said that both he and Annie Mae had eaten the grits before leaving and from the beans, rice, and hogshead for their previous night's dinner.

Richardson then told the men they had his full cooperation, that they could look anywhere in the apartment, and that the building had a shed they could search, but all that was in it was an old bag of lime. Lime was a caustic but not very dangerous rock powder used in gardening. In all, Cline visited the Richardson home five times that day. He collected two pots, a frying pan, and a pot lid and gave the items to the State's Attorney's Office in Sarasota for testing, as well as what he described as an insurance receipt from the Union Life Insurance Company.

The receipt, though, was actually a yellow business card from a white traveling salesman named Gerald Purvis, who had written the names of the Richardson children and the amount each would be insured for on the back. Although not a legally binding business document by any means, the

Frank Cline examining a refrigerator in the Richardsons' apartment, 1967. The DeSoto County sheriff claimed that the smell of parathion was so strong when he entered the residence he could taste it. Courtesy *Sarasota Herald-Tribune*/Imagn Images.

card, to Cline, was a smoking gun, proof that Richardson had poisoned the kids for profit.

Never mind that Richardson had given the card to Cline willingly and that neither Cline nor Hays or any of the deputies present found the source of the parathion. They'd searched the apartment, the shed, the stairwell, and the yard, but not the apartment of next-door neighbor and babysitter Betsy Reese. One would think that Reese was a prime suspect. After all, the curt, forty-five-year-old mother of three, known as Big Mama, had first denied babysitting the kids or even being in the apartment and was the last person to see all seven children alive. Reese was also a parolee who'd spent four years of a twenty-year sentence at the Lowell State Women's Prison near Ocala for shooting and killing her second husband. She also was rumored to have poisoned the first; the twenty-six-year-old man "had mysteriously dropped dead," wrote one reporter, "after eating her beef stew."[34]

Reese had also had a tempestuous relationship with Richardson, who in turn had an equally tempestuous relationship with Annie Mae, his wife. A semiliterate, partially deaf, slightly built man in his thirties, Richardson was a lothario, known for affairs throughout the Quarters and for fathering upward of a dozen children with three wives. Richardson had married Annie Mae without divorcing either of his first two wives—a product, perhaps, of his poor itinerant lifestyle—while Annie Mae was herself still married to Richardson's stepbrother Leonard Bryant. Thus, theirs was a blended family, with Vanesa, Diane, and James Jr., the youngest three children, the product of Annie Mae's marriage to Richardson and the other four of Annie Mae's marriage to Bryant. However, as Annie Mae would attest, Richardson "was a father to all of them. He loved them all."[35]

Richardson often failed to pay for their upkeep, though. Annie Mae and Richardson's second wife, who lived in Jacksonville, had had him arrested for his failure to pay child support. They "were a very dysfunctional family," wrote one observer. "Migrant farmworkers, constantly moving, with both wife and husband habitually walking away to adulterous liaisons, then returning."[36] It was rumored too, though not proven, that Annie Mae had also had a romantic relationship with Betsy Reese on the side and that Reese had been competing with Richardson for Annie Mae's attentions.

Others said Reese had been angry at Richardson for giving her third husband a ride to Jacksonville, where he had shacked up with Richardson's cousin and chosen not to return. Still others claimed that Sheriff Cline had protected Reese for a piece of Arcadia's *bolita* racket; the bingo-like game was illegal in Florida, but Reese was rumored to have run it in the Quarters. And finally, members of Arcadia's Black community whispered the biggest rumor of all: that Cline had a baby, a mixed-race girl, with Reese's daughter in 1965 and refused to arrest Reese for fear the truth would come out.[37]

This last rumor—that a white sheriff in a segregated town in the heartland of Florida fathered a child with a Black woman—would dog the lawman and his family for decades. It became a joke in the Quarters, almost a truism, and as the child grew into adulthood and developed a drinking problem, she'd sometimes shout, "Sheriff Cline is my daddy! Sheriff Cline is my daddy!"[38]

The African American community used it as an "epithet," wrote *Miami Herald* journalists Charles Flowers and Peter B. Gallagher, who investigated the case in 1988. Many blamed Reese for the murders, calling her "Abdullah the Butcher" in reference to a bloody character of then pro wrestling fame, but some saved the most vicious barbs for the granddaughter, who grew into a "stout, mannish woman with Black features and fair skin," the reporters wrote. One person even told reporters, "If you stick a pipe in her mouth, she looks just like Frank Cline."[39]

The sheriff, for his part, firmly denied that he had a baby with Reese's daughter and would, in time, pass a DNA test to prove it.[40] But back in 1967, at the very beginning of the case, there was something odd in how he treated Betsy Reese. She simply wasn't a suspect. She wasn't even a suspect when, a day after the murders, in a bizarre development, Reese and a reported town drunk named Charlie Smith together searched for and found an open bag of parathion in Richardson's shed. This was the same shed that Cline himself searched a day earlier, finding nothing. The bag just "appeared in plain sight," stated Cline, who on Thursday, October 26, interviewed Reese, then Smith, together with Assistant State Attorney John H. "Red" Treadwell III.[41]

Their story, as unbelievable as it was, was this: Smith had heard gossip on Orange Avenue, the main thoroughfare of Arcadia's Black neighborhood, but from whom he couldn't remember, that somehow, in spite of five police searches including several by Cline, there was a bag of parathion in the shed behind the Richardson duplex. So, not wanting Reese's kids to get into it and die, presumably, a concerned Smith went to the woman's apartment and asked her if she'd help him look for it.

They went to the shed, pulled a board from the window for some reason, though the door was open, and found a two-pound bag of Ortho parathion on the floor. At least, that's what they said. It was half full and old—Ortho had been acquired by a competing company, and its insecticides hadn't been sold in Arcadia for more than a year—and the wrapper lacked fingerprints. Yet to Cline, this was the murder weapon, and Richardson, who hadn't been seen by anyone anywhere near the shed and had been staying at a neighbor's, had somehow put it there.

The scenario made no sense, for even if Richardson had murdered the kids, why would he risk bringing a bag of parathion back to the murder scene when a bag hadn't been found? What would he gain from it? And how would Smith even know? The middle-age African American man was severely alcoholic; he rambled incoherently, denying at first he even knew Reese when Reese said they were dating, then telling Cline that two . . . no, three . . . no, six people had told him about the bag.

Smith seemed to fear Reese, observed Cline, but neither the sheriff nor the assistant state attorney bothered to ask him why. Why was he afraid of Betsy Reese? Had she threatened him? Or had she killed the kids and somehow ordered Smith to place the parathion in the shed? It's impossible to know. But that would explain why the pair had concocted such an outlandish story, that Reese had the bag in her apartment and told Smith to move it. She might have feared being searched. Nevertheless, when Cline and Treadwell interviewed the two separately, they took what Reese said at face value. Indeed, they didn't ask the woman if she'd had a hand in the murders, while accusing Smith of conspiring with Richardson.[42]

FOUR

A STUBBORN AND PURPOSEFUL MAN

Cline's theory that Richardson must have killed his children depended on the testimony of Gerald Purvis, the insurance salesman, who on October 26 sat for an interview with State Attorney Frank Schaub. A native New Yorker who'd come to Florida by way of Idaho and a stint in the Navy, Schaub was a 1948 graduate of Stetson Law School in DeLand, Florida, and was as tenacious as he was tough. "Frank [Schaub] is dedicated," said a friend and fellow district attorney, "maybe too much so. He can be stubborn.... Once he's made up his mind, no amount of logic, emotion, or reason is going to change it."[1]

The forty-five-year-old prosecutor had been state attorney since 1960 and oversaw an eight-county mostly coastal territory stretching from Bradenton in the north to Naples in the south, with three landlocked counties to the east: DeSoto, Hendry, and Glades. It was a big district; at 8,809 square miles, Florida's 12th District was bigger than Delaware and Connecticut combined. With six assistant state attorneys to help him, men with private law practices who worked for the state part time, Schaub traveled the circuit, prosecuting on average about a thousand felonies a year.

In 1967 he handled cases in the New South cities of Bradenton and Fort Myers; cases in the rough-and-tumble, Old South, orange and cattle communities of Arcadia, Immokalee, and LaBelle; cases in the northern-retiree enclaves of Cape Coral and Port Charlotte; and cases in the wealthy waterfront villages of Naples and Longboat Key. It was a murder on Longboat Key, the famed poisoning of thirty-two-year-old Carmela Coppolino by her anesthesiologist husband, Carl, that thrust an otherwise impassive Schaub into the national spotlight.

An aquiline-nosed New Jerseyan in his thirties, in 1965 the narcissistic Carl

Coppolino had moved with Carmela as well as his lover, Marjorie Farber, from Monmouth County, New Jersey, to Longboat Key. Farber lived in the same neighborhood as the Coppolinos in 1965 when Carmela died unexpectedly of a heart attack. Six weeks later, Carl dumped Farber by marrying a woman from his bridge club. Angry and hurt, at the urging of a priest Farber went to authorities with a story: back in New Jersey, her recently deceased husband had not died of a heart attack but had been knocked out by a paralytic muscle relaxant, then choked to death, by Carl. That led to two police investigations, one in New Jersey and one in Florida; circus-like murder trials ensued in 1966 and 1967 in which famed defense attorney F. Lee Bailey represented Coppolino.

A skilled interlocutor who'd defended both the "Boston Strangler" and Sam Sheppard of *The Fugitive* fame, Bailey had the "elegant and articulate ability to select the exact word and the most telling phrase."[2] He won an acquittal for Coppolino in the New Jersey case by pointing out that succinylcholine chloride, the muscle relaxant prosecutors claimed he had used to kill Farber's husband, wasn't detectable in autopsies and that the victim's broken hyoid bone hadn't come from strangulation but from rough treatment by cemetery workers as his body was disinterred.

Then the silver-tongued Bailey eviscerated Marjorie Farber on the stand, calling her a "Dr. Jekyll and Mrs. Hyde" who wanted Carl Coppolino "so badly, that she would sit on his lap in the electric chair while somebody pulled the switch, just to make sure that he dies." He told the jury, "This is not a murder case at all. This is monumental and shameful proof that hell hath no fury like a woman scorned."[3] However, in Coppolino's Florida trial, in which State Attorney Schaub had reams of circumstantial evidence that the now-infamous doctor had poisoned his wife, the prosecution could construct a case that didn't rely on Farber. That made Schaub's job easier, for the sullen prosecutor had none of the wit or bombast of Bailey, who, in early 1967, represented Carl at preliminary hearings in Sarasota for this second trial. By that point, the thirty-three-year-old Bailey had won an astonishing nineteen homicide cases in a row. He was a celebrity attorney, to some a hero, who case after salacious case became the "longest ball hitter in the lawyer league."[4]

Bailey seemed unbeatable, but in Florida he faced a surprisingly staunch, no-nonsense, and resolute opponent in Schaub. Novelist John D. MacDonald, famed author of the Travis McGee detective series, described the state attorney in his 1968 account of the case, *No Deadly Drug*. Schaub was "a stubborn and purposeful man," observed MacDonald, a single-minded man who gave "the impression of being wary and suspicious of all those around him." Schaub was irascible and abrupt and had "a compulsive urgency to get on with the job at hand . . . with a minimum of flap."[5]

But Bailey enjoyed the flap; he reveled in flap and requested a change of venue due to prejudicial pretrial publicity that he and his client had caused. Bailey wanted Miami, a big city in Florida's 11th District where news of the case wasn't so encompassing; instead the case was moved to ritzy Naples, which Bailey claimed was a mistake.

"Naples was then and continues to be a well-to-do community of older people, many of whom were retired," explained Bailey in 2008. "I did not like that venue for the trial of Carl Coppolino, an admitted philanderer whose accuser was an older woman herself."[6] Bailey could have added that Naples was full of WASPs: conservative, mostly Midwestern, white, Anglo-Saxon, Protestants who as a jury pool might have detested Coppolino, a Brooklyn-born, Italian Catholic social climber who had cheated on his wife.

Coppolino wasn't a good defendant, at least not in Naples, where in April 1967, a large contingent of the nation's press filled the city's bars and hotel rooms and lined up at 2:30 in the morning for tickets to the trial.[7] Joining the press were courtroom groupies, mostly housewives and women tourists who'd traded a day at the beach for a chance to see Coppolino, an immaculately dressed, darkly handsome defendant who resembled the film star Danny Thomas.[8]

Coppolino didn't testify, claiming the Fifth Amendment, while Bailey and his team tussled with Schaub from the get-go. During the *voir dire* portion of the trial, they nixed potential jurors and sought to influence future ones by taking not-so-subtle jabs at Schaub. The state attorney choked and turned purple, wrote a reporter, when Bailey asked a potential juror who happened to know Schaub personally if he could maintain his objectivity even if Schaub had "manufactured" the case. Manufactured the case?

An enraged Schaub jumped to his feet, yelling, "I object that there is any evidence that I manufactured this case! I am not on trial here!" Schaub then collected himself, telling Bailey that he could dismiss the juror if he wanted to by using a preemptory challenge—he had ten—to which Bailey replied, smartly, "*You* want to keep him! You [two] are chums!"⁹

Indeed, as Schaub brooded and complained, Bailey told jokes, even teasing a potential juror who had identified herself as "Mrs. Waples from Naples." Under Florida law at the time, women could serve as jurors but weren't issued summonses; they had to volunteer, and people who volunteered for jury duty were often seen as too eager by both the prosecution and the defense. So, when Mrs. Waples claimed that she came from a family of lawyers and that her late husband had once been the attorney general of Michigan, Bailey couldn't resist asking, "Are you truly Mrs. Waples from Naples?" "I am," she replied. "Well," Bailey told her, "this gentleman is Coppolino from Portofino, and you are excused."[10]

Bailey's word play notwithstanding, as testimony began, the talented defense attorney didn't have an answer for Schaub. Slowly and methodically, reading from a prepared script, Schaub addressed each of his witnesses in a dull, gravelly voice, his words unvarying: "If you will speak loud enough for me to hear you, then the jury will be able to hear you too. Tell us your name and where you live"—eleven witnesses, the same introduction eleven times. Schaub plowed through two full weeks of testimony, rephrasing questions over and over to get just the right answers in a "one, two, three approach to the law."[11]

The evidence was circumstantial. Carl Coppolino had ordered a small amount of succinylcholine chloride from a drug company for experiments on cats; Carmela, an otherwise healthy woman with a $65,000 life insurance policy, died with a one-inch-deep needle track on her buttocks. Was she poisoned? Two New York medical examiners, a boss and his assistant, said yes, claiming that in the six months since Coppolino's first murder trial, they'd devised a method for detecting excess succinic acid, a key component of succinylcholine chloride, in Carmela's brain.

The drug is what killed her, they said. And though the new technique had yet to be tested by anyone anywhere, neither man budged. Bailey grew frustrated, at one point shouting at medical examiner Milton Helpern, "Whatya' doing? Taking a flyer?" Schaub objected, but before Judge Lynn Silvertooth could respond, Helpern shouted back, "I object to you using that word. I never take a flyer. My feet are on the ground."[12]

As temperatures rose in the courtroom, Schaub stunned observers by wrestling, physically, with Bailey co-counsel James Russ after Russ grabbed an autopsy report that Helpern was reading to the jury and refused to give it back. Schaub tried to snatch the report, and as he and Russ engaged in an angry tug-of-war, a disbelieving Silvertooth slapped his hand on the bench and yelled, "Gentlemen, if I hear one more argument between you two, I'm going to put you both in jail."[13] Schaub apologized, embarrassed, but his impromptu aggressiveness in the courtroom showed this was a prosecutor who wouldn't give Coppolino an inch. The doctor was in trouble.

Indeed, when the accused man's main rebuttal witness, a British biochemist described in the press as so soporific and boring he put jurors to sleep, failed to refute Helpern, Coppolino suffered a sudden case of angina.[14] The court broke early for lunch and delayed the expert's testimony so Carl could recover, but the damage was done; the all-white, all-male jury convicted Coppolino of murder.

When the news broke, most of America's media outlets covered it: *Time, Life, Look,* the *New York Times,* the *Washington Post,* even Walter Cronkite of the CBS *Evening News*. Most improbably, "a hick attorney from Florida," as one writer quipped, had beaten F. Lee Bailey, the Perry Mason of American defense counsels who once had his own TV show.[15] Bailey left Naples in a Learjet, accompanied by a press agent, and Schaub drove his own car 130 miles up the Tamiami Trail to Bradenton. He had five new murders to try that summer and had to get home.

Unlike F. Lee Bailey, district attorney Frank Schaub wasn't a publicity hound. In the months following the Coppolino verdict, he traveled to New York to speak on "glamour trials" at a professional meeting of the National District Attorneys Association; when he returned, he addressed the Sarasota Sertoma Club and the Sarasota Marine Corps League, but that was it. He had few hobbies other than lawyering, he said, and seemed to relish sending people to prison. It's what he did.

Between June 1, 1968, and June 30, 1969, a period of thirteen months, Schaub and his associates handled some 1,259 felony cases, managing a near-perfect conviction rate of 95 percent.[16] Schaub cherry-picked the most win-

State Attorney Frank Schaub, 1968. Described as a "stubborn and purposeful man," Schaub oversaw the Richardson case. Courtesy Manatee County Public Library Historical Digital Collections.

nable cases, but the 12th District's bulldog prosecutor pursued his prey with the dogmatic zeal of an inquisitor. "I've always thought he was conscientious but pigheaded," said a former judge. "He assumes that if someone's arrested, it means they're guilty. There's no gray. It's all black and white."[17]

Because Schaub had such a huge territory to cover, he relied on local law enforcement officers and a handful of staff investigators to do the legwork and gather evidence. In October 1967, in the small chapel of Arcadia's general hospital, Sheriff Cline decided that that evidence pointed to Richardson. Except for one thing: the day after the murders, Schaub and his lead investigator, James Foy, interviewed Union National Life Insurance salesman Gerald Purvis in Arcadia.

A balding, somewhat heavy-set man in his thirties, Purvis sold policies door to door from an office in Tampa. He met Richardson the evening before the murders by chance. Purvis had been combing the neighborhood selling insurance, stopped on Watson Avenue, and knocked on the door of the Richardson apartment sometime around 7 p.m. As Purvis recalled, Richardson invited the salesman in. He'd been watching a show about Wyatt Earp on television, and as the two men discussed insurance, both Annie Mae and Betsy Reese passed into and out of the kitchen.

Richardson listened intently as Purvis described a family group plan in which Richardson would get a $2,000 policy for himself, a $1,500 policy for Annie Mae, and $500 policies for each of his ten children, presumably the seven he and Annie Mae had in Arcadia and three from a previous marriage in Jacksonville. The cost, said Purvis, was $1.40 a week. Richardson asked if he could double the payouts by doubling the premium, to which Purvis answered yes. If he paid $2.80 a week, he would have twice the insurance, $4,000 on himself, $3,000 on Annie Mae, and $1,000 on each of his children.

However, at no point, said Purvis, did Richardson inquire about "double indemnity" life insurance, that is, insurance in which Union National would pay double the amount of the policies on either Annie Mae or the children in cases of accidental death. Theirs were for natural deaths from illness or disease and wouldn't have paid out for poisonings. The following is an exchange from Purvis's interview by Foy on October 26, 1967:

Foy: "Now, as to the coverage . . . what did he ask you?"

Purvis: "He [said] you mean I can cover my whole family for just this much money, just this much in premium?"

Foy: "Did he mention anything about double indemnity?"

Purvis: "Sir, the only thing was, toward the interview's end, as I was standing up, he wanted to know about doubling the coverage on the family."

Foy: "But he didn't. . . . [He talked about] doubling the coverage, but not double indemnity? Did you discuss double indemnity with him at all?"

Purvis: "No sir. I didn't."

Foy: "Now there was some discussion concerning accidental death, is that right?"

Purvis: "No sir. He would have had accidental death on himself, not the rest of the family."[18]

The next day, during a follow-up interview with Assistant State Attorney Red Treadwell, Purvis said the same thing. Richardson had not asked for double indemnity life insurance, and the group plan Purvis wanted to sell him had "no accidental death on the children or the wife."[19]

So what gives? Judge Hays claimed that Richardson told him he had double indemnity life insurance, and Purvis, the insurance salesman, said he did not. Curiously, there's no transcript of Hays's conversation with Richardson, and out of more than 2,500 pages of court records and investigative documents from the Richardson case, the transcript of only one Richardson interview remains. There were, reportedly, several. Conducted by Schaub and Foy, the interview took place in the hospital, shortly after Richardson learned of his children's passing, and in it, Richardson claims to have asked Purvis for "double the insurance." He made no mention of a double indemnity "rider," as it was known, and neither Schaub nor Foy asked what kind of insurance he may have had on the children.

Yet in statements to a reporter on Friday, October 27, Schaub and Treadwell claimed, with no firm evidence, that Richardson had purchased "$1,000 double indemnity life insurance policies" and had asked Purvis to lend him the premium.[20] But Richardson said he hadn't done that. He said he'd asked Betsy Reese, not Purvis, to lend him the premium, and when she said no, that she was broke, Purvis offered to come back the following Tuesday. Purvis would state—as would Reese and Annie Mae and James Richardson, all independently of each other—that Richardson hadn't paid for the insurance *at all,* as Purvis said in his interview by Treadwell on October 27:

Treadwell: "You say he asked this other lady that was in there? Did he ask her if he could borrow some money from her?"
Purvis: "Yes sir, he certainly did."
Treadwell: "Did she loan it to him?"
Purvis: "No sir. She dug in her pocket. She was wearing dungarees. She dug in her pocket and pulled out some change, and said that was all she [had]."[21]

Richardson then asked Annie Mae for the money, but she didn't have it, so he told Purvis to come back on Friday, when he got paid. Purvis said no, explaining he only came to Arcadia on Tuesdays, so Richardson could pay the premium and thus put the policy into benefit then.

> Treadwell: "Did he act like he wanted to get the insurance anyhow? Some way or another, if he could go borrow the money or whatever it took?"
> Purvis: "No sir, I wouldn't say that, because he ... [asked] me to come back on Friday."
> Treadwell: "You didn't leave him a copy of this application did you?"
> Purvis: "No sir."
> Treadwell: "Did you leave a receipt?"
> Purvis: "No, not to my knowledge."
> Treadwell: "Do you think James thought he was insured when you left?"
> Purvis: "No sir. I don't think he could get that impression. Because I told him these benefits did not go into effect until the first premium was received."[22]

As proof, Purvis showed investigators his weekly "Agent's Report to Manager," a lined document listing the names and addresses of customers Purvis had sold insurance to. There were eight entries for "writing, revivals, and advance deposits," but not one of them was for Richardson.[23]

Still, Schaub and Treadwell felt Purvis was lying. They theorized again that Purvis had fronted Richardson the money, that he had paid the man's first premium to get him to buy insurance. That was illegal, said Treadwell, but was a practice "common in Negro slums where high premiums are asked on short term insurance."[24] At one point, Schaub, Treadwell, and Cline even questioned Purvis in the presence of his district manager, but Purvis didn't waver. For the third time in five days he'd told the men that Richardson didn't have insurance. They "were trying to persuade me, you know, to say that Richardson thought he was covered. Or that I led him on to believe that," explained Purvis. But "I stuck to the truth.... I don't think there was any way he thought he was covered."[25]

Annie Mae Richardson faints at her children's funeral, October 1967. At a packed school gymnasium in Arcadia, ushers hold the distraught mother. Annie Mae maintained her husband's innocence for the rest of her life. Courtesy *Tampa Bay Times/Zuma Press Wire*.

On Sunday, October 30, 1967, a crowd of some 1,500 people filled the gymnasium at Smith-Brown School. There were more outside, hundreds even, who'd braved a hot autumn day and no air-conditioning, to pay their last respects at a funeral for the Richardson kids. The seven white coffins, with satin coverings and ornate flower arrangements, were lined up end to end in a row. Funeral director Eugene Hickson said community members, both Black and white, had raised more than $2,000 for the funeral, where three African American ministers as well as Smith-Brown Principal Louis Anderson delivered the eulogies.

Stricken, Annie Mae stared off into nothing, lost in thought, while Richardson sat next to her and cried. He cried all through the opening remarks, then through various hymns and a reading of Psalm 27—"the Lord is my light and my salvation; whom shall I fear?"—but started to wail uncontrollably when, "in a bell-like, soprano voice," an eleven-year-old African American girl named Sharon Thomas sang "How Great Thou Art." A shudder passed through the crowd, wrote the *Miami Herald* reporter, "rippling outward," and soon others began to wail. Described as "hysteria" by an observer, the raucous mourning stopped when a neighbor gave James Richardson smelling salts to revive him, and Reverend C. S. Felder, the pastor of Arcadia's Elizabeth Baptist Church, read a poem by Longfellow.[26]

Mourners waved fans and sweated profusely but yelled their assent when Felder, in a black frock coat, thundered that the poisonings had been God's way of saying, "Arcadia, set your house in order!" To which voices in the crowd replied, "Amen! You're right!" and "We've gotta do it!"[27] At that point, pallbearers opened the caskets for the viewing. The children, ages eight to two, wore brand new clothes, the girls in dresses with matching gloves and tiny James Jr. in a suit. For roughly forty-five minutes, Arcadia's Black residents and maybe a hundred whites filtered through, but when Annie Mae passed the fifth coffin and saw her daughter Susie, she shrieked.

Unable to stand and overcome with emotion, she passed out, after which pallbearers rushed her to a waiting car and on to the hospital. That's when the wailing resumed; the crowd again turned hysterical, seemingly unhinged by the grieving mother. Mourners drove in an orderly procession to the Negroes Only section of Arcadia's Oak Ridge Cemetery. The services there were brief. Annie Mae rejoined the family, a zombie, and watched impassively as pallbearers placed the seven small caskets in front of seven empty graves, and Reverend Felder intoned, "It becomes our sad duty to commit these bodies to the earth. Ashes to ashes, dust to dust."[28]

FIVE

NO WORKINGHARD MAN

In the weeks and months following the Richardson murders, several leading news correspondents, including Richard Nellius of the *St. Petersburg Times* and Dave Behrens and Jon Nordheimer of the *Miami Herald,* came to Arcadia. There they were joined by perhaps two dozen other Florida reporters, various photographers, and radio and TV crews from stations throughout the South, plus freelance writers known as "stringers" for the Associated Press (AP).

The AP is a news service that began in 1846 as a nonprofit cooperative of newspapers for the purpose of disseminating news. Communications technology evolved, and by 1968 it had grown to some 1,750 daily and Sunday publications and close to 3,000 radio and TV stations nationwide as well as internationally. Thus, readers in Tucson, Arizona, for example, saw news of the poisonings at the same time readers in Florida did.[1] The children fell ill on October 25, 1967, and the AP ran the story on October 26.

But, when an unnamed reporter referred to Arcadia as "a small agricultural community on the edge of the Everglades," which it wasn't—the town was at least ninety miles from the swamp, and wasn't itself wet—Arcadians bristled.[2] They didn't like being mischaracterized, and though editor Bill Hackney of the *Arcadian* newspaper teased the town's chamber of commerce for getting its dander up, Hackney had no idea of the gigantic media firestorm that was to come.[3]

At first, the media's descriptions of Arcadia were benign. *Miami Herald* reporter Jon Nordheimer, who later became a prize-winning writer and bureau chief for the *New York Times,* wrote that there was a "black-white thing" going on "in that ghetto," but that as far as neighborhoods went, the Quarters looked like any other poor neighborhood in the South. He described it as a "sleepy... Negro district."

> Shotgun shacks and sleezy apartments line the dusty streets, but many trim little cottages with hibiscus and tomato plants... stand triumphant over time and circumstance.... Dogs, like all dogs in poor neighborhoods, roamed the streets sniffing at garbage cans.... Children, like all children in poor neighborhoods, skipped to school, laughing, singing, gamboling—unconcerned with poverty.[4]

In Nordheimer's depiction, nothing much had happened in Arcadia since the range wars of the 1800s. It had "slumbered uneventfully," he wrote, but was now the "scene of one of the worst crimes of the century."[5] Initially, Nordheimer and most of the press took what Sheriff Cline said at face value, namely, that Richardson had given a sworn statement in which he "told of arranging for $1,000 double indemnity policies... [and] believed the policies were in effect."[6]

But when Cline made the wildly false and quickly disproven claim that Richardson "may have had at least twenty-one children" through three marriages and that more than half of the children had died, possibly from parathion, reporters started to view Arcadia and Cline in particular with mistrust. In February 1968, *St. Petersburg Times* reporter Nellius did a feature on Arcadia for the newspaper's Sunday supplement, *The Floridian*. Headlined "Arcadia: Profile of a Small Florida Town," it began with an editor's preface, which grimly opined,

> Florida's palmetto and pine-fringed face is freckled with hundreds of small towns.... Motoring from one metropolitan area to another, chances are you'll drive through one of these small towns. You'll be charmed by it, startled by it, or puzzled by it... sometimes even repelled by it. Arcadia is such a town. It is a sleepy little south-central Florida town, where... massive live oaks, shrouded with Spanish moss, loom over the streets. Beneath its tranquil surface, Arcadia seethes with violence, frustration, and racial tension.[7]

As proof of the editor's description, Nellius cited the police blotter for 1967, which included not only the Richardson murders but also fifteen break-ins, four safe-crackings, two domestic violence killings, a pair of suicides, and a breakout at the jail. Nellius quoted Cline as saying, "We had some of everything last year. You name it, we had it. Activities in the sheriff's office, overall, were up 25 percent."[8]

Cline didn't say why in the article. But in Nellius's *Floridian* exposé, his deep dive into the people and culture of Arcadia, the reporter implied that there were several reasons. The town's conservative to ultraconservative politics were one; its low-wage industries, lack of job and educational opportunities, and free-wheeling gun culture were others, as was race. Race, to Nellius, was the big one. For, as he observed, this was a town whose sheriff openly claimed that African Americans' brains were smaller than whites' brains and whose school superintendent publicly opposed integration. "Why, I'm from Brunswick, Georgia," the superintendent told Nellius, "so you know how I personally stand."[9]

Nellius noted that in 1968 Arcadia's white voters were crazy for George Wallace, the former Alabama governor and third-party presidential candidate known for his "segregation now, segregation tomorrow, segregation forever" speeches and who in 1963 physically blocked the entry of African American students to the University of Alabama. A *Tampa Tribune* reporter observed, "There are so many huge Wallace billboards in DeSoto County, that an observer can't help wondering whether some of them couldn't have been more effectively placed in urban areas. Putting up more Wallace signs in DeSoto is like sending an evangelist to speak to the Ministerial Association."[10]

DeSoto County was so pro-Wallace and so right of the American center that in the elections of 1968, Wallace received more votes there (2,054) than Republican Richard M. Nixon and Democrat Hubert L. Humphrey combined (2,040). Overall, 28.5 percent of Florida voters opted for Wallace that year, while a whopping 50 percent of DeSoto voters did. Clearly, white Arcadia residents disliked integration. "The white fears the Negro" here, wrote Nellius, so much so that by the late 1960s, the city council had closed the town's swimming pool rather than have Black kids swim with white kids, and most of its rich white families, who were Protestant, began busing their elementary schoolchildren thirty-five minutes away to a private Catholic school in Port Charlotte.[11]

Lost in Nellius's *Floridian* piece, as damning as it was, was a gossipy tidbit regarding the Richardson case and the relationship between Assistant State Attorney Red Treadwell and Sheriff Cline. Nellius reported that Cline didn't get along well with Treadwell because Cline wanted to charge Richardson with first-degree murder and Treadwell didn't.[12] Yet Cline was adamant, and on October 31, the day after the children's funeral, he asked the Richardsons as well as Charlie Smith, Gerald Purvis, and Betsy Reese to take polygraph tests administered by a Florida Bureau of Law Enforcement expert, Clifford Powell.

The test was voluntary, not to mention inadmissible in court because it sometimes gave false positives, but everyone except Purvis agreed to take it. Annie Mae said Richardson was hard of hearing, so "when they called him, I tried to tell him 'You got to try and hear what they are saying 'cause if you don't the needle will move. You must tell the truth.' Well, he wasn't in there five minutes when they started hollering about 'We got him! We got him! He killed his children!'"[13]

Still, the evidence was slight, so Cline arrested the Richardsons on child neglect charges in order to hold James and announced there'd be a press conference with coroner Judge Hays the following day. On November 1, in front of a throng of reporters, a triumphant Cline stated that Annie Mae and Betsy Reese had passed their polygraph tests—Smith's was pending and he passed too—but that James had shown a "guilty knowledge" of the crime. "The motive," Cline said, "was remuneration for life insurance," specifically seven $1,000 double indemnity policies Richardson thought he had purchased the night before the children were poisoned.[14] That wasn't what Purvis had said or what Richardson, Annie Mae, or Betsy Reese had said; the questions Powell asked Richardson and his responses during the polygraph weren't transcribed.

Nevertheless, Cline and Hays claimed they had enough evidence to file murder charges, while State Attorney Schaub and Assistant State Attorney Treadwell said they did not. Schaub specifically wanted a grand jury indictment before he would act, but Hays chose a faster route, a so-called coroner's inquest. A product of medieval England, where kings appointed locals known as "crowners" to preserve evidence and investigate suspicious deaths, in Florida, the coroner's inquest included a six-person jury of "good and lawful men" from the district. These men should have been chosen at random, from voter rolls, but Cline handpicked the jury himself. Then, with lightning speed, Hays summoned witnesses, and the inquest met on Thursday, November 2.

As a judicial body, the inquest's role was investigative; it was to meet and hear testimony, and if it found evidence that a murder had been committed, the coroner, Judge Hays, could issue a warrant for the suspect's arrest. A DeSoto County institution in his own right, Hays was first elected judge as a twenty-one-year-old Stetson law school student in 1924, becoming the youngest elected judge in Florida history. He'd been so busy campaigning, it was said, that instead of attending his school's graduation ceremony in DeLand, he had his diploma mailed to him in Arcadia.[15] There, he served as county judge, small claims court judge, probate judge, and juvenile court judge as well as coroner until 1936, when he lost unexpectedly and entered private practice. He won again in 1948, and ran unopposed for the next twenty years, hearing hundreds of cases and traveling with sheriffs to crime scenes as coroner to determine causes of death.

That's why Hays accompanied Cline to the hospital that day as coroner and why there were photographs of Hays examining the Richardsons' apartment. Through the years, Hays had studied dozens of deaths, including the murder in 1955 of a Nocatee man named Eddie Reese, the ill-starred first husband of Betsy Reese, but only on rare occasions in over thirty years as a judge had he convened a coroner's inquest.[16] Held at the DeSoto County Courthouse in an un-air-conditioned room packed with journalists, the Richardson inquest had the appearance of a show trial. Called were twenty-two witnesses, mostly teachers and medical professionals, who described for the jury the specifics of how the children had died at school or at the hospital and with lethal doses of parathion in their blood, urine, and other bodily fluids and in food found in their stomachs.

Then, a chemist from the state board of health testified to finding two pots in the Richardson home containing cooking grease and food scraps laced with parathion. Betsy Reese, dressed in a "mod" hat, a button-down men's shirt, and dungarees, testified that she had served the children the food. The testimony took hours, but only Purvis and Cline mentioned Richardson. Under questioning from Treadwell, Purvis explained that he had dropped by the Richardson home while selling insurance and that Richardson had wanted to buy a family group plan but didn't have the money, so Purvis told him, "James, I tell you what I'll do. I'll take care of this and be back next week to pick up the premium."[17]

What Purvis meant was that he'd handle the paperwork. But Treadwell jumped at the line "I'll take care of this" to ask Purvis if Richardson thought he was insured. "You left him with the impression that he was covered by the policy?" asked Treadwell. Purvis replied, "Maybe, sir, but not intentionally."[18]

Cline took the stand, the last witness. Carrying a folder full of documents that he picked through during questioning but didn't give to the jury, the sheriff said that on the Tuesday before the murders, Richardson had *bought* insurance. Cline made this claim under oath. He then described coming into the Richardson home and smelling parathion, and he explained that while he hadn't found the source of the poison, he'd found traces of parathion on a flower pot in a direct line between the apartment and the bag that Smith and Reese had found in the shed.[19]

Cline's bombshell, however, and something he'd left to the end, involved a call he'd received from Jacksonville, from detectives at the Duval County Sheriff's Office who told him that at least three other children named Richardson had died there in recent years from poisonings. And though they couldn't be sure if the children belonged to James, Cline would be flying to Jacksonville to find out.[20]

The only problem was that Duval County Sheriff J. L. Hamlin denied that his office ever made such a call; the *Tampa Tribune* reported that while, yes, three children named Richardson had died in Jacksonville, only two of them belonged to James.[21] An infant girl named Annie Laura perished in 1959 of "encephalomalacia," a softening of the brain tissue due to infection, and a two-year-old boy in 1963 named Sampson Jehovah died from an "electrolyte imbalance associated with prolonged vomiting."[22] In neither instance was foul play suspected, nor did Richardson have or file claims for insurance. But the jury didn't know that. The jury took Cline at face value, ignoring Purvis and finding that Richardson had poisoned the kids "with premediated design." Hays then signed a coroner's warrant charging Richardson with murder.

Jon Nordheimer of the *Miami Herald* was at the DeSoto County jail when Cline showed Richardson the warrant. The prisoner "stood unflinching," he wrote, as Cline "read a legal document this negro with a sixth grade education couldn't understand. But as the realization seeped in, Richardson shook his head... [and cried,] 'I loved my children very hard.... People that know me know I loved them and took care of them and now they say I killed my own children. No workinghard man ever killed his children. Never heard of any man would kill his children. No man.'"[23]

Nordheimer then followed Richardson to his cell. There were six other prisoners, all African Americans, who sat quietly on their bunks. Still being held on child neglect charges, Annie Mae was in a different cell but within earshot.

"You hear that, Annie?" he yelled. "They say I killed the children!"
"What? What's the matter?" she replied.
"They got me charged with the murder of my children!"
The grieving mother went mute, and Richardson grew quiet.[24]

In November 1967 the recently elected president of the Florida chapter of the NAACP was a diminutive Baptist reverend named Joel Atkins. He had grown up in Arcadia, a town he described as "deeply entrenched with segregationists," before graduating from college and seminary and becoming preacher of the Zion Hill Baptist Church in Winter Haven.

Dubbed a "pint-sized Orson Welles" whose "stick-to-itiveness some would call stubborn," Atkins didn't like the news he'd been hearing from Arcadia.[25] Was Richardson guilty? He didn't know, but the sheriff there just wouldn't shut up. For, as Atkins knew, there were limits to what authorities could say before prejudicial pretrial publicity negated the accused's right to a fair trial. Therefore, shortly after Richardson's arrest, Atkins wrote a letter to then–Florida governor Claude Kirk demanding that Cline, whom the NAACP said in statements to the press had acted "irresponsibly and prejudicially," be suspended.[26]

However, the governor demurred. The jowly Jacksonville Republican had campaigned through 1966 as being tough on crime, and besides, Cline hadn't broken any laws. That's because, as far as pretrial publicity went, *there weren't any laws*. There weren't any guidelines then as to what sheriffs or state attorneys could say to the press or publicly disclose, only the vague understanding that if excessive media attention tainted a jury pool, then judges could move trials to different venues or, in rare instances, throw out convictions on appeal. In the summer of 1967 the American Bar Association released widely publicized draft recommendations for "mandatory state codes restricting lawyers, court officers, and law enforcement agencies from giving information to the press on criminal cases before or during a trial."[27]

The recommendations made sense: Do not make any extrajudicial statement concerning "the prior criminal record . . . or reputation of the accused." Don't discuss the contents of any confessions or admissions made by the accused. And don't give out test results, identify witnesses, or share an opinion as to the guilt or innocence of the accused.[28] In short, everything that needs to come out will come out at trial.

But Cline had been egregious, even by Florida's low legal standards, in declaring not only the substance of his interviews with Richardson and his lie-detector test but also a motive. Richardson was "a psychopathic miser," stated Cline. "[His] motive was to collect benefits on a life insurance policy. . . . [He] is guilty of the crime."[29] In fact, the day of the coroner's inquest, before any evidence had been presented, the *Fort Myers News-Press* blared, "Sheriff Sees Insurance Plot."[30]

Other early headlines included "Poison Motive Established" (*Pensacola News*), "Kids Killed for Insurance" (*Miami News*), and "Sheriff Sees Poison Death Plans Motivated by Insurance Benefits" (*Panama City News*).[31] Meanwhile, in Arcadia, Cline gave damning extrajudicial statements to the local *Arcadian* newspaper, the town's only newspaper, whose editor, Bill Hackney, served on the coroner's inquest jury.[32] Both Cline and Hays spoke to TV reporters, continually, which drew the attention of a white Daytona Beach-based personal injury attorney named John Spencer Robinson.

A graduate of Florida Southern College in Lakeland and the then barely accredited Cumberland University School of Law in Lebanon, Tennessee, the just thirty-year-old Robinson had proven himself as both a businessman and an attorney and was a philanthropist, community organizer, and Democratic Party campaign manager to boot. In high school, the muscular Robinson had been an all-state football player. He flew planes and raced cars and spent much of his time, when not lawyering in Daytona, doing good deeds, receiving the President's Award, for example, from the historically Black Bethune-Cookman

College for managing its scholarship fund. Robinson taught courses on citizenship for immigrants at Daytona Beach Junior College, founded and chaired the Volusia County Big Brothers Association, and sat on the Daytona Beach Inter-Racial Advisory Board, a body of twelve whites and twelve Blacks appointed by the mayor to work to integrate the city.[33]

In 1964 and 1966, Robinson held leadership positions in Miami Mayor Robert King High's two gubernatorial campaigns, where he met the African American activist and preacher Joel Atkins. The two men stayed in touch, and Robinson called Atkins in a huff after seeing Cline and Hays disparage Richardson on TV. "I'm concerned about what's being done to this man, Richardson," he told Atkins. "Everyone's talking about how guilty he is; it's in the newspaper every day. [And] I just saw those two clowns on television again tonight."[34]

Robinson then asked Atkins if the NAACP intended to defend Richardson. The preacher said yes. The organization planned to give Richardson a list of attorneys willing to serve as his defense. Should the NAACP add him to the list? asked Atkins. To which Robinson replied, yes. The next day, NAACP representatives met with Richardson at the jail. They gave him a list with Robinson's name on it, and because Richardson resembled Robinson on the page, the down-on-his-luck fruit picker chose him. The two men met, and Robinson agreed to be his lawyer.

"I was incensed by the denial of Richardson's rights," said Robinson in 1970. "It represented the most extreme annihilation of a man's right to a fair trial that I had ever seen in this state. The sheriff and the judge were condemning the defendant every day, it seemed. A headline a day. A newsbreak in the evening for the television audience. Where could he get impartial jurors?"[35] Probably not in Arcadia, where on Monday, November 13, Robinson filed a petition with the court for a writ of habeas corpus on behalf of Richardson, thereby requiring the state to produce actual evidence as to why Richardson should be in jail. But as Robinson was leaving the courtroom, a grizzled old white Arcadia resident in coveralls called him a "n****r lover" and spat in his direction.[36] Said Robinson's law partner, "Those rednecks have tried him already."[37]

Nevertheless, Robinson's habeas corpus petition effectively upped the ante for Cline, who quickly realized that his circumstantial evidence might not hold up in court. At one point, Schaub reportedly yelled at Cline, "You got me into this mess. Now you better get some evidence to get me out of it."[38] Enter John Boom. "Bad Boy" Boom. A powerfully built, 255-pound, African American deputy from Immokalee, in nearby Collier County, a farming and cattle town similar to Arcadia.

Schaub knew Boom from cases he'd tried; Collier was in Florida's 12th District, and Boom was adept at extracting information from Immokalee's migrant community, so adept that he'd been loaned out to sheriff's offices throughout the state. Boom's "got a way of talking to them [Black people] that really gets results," explained Cline. "He's questioned men no one else has ever gotten a thing out of, and comes back with answers. They never complain of bruises or anything, so we never ask."[39]

A practitioner of hands-on policing, the forty-eight-year-old Boom was the abandoned son of a Georgia sharecropper. He migrated to Florida and worked as a laborer until 1957, when Collier Sheriff E. A. "Doug" Hendry hired Boom as one of the first Black deputies in the state. His job was to police the ghetto, and Immokalee was one large migrant ghetto, the home of barracks and shanties and beat-up buses that drove migrants down State Roads 82 and 846 to work in the region's famed tomato, cucumber, pepper, and watermelon fields. And while the town had maybe 3,000 residents year round, the number swelled to upward of 12,000 residents in the winter, when crops were picked.[40] Living without indoor plumbing and preyed upon by white store owners who raised prices whenever paychecks were received, Immokalee's migrants drank and got into fistfights, which Boom considered his specialty.[41]

"I've fought up and down all these streets," he claimed in a 1974 interview, "all night and all day. You've got to be tough when you live around these people. If you have one soft spot in you, these people will find it."[42] Boom preferred to patrol at night, alone, walking from bar to bar, and camp to camp. He'd break up fights, make collars, and "carry ten to fifteen people to jail on foot," by himself, while he told others to report to jail on their own. "In the old days, I'd tell a man to go to jail and tell the jailer that I sent him," said Boom, "and he'd be there when I checked in later.... I don't think most people want to mess with me now."[43] In cases where migrant crimes required investigations, Boom would grill suspects using what deputies called "the Boom method." It was described by a deputy as follows:

> A truck had been stolen, and Boom come to talk to the man we thought had done it.... [He] comes in and just looks at him for a minute, then says, "Alright, boy, where the keys?" He gets back a lie. He asks again.... "Where them damn keys?" He gets another lie.... [Boom] slaps him out of the chair. He picks him up, puts him back in the chair and asks again. Another lie. Then he slaps him—off the chair and through an open window onto the ground outside.... [Boom] walks on out the door and calm as you please throws him back in through the window. By the time he comes back in, the man is talking, telling the truth. We got the keys and got the truck.[44]

Although the hulking Collier deputy Boom denied it under oath, sometime in early November 1967, in Arcadia's small jail, he beat Richardson, too.[45] It'd been a week since the children had died, and Cline lacked even a scintilla of evidence linking the father to the crime. So he called Boom. Richardson recalled Boom's arrival at the jail.

> Someone looked out the window and said, "Bad Boy is here." The place got silent. Everyone was afraid.... [Then] Bad Boy said to me, "You sick? Something wrong with you Richardson?" Bad Boy had a big gun in his belt, not in his holster. He called me into a little room ... [and said] "I want to treat you nice if you let me. If not ... I'm going to fuck you up."[46]

At one point, claimed Richardson, Boom promised to release Annie Mae if Richardson confessed; when he didn't, Boom put an unloaded gun in Richardson's face and cocked the trigger. Years later, the investigative reporters Flowers and Gallagher visited the retired Boom in Immokalee. Among other things, Boom admitted to being in the room, essentially menacing Richardson, during the lie-detector test and to beating not only Richardson but three other inmates in hopes of gaining "snitch testimony" that Richardson had confessed. "Sure, it could have happened," said Boom. "It was a different time back then. If the sheriff said to do something, you did it. Those were frontier times. It was my job. Anyway, Richardson was guilty. He had to be."[47]

SIX

QUID PRO QUO

Unfortunately for Deputy Boom, the arrival of John Robinson as Richardson's defense attorney meant his two-fisted interrogations of Richardson came to an end. He and Cline still questioned Richardson incessantly, without Robinson present, but the jailed man said again and again he hadn't killed his children. And with only circumstantial evidence that he did, on Thursday, November 16, following a closed-door meeting with Circuit Court Judge John Justice of Sarasota, Robinson and Schaub negotiated Richardson's bail, a paltry $7,500 for the murder of seven kids.

Robinson surmised that Schaub feared he didn't have sufficient evidence to keep Richardson in jail, so rather than reveal what he had in court, he let the defendant bond out. That, in and of itself, was unheard of. Bail, for the premeditated mass murder of children? Then, there was the amount: $7,500. In 1966 a judge set Carl Coppolino's bail at $15,000, which at the time Schaub said was too low. So clearly, the state attorney didn't want to show his cards.

As for Robinson, the Daytona Beach attorney used the threat of a habeas corpus hearing to get Richardson out of jail and claimed to have bargained Schaub down from an initial offer of $100,000. Robinson reasoned that once Richardson was out of jail and out of Arcadia, Schaub would drop the charges. He'd have to. He just didn't have the evidence. But two days later, Cline and Boom interviewed Richardson's cell mate, a small-time crook named James Dean Cunningham, at the jail. Cunningham conveniently told the two men that Richardson had confided in him, in tears, immediately after his October 31 lie-detector test. According to Cunningham, Richardson said he'd killed the kids for $7,000 in insurance because he wasn't making enough money to take care of them.

However, in that same interview Cunningham also said that Richardson didn't do it and that the babysitter put the poison in the food.[1] So, which was it? Why had Cunningham contradicted himself, and why would Richardson admit to murdering the kids and confide in an inmate he'd just met? It made no sense. But the crafty Schaub decided to use Cunningham as a witness, a jailhouse snitch, but the transcript of Cunningham's November 18 interview with Cline never made it to the defense.

Thus, as Richardson's attorney, the inexperienced Robinson had misjudged Schaub, badly, because this so-called bulldog prosecutor wasn't dropping the case. In fact, he took it to a grand jury to seek a first-degree murder indictment, while finding two additional snitches and burying a December 1 interview with Minister Fagan. Since the murders, Fagan had been transferred to Puerto Rico. He'd sold his house in Arcadia and was flying to San Juan the day after the interview, which was conducted on December 1, 1967. The transcript doesn't give the interviewer's name; presumably it was either Assistant State Attorney Red Treadwell or Schaub.

> QUESTION: "In the course of your conversation, was there anything mentioned about insurance proceeds for the children?"
> FAGAN: "Yes. One of the secretaries in the hospital came in to make out the usual admission statements . . . ages, names, and so forth. And during the questioning, either she or I, we were both trying to console the mother, asked if they had any hospital insurance. Mr. Richardson said that they didn't have any. They had signed up for it the night before but didn't have the money to make the down payment. . . . There was some lady present, a colored lady, a large lady [Betsy Reese]. 'I tried to borrow a dollar from her last night to put the insurance in force, but she wouldn't let me have it.'"
> QUESTION: "Did you get the impression from talking with James Richardson that he wasn't covered with insurance?"
> FAGAN: "As far as he was concerned, he had no insurance."
> QUESTION: "He had no insurance?"
> FAGAN: "Right."[2]

Fagan's statement to authorities didn't absolve Richardson of the crime. The minister could have misheard the man or gotten his facts wrong. But under

Florida law, when Richardson went to trial, transcripts of Fagan's interview as well as the Purvis and Cunningham interviews should have been provided to the defense. That wasn't negotiable. In fact, that was a ground rule applicable to every court in the state and backed by a US Supreme Court ruling in 1963.

If Schaub possessed exculpatory evidence that would have helped Richardson, he had to give it up. But he didn't. Instead, on December 5, Schaub presented evidence to a grand jury in Tampa, where he asked for a first-degree murder indictment of Richardson for the killing of eight-year-old Betty Jean.[3]

Schaub wanted the indictment for just a single count because if he tried Richardson for Betty Jean's murder and lost, he'd still have six more bites at the apple. It was a devious ploy, and after hearing witnesses in a closed proceeding lasting some ten hours, the jury gave Schaub what he wanted, a true bill charging Richardson with the child's murder. He stayed free on bond but faced a May 1968 trial in Fort Myers conducted by Judge Justice.

There were preliminary hearings, including one in which Robinson tried unsuccessfully to have Cline sanctioned for talking to the press and another to throw out testimony from the two additional snitches, Earnell Washington and James "Spot" Weaver. Both were African American street toughs and penny-ante gamblers who, Weaver later claimed, had received reductions in their sentences for stating under oath that Richardson had admitted to the crime. Richardson claimed he hadn't, though, and in a fit of rage yelled "YOU'RE LYING!" at the men before the judge ruled they could testify.[4]

Then, Justice ruled that Washington's earlier statement to Cline could be used as evidence at Richardson's trial, though in April 1968, Washington had been shot and killed in an unrelated event at an Arcadia bar.[5] Washington would die just two weeks before Judge Hays died. Hays had suffered a heart attack at work, but Justice also allowed his testimony as coroner at the preliminary hearing into court.[6]

A clean-cut, bespectacled man in his fifties described as stern but fair, Justice wasn't wrong—sworn testimony from witnesses who had died could be offered into evidence—but the Sarasota judge ruled against Robinson at least a dozen times. In fact, Justice agreed to just one of Robinson's motions, namely change of venue, which is how the Richardson case landed in Fort Myers. Famed for being the winter home of inventor Thomas Edison, Fort Myers was the bustling seat of Lee County, so named for Confederate General

Robert E. Lee. Through tourism to its beaches and the building of northern retiree home developments such as Cape Coral, Fort Myers had doubled in population, from 50,000 to 100,000, in ten years. It had a modern indoor shopping mall, a glistening new community college, and direct flights daily to and from New York.

However, like Arcadia, Fort Myers had only recently and only partially desegregated. In 1968 it still had a Blacks-only high school; the city-run Teen Club and three city swimming pools were segregated; and Black police officers could only work and arrest people, in Safety Hill, the city's Black neighborhood.[7] "We were still confronted with all of the ills of a segregationist government," said Veronica Shoemaker, an African American community activist and Fort Myers city council member who first ran for office in 1968.[8] "Back then we were negroes," so, when campaigning in white neighborhoods, she said, "I always went to the back door."[9]

Shoemaker wasn't exaggerating. The worst of Jim Crow had ended in Fort Myers, but as late as 1963, the city's code of ordinances had made it "unlawful for persons . . . of the colored race . . . to loiter upon the streets, patronize establishments serving food and beverages, use lavatory and sanitary facilities, [or] attend theatres and places for public gatherings . . . in the divisional area for the white race."[10] Schools were a flashpoint. Beginning in 1964, Lee County started to integrate, gradually, but when its all-white school board proposed integrating schools one grade at a time, over a decade, the African American community complained. "The school board in those days had no intention of integrating the schools," remembered Reverend Isadore Edwards, then head of the Lee County NAACP. "They thought they were protecting the little white girl from the dangerous black boy."[11]

When Edwards and other Black leaders planned a march in Fort Myers to protest what they saw as the intransigence of the board, Edwards was escorted downtown by the white sheriff, Flanders "Snag" Thompson, who wanted to show Edwards what awaited people if they marched. "First Street was lined with rednecks from Alva," a rural area to the east of Fort Myers, Edwards said. They "were armed with chains and baseball bats just waiting for us. Snag told me there was no way he and the city police could guarantee our safety, . . . [so] I called off the march."[12]

Eileen Bernard, a white northern transplant office manager for the company that built Cape Coral, recalled attending mixed-race civil rights meetings in Fort Myers and being harassed by the police. She said deputies would run license plate numbers over their radios, then read out the names of car-owning attendees through a loudspeaker. "I'd get phone calls at night," she said, and people would hiss, "Why don't I go back home and take my baboons with me?"[13]

In August 1968 the Lee County NAACP asked the US Justice Department to investigate Sheriff Thompson for a host of racist practices, then complained, too, that Lee County's court system "discriminates against negroes."[14] There were, after all, no Black lawyers in Lee County, no Black judges, and an all-white, five-member board called the Jury Commission that personally selected jurors. For more than eighty years, up to that point the entire history of Lee County, the commission had excluded African Americans entirely.

However, in 1947 the US Supreme Court ruled that in cases involving African American defendants, jury venires, the lists drawn from voter rolls jurors were chosen from, had to include African Americans or they violated the Equal Protection Clause of the Fourteenth Amendment. So Lee County's Jury Commission began including Blacks, grudgingly; well into the 1970s, when finally jury venires were chosen randomly by computer, the number of African Americans in local jury pools remained pitifully small. In 1960 the *Fort Myers News-Press* reported that 1,200 people were in that year's potential juror list, but just 30 of them were Black.[15]

The numbers hadn't improved much by the May 1968 Richardson trial, and during jury selection, five of the six African American jury pool members present were excused for cause. The reason was that *State of Florida vs. James Joseph Richardson* was a death-penalty case, and at the time, states had the right to remove potential jurors who opposed capital punishment. Thus five Black objectors were dismissed along with ten white objectors, plus three whites who claimed they couldn't convict a person using circumstantial evidence and one who said he'd already formed an opinion of the case.

That left one African American man, an electric utility worker whose boss and two of his coworkers had been called for jury duty too. Jurors weren't supposed to know each other. They could form cliques or have an undue influence on each other, especially in cases of white bosses and Black workers, so Robinson removed all four. The result was a completely white jury

James Richardson leaving the Lee County Courthouse, 1968. Defense attorney John Robinson (*top left*) accompanies Richardson as he is escorted outside after a hearing. A judge moved the proceedings from Arcadia to Fort Myers in Lee County due to massive pretrial publicity. Courtesy *Tampa Bay Times*/Zuma Press Wire.

of eleven men and one woman whom Robinson considered biased toward Blacks. He offered no evidence but griped, "What does a challenge for cause mean in a case like this? Why, you ask some redneck if he is prejudiced, he answers, 'No sir, I'd believe a n****r if he was telling the truth,' and the judge rules that he's impartial."[16]

One person who wasn't impartial was Frank Cline, who in late 1967 appeared in DeSoto County court as a character witness for Earnell Washington, the jailhouse snitch who'd testified before a grand jury against Richardson. This was the quid pro quo, presumably, the favor for a favor, and though James and Annie Mae Richardson weren't even in Arcadia when Washington died, Cline hinted publicly that Richardson had killed him.[17] He hadn't. A thirty-four-year-old woman named Beatrice Cosey had shot Washington in a bar; she pleaded guilty to manslaughter in 1969.

Yet Cline's biggest chicanery was to come, at the May 1968 Richardson trial, where Robinson's lack of experience as a criminal defense attorney was clear. He and his partner, Richard Whitson, specialized in car wrecks and product-liability suits and divorces and didn't know, for example, that they had to petition Judge Justice to have a court reporter record all of the proceedings. As it stood, Justice had only asked the reporter to write down witness testimony; therefore, there is no record of the preliminary arguments, the jury selection, or the opening and closing statements of Robinson and Schaub. According to the press, though, Schaub vowed that the evidence would prove that Richardson had been "looking for a way out" and had grown "disenchanted with Annie Mae." That's when Richardson received a visit from the insurance salesman Gerald Purvis and immediately hatched a plan. He would poison the kids with parathion, which he "very carefully put . . . in food his children were to eat."[18]

Then Schaub called his witnesses: Myrtice Jackson, Ruby Faison, Louis Anderson, and other Smith-Brown teachers who'd witnessed the children blanch and sicken before rushing them to the hospital. Then came three Arcadia doctors. One of them, Elmer Schmierer, had quickly guessed organophosphate poisoning and administered massive amounts of atropine and protopine, to no avail. Schmierer had no idea how the kids had ingested the parathion, but after speaking with Judge Hays, he had taken the unusual step of listing their manners of death on their death certificates as not just homicide but "premeditated murder." Official manners of death in those days included terminal illness, accident, suicide, and homicide—the attending examiner actually checked a box—but premeditated murder was a legal conclusion for a judge or jury to decide, not Schmierer.

But in what was called "a defense lapse," Robinson didn't object, essentially conceding to Schaub and the jury that the children had been poisoned on purpose.[19] It wasn't a case-ending mistake, by any means, but one of several instances in which Robinson and Whitson dropped the ball. They argued doggedly, to be sure, at times screaming at Schaub and pounding their hands on the table angrily, but seemed not to see the forest for the trees. They objected to the submission of the children's medical records as evidence because the nurse who brought them to court hadn't been the one who prepared them. They objected to Schaub's description of a Sarasota pathologist as a "medical scientist," saying "medicine is an art... not a science," and they badgered Schaub and Assistant State Attorney Leroy Hill for failing to phrase their questions correctly.

However, when Cline took the stand and perjured himself by calling the yellow card Purvis had a given to Richardson a "receipt," the defense said nothing. As Cline knew and Purvis had told investigators repeatedly, the card wasn't a receipt. It was a business card with insurance amounts handwritten on the back that Schaub hadn't entered into evidence. And though Schaub didn't have to prove a motive to convict, jurors were human. They, like everyone else, wanted to know why. Why had Richardson committed the crime? Schaub said insurance, that Richardson was looking for a way out, but the coy state attorney failed to present evidence of an active policy. He also withheld Purvis's "Agent's Report to Manager," which didn't list a Richardson policy, and he decided not to call Purvis to the stand.

Legally, Schaub could call or not call Purvis if he wanted to. But why didn't Robinson put Purvis on the stand? It seems like a bad mistake, a miscue, as Richardson's inexperienced defense attorney missed a golden opportunity to undermine Schaub's case. The same could be said for the murder weapon; there wasn't one, only the dampish bag of old parathion that Reese and Smith claimed to have found in Richardson's shed. As evidence, it had no probative value, no connection to the accused, but Robinson failed to ask Judge Justice to exclude it. That was a mistake because a theatrical Cline brought the parathion into the courtroom while wearing oversized yellow gloves. He didn't need the gloves; he actually put them on in the hallway and had packed the parathion in sealed glass jars inside cardboard boxes.

Yet Cline acted as if he'd been poisoned. He slurred his speech and mumbled, while Hill blared, "[These jars] can only be handled at your peril.... [They contain] almost pure parathion and I want counsel to be aware of the fact that I am not going to handle them anymore than necessary and he can do likewise.... The sheriff had some problem with [them] already."[20] It seemed like a fair warning, but why, if the boxes were so dangerous, had Cline brought them into the courtroom at all? And if Cline had truly been poisoned, as Hill implied, why didn't Hill or Schaub rush the ailing sheriff to the hospital? The answer is they were acting, trying first to inflame, then distract jurors from realizing that the evidence they'd been given wasn't evidence at all.

Naturally, Robinson was apoplectic. He jumped up and demanded a mistrial. But when Justice refused his request, the attorney did a poor job of questioning Cline. First, he let the "receipt" thing slip, then needled the sheriff unremittingly over the smallest of details. When had he visited the apartment? How many times had he visited the apartment? "Was it after two or before two?" Or "could it have been two?" Or, "a quarter to two?"[21]

Robinson wanted specifics, probably to show that Cline was an unreliable witness, but the questions didn't lead to anything. They didn't impeach anything, and when Cline admitted that Betsy Reese and Charlie Smith had found the parathion in a shed he'd already searched, Robinson let it pass. Sure, he asked about it, but at no point did he make Cline admit the absurdity of it, nor did he point to Betsy Reese as someone besides Richardson who could have committed the crime.

Robinson's entire defense could be summarized thus: Richardson was a good man, a family man, as Annie Mae and six friends and relatives and even a minister would attest. They came from Jacksonville, where the Richardsons had lived before moving to Arcadia in 1966 and where James worked as a garbage man from morning until night. He came home reeking of garbage, testified Bernice Hartley, a friend and former neighbor. But the kids would run out to meet him. They'd "be on his legs and shoulders just dragging him [into] the house," and there was "never no fussing, cussing or raising sand. . . . That boy loved his children."[22] Sarah E. Jones, the minister of Sunshine Spiritual Church, which the Richardsons had belonged to before moving, insisted that "the children were wonderful" and that "a white or colored man couldn't be any better to that family than he was to them."[23]

Richardson's biggest defender was Annie Mae, who insisted that "he loved every last one" of those kids and treated them all "equal right." He'd even gone shopping shortly before the murders and bought the kids Christmas presents on layaway, paying a bit each week so that Susie would have a tea set, James Jr. would have a tricycle, and so forth. And besides, Annie Mae, not James, was the one who'd cooked the food, and she said she was in her husband's presence the entire night. He'd gotten up at 4:30 in the morning and gone into the kitchen for breakfast, where he ate the same rice, beans, and hogshead that the children did. He put nothing in the food, she testified, nor had he purchased insurance the night before. "I will ask you one final question," Robinson said, for effect. "Do you think your husband poisoned your children?" "No," she answered, "I do not think my husband poisoned my children."[24]

For his part, State Attorney Schaub relied almost entirely on circumstantial evidence, the jailhouse-snitch testimony of Spot Weaver and James Cunningham, and the preliminary hearing testimony of the late Judge Hays. He didn't have much, but since Robinson blew it by not calling Purvis to the stand, the jury ignored Richardson's own dramatic testimony and voted to convict. The all-white body deliberated for just an hour and a half after closing arguments in which Schaub called Richardson a "sanctimonious hypocrite" and Robinson tried to reason with jurors by declaring, awkwardly, "I'm dealing with a poor, illiterate n****r. . . . I wouldn't want to socialize with him and neither would you. But he has equal rights."[25]

At that point, Robinson intentionally and very dramatically swept several piles of evidence, a few boxes of parathion, and some pots and pans onto the floor. There was a terrific crash, then pandemonium, over which Robinson yelled, "Has the state ever linked James Richardson to that parathion?!"[26] The answer was no. But on that hot Florida day, in the case of a Black man tried in a courthouse under a portrait of Robert E. Lee, no one cared.

SEVEN

THE LAWYER-TURNED-PAMPHLETEER

Reporters dubbed him the "attorney-writer," the "investigator-lawyer," and the "lawyer-turned-pamphleteer," the swarthy, bespectacled, fortyish former New York state assemblyman and "grassy knoll" conspiracy theorist Mark Lane. He had served in Army intelligence during World War II and in 1951 received his Bachelor of laws degree from Brooklyn Law School. In law school, instead of studying, Lane spent most of his time volunteering for the über-progressive National Lawyers Guild, then a kind of antidote to the politically conservative American Bar Association, which had only recently admitted Blacks.

As Lane's former campaign manager and City University of New York professor Stanley Aronowitz explained, Lane "wasn't an ordinary liberal. He was like Bernie Sanders . . . [always challenging] the received wisdom. . . . He was a lefty liberal."[1] In 1952 Lane opened a one-man law firm in the Puerto Rican enclave of East Harlem, where he gained a reputation as a tenants' rights activist and pro bono criminal defender whom residents called "the good Jew."[2] He defended gang members, took on the New York Department of Mental Hygiene over horrific conditions at its Wassaic hospital, and opened a heroin addiction clinic, the first in New York state, at a church in Harlem.

In 1960 Lane ran for and won a state assembly seat as a Reform Democrat, earning the endorsement of Eleanor Roosevelt, among others, while positioning himself as an "insurrectionist candidate" to the left of the Democratic Party. "Lane, whose extreme liberalism has made him a maverick [among Democrats]," wrote an Albany reporter, "never has been one of the boys here. . . . [He is] the lonesomest man in the capital."[3] In 1961 Lane attacked state Republican leader Joseph Carlino for serving on the board of a fallout shelter manufacturer while pushing for legislation requiring fallout shelters in New York schools. In doing so, he drew the ire of both parties, whose members, fearing conflict-of-interest investigations into their own affairs, exonerated Carlino 143 to 1.[4]

Soon, politically inspired anti-Lane headlines read, "Lane, Not Carlino, the One out on Limb" and "Colleagues Shun Carlino-Baiting Lane as Upstart."[5] Yet that was Lane: always the upstart, the pot-stirrer, the man who didn't do much as an assemblyman but who in 1961 flew to Jackson, Mississippi, with New York City NAACP head Percy Sutton to be arrested on purpose for refusing to leave a segregated bathroom.[6] Thus Lane, a Harlem lawyer and New York state assemblyman, was a Freedom Rider.

He had a "crusader's zeal," wrote an observer, and "his soft manner of speaking and horn-rimmed glasses belied the idealism... that earned him the labels 'firebrand' and 'Commie'... beyond the New York Assembly."[7] But it was in the New York Assembly where Lane was most dangerous. Not only had he attacked a powerful Republican leader whose fallout shelter project was, in turn, the pet project of New York governor Nelson Rockefeller, he'd attacked the assembly itself, questioning its no-show party jobs and its lack of ethics and oversight and calling his colleagues "a disgrace."[8]

Lane might have returned to Albany for a second term, had it not been for a racy, sadomasochistic sex photo of Lane taken by a former girlfriend and leaked to the press. The press didn't publish the photo, but in May 1962 Lane announced that he was quitting politics to make a "meaningful contribution" to the world by writing a book.[9] What that book was he didn't know, but when in November 1963 Lee Harvey Oswald shot and killed President John F. Kennedy in Dallas, Lane had his topic. He'd been watching the news, he said, when just three days after the murder he'd heard Dallas District Attorney Henry Wade say to a "moral certainty" that Oswald had committed the crime.

"At that point, I'd been a defense attorney in criminal cases for a decade," wrote Lane, and knew that cross-examination was "the heart and soul... of due process." But since Oswald himself had been murdered, there wouldn't be a process, and no one would examine Wade's claims.[10] Therefore, in December 1963, he published a 10,000-word "defense brief" in the progressive-liberal publication *National Guardian*. The article wasn't so much an "innocent until proven guilty" brief as a doggedly conspiratorial, "Oswald didn't do it" brief attacking the FBI.

Mark Lane, 1989. The circumstances surrounding Richardson's 1968 murder conviction drew the attention of the publicity-seeking activist and lawyer. Courtesy Tanman Films.

"This remarkable law enforcement and investigatory agency," he jabbed, "unable to solve a single one of more than forty Birmingham bombings, is now able to function as investigator, prosecutor, judge, and jury, ... [while its] verdict, deftly and covertly divulged to the press ... [is clear:] 'Oswald is the assassin. He acted alone.'"[11] However, evidence suggests that Oswald did act alone, contended former Charles Manson prosecutor Vincent Bugliosi in his voluminous 2007 work *Reclaiming History: The Assassination of President John F. Kennedy*. Bugliosi penned a remarkable 1,600 pages refuting virtually every conspiracy theory he could think of, and, in particular Mark Lane's. What with his *National Guardian* article, wrote Bugliosi, Lane fired "the first literary shot" of a movement, a conspiracy-theory movement that from that point forward gained tens of thousands of adherents and made Lane, an out-of-office though still very ambitious lawyer, a star.[12]

Lane "almost singlehandedly invented the lucrative JFK conspiracy industry," wrote Kennedy expert and *Dallas Morning News* reporter Hugh Aynesworth. Lane's early writings were "a publishing homerun" and "showed the way for hundreds of other buffs ... to advance their bogus claims, grab their fifteen minutes of notoriety, and also make a buck."[13]

And in telling his JFK assassination story, first to European progressive groups, then to college assemblies nationwide, Lane made some bucks. He charged speaking fees, sold pamphlets, and in 1966 published the book *Rush to Judgment,* which spent six months on the *New York Times* bestseller list, before starting a nonprofit assassination investigation committee in New York. Lane even represented the killer's mother, Marguerite Oswald, for a time, and in 1964 made $6,000 selling tickets to a Broadway discussion of hers titled "Did Lee Harvey Oswald Kill President Kennedy?"[14]

Yet Lane "was not one to be fastidious with data," wrote critic Bob Katz in 1979. "The glaring errors and extravagances in some of his statements cast unfortunate doubt on the rest of them. . . . But when the media wanted a spokesman on the issue—someone to refer to or just pillory—it was invariably Lane. He was brash, assertive, and, in his success, easy to portray as exploitive and greedy."[15] In 1968 Lane published a second Kennedy book, this one called *A Citizen's Dissent,* but when Americans moved on from the topic culturally, so did Lane. He reemerged as a semiserious vice-presidential candidate on the hippie-liberal 1968 Peace and Freedom Party ticket with noted Black comedian Dick Gregory.

The two men toured the country, speaking at anti–Vietnam War rallies and handing out fake dollar bills with Gregory's face and a peace sign on the front and the lines "Express your free choice" and "This country is redeemable" on the back. Then, in the run-up to November, Lane appeared on *The Tonight Show Starring Johnny Carson* and traveled with a photographer to the 1968 Democratic National Convention in Chicago, where he sought just the right photo as frenzied Chicago police bludgeoned demonstrators and shot teargas into the streets.

That's when columnist Garry Wills happened to see him. The air was filled with teargas, wrote Wills, and "young people came out of the thicker clouds, sneezing and gasping, with their faces mucus-smeared. . . . As the process went on, I heard a dry-eyed man say to a girl beside him, 'Get my picture with them.' He got in line, as if he were one of the victims just emerged from the ordeal."[16] The Democratic National Convention was in August 1968. In the coming months, Lane wrote a book on the subject, *Chicago Eyewitness,* then did a series of talks between Sacramento and Los Angeles.

He was staying at the Big Sur Inn in a cabin off California's Highway 1, where he found a year-old copy of *Newsweek* and the story of James Richardson. "I wasn't seeking another windmill," he wrote, but "for a reason I cannot define or explain, the charge [against Richardson] had a disquieting effect upon me, and I thought I should visit the area and look about."[17]

In November 1968, after yet another speaking engagement, this one at the University of South Florida in Tampa, Lane met with attorney John Robinson in Daytona Beach. The two men didn't know each other, but Robinson had read Lane's books and knew instinctively that the "éminence grise of Kennedy conspiracists" could only help with Richardson's case.[18] The condemned man had been sent to the maximum-security unit of the Florida State Prison in Raiford and had an appeal scheduled for 1970, so Robinson told Lane what he knew.

Robinson "was convinced that his client was innocent," recalled Lane, and that "the state's claim, repeated over and over, that James murdered his children for the proceeds of an insurance policy, was never established."[19] Lane read the trial transcript, then asked if he could visit Richardson at Raiford, north of Gainesville, where approximately sixty death row inmates, including a seventeen-year-old, lived in six-by-nine-foot cells in a separate block in the prison's maximum-security east wing, in desolate Bradford County, while the rest of the prison and its administration buildings known as the main wing were across a river in equally desolate Union County.

Both wings had fences topped with concertina wire as well as touch-sensitive pressure wires, and patrolling the ground between them were dogs—angry, man-killing dogs that not even the prison guards would touch. As one person put it, those animals were "nuttier than hell."[20] Richardson had a cot, a table, a window, a drinking fountain, and a toilet and got two, two-hour outdoor exercise periods per day. Not bad for Florida prison standards at the time, especially for a death row inmate. But down the hall just feet from Richardson was Q block, the east wing's windowless punishment section containing the "Death Room," which had seats on one side and Florida's famed electric chair, "Old Sparky," on the other.

That is what awaited Richardson: a wooden chair with thick leather straps, a black hood, and a *seven-minute* electrocution period in which the prison's executioner, who, by law, was the "chief electrician" of the Florida state prison system, would give the condemned man 2,400 volts and 500 amps for three minutes, pause for one, then give him 2,200 volts and 300 amps for three more minutes.[21] The prisoner could speak if he wanted to—most praised the Lord or begged forgiveness from their victims—though one in 1964 said simply, "Shoot the juice, Bruce."[22]

Authorities at Raiford abhorred having visitors, permitting inmates just a single short meeting a week with family, and visits from authors and members of the media were a no-go. Therefore, Robinson told Raiford officials that Lane was Richardson's attorney, his third co-counsel, and on Friday, November 29, 1968, the two traveled to the prison to meet Richardson. "We signed the registration book," wrote Lane, then were "ushered into . . . a room not far from death row." Richardson "was there, waiting for us. . . . He looked so much like [African American author] James Baldwin that I was struck by the resemblance. Medium height; dark-Black, close-cut hair; slight, with a head that appeared just a bit too large for the rest of him."[23]

Lane and Richardson exchanged pleasantries, then Richardson told Lane his story. Betsy Reese had agreed to watch the kids while the Richardsons were in the groves, he began. They'd filled fifteen boxes that day and had stopped to take a break, when the manager came running up to them. "Richardson! Richardson!" he yelled. "Hurry up! . . . Someone of your children are sick."[24] Their hearts racing, the startled parents jumped into the manager's truck, Annie Mae in the front seat and Richardson on the flatbed in back. As they raced into Arcadia and came to the hospital, they saw Betsy Reese just "standing there looking scared," like "she was going to run." That's when Richardson asked her what happened. "I don't know," she replied, nervously. "Go inside and they'll tell you."

Next came Minister Fagan, then Hays and Cline, then a white nurse, who nearly broke the stunned father by telling him that one of his girls had sobbed, "I want to go home with my mom and dad" before "she laid down and died." With Lane and Robinson sitting quietly, Richardson started to weep. He then stared at the ceiling and moaned, "Oh, Lord, oh Lord, if only you knew, if only you knew what they meant to me!" He blubbered uncontrollably for the next fifteen minutes, until Lane said firmly, "Listen, Mr. Richardson. I am here because I think I can help you, but if you don't stop crying and if you don't continue to tell me what happened that day . . . I won't be able to."[25]

Thus began lawyer-author-provocateur Mark Lane's first early involvement in the Richardson case. The grieving father told Lane his story, and for the next eight months Lane made several long trips to Florida in which he interviewed at least twenty people and toured Arcadia. This was still Lane, though. He jetted out periodically for Kennedy lectures and in February 1969 sat with the prosecution at the bizarre show trial of New Orleans businessman Clay Shaw.[26]

Shaw had been brought up on pie-in-the-sky conspiracy charges by a publicity-seeking New Orleans district attorney named Jim Garrison, who claimed with virtually no evidence that Shaw had conspired with Lee Harvey Oswald and anti-Castro Cuban activists to kill Kennedy. The jury took just fifty-four minutes to acquit Shaw, but the trial formed the basis of the 1991 Oliver Stone film *JFK*.

That same month, Lane made his first public statement regarding Richardson in the "Forum" section of *Playboy*, which was, in those days, a kind of discussion board for issues and events. "In the firm belief that the deprivation of one man's civil liberties is an affront to us all," he began, "I am writing... to bring public attention to the largely unheeded plight of James Richardson, a Southern Negro."[27]

Richardson had been railroaded by a deceitful sheriff and an overzealous district attorney, insisted Lane, and together they had created what Lane called a "lynch atmosphere" that had riled the all-white jury and sent a good man to death row. He was convinced, he wrote, that Richardson was innocent and "that his innocence is demonstrable beyond any doubt." Now Lane was writing a book about it, asking Florida Governor Claude Kirk and the Florida Supreme Court to reopen the case and doing all he could to help.[28]

In June 1968, shortly after Richardson's conviction, Robinson filed a forty-four-point motion for a retrial that Judge Justice denied. The next step was the Florida Supreme Court, which planned to hear the case in the summer of 1970. That gave Lane time to write his book, which the New York press Holt, Rinehart, and Winston published just before the ruling for maximum effect.

Titled *Arcadia*, Lane's book came out in March 1970 and was, compared to his earlier books, a dud, both sales-wise and in the press. Two-hundred-and-eighty-pages long, more than half of it an annotated and selectively chosen trial transcript, *Arcadia* just wasn't any good. Reviewers called it "sloppy," "unfocused," "variable in its readability," and a "panache of trial tapes and interviews" instead of original text.[29]

The proofreading, critics noted, was horrific. Lane wrote DeSoto as De

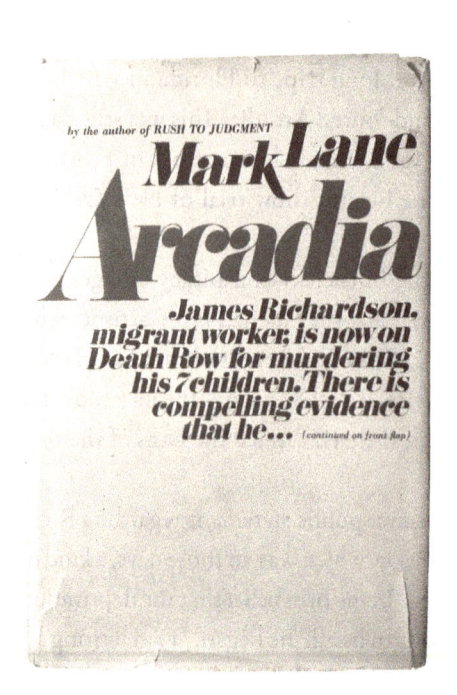

Cover of Mark Lane's 1970 book, *Arcadia*. In his book on the James Richardson case, Lane criticized the town for racism and insisted that babysitter Betsy Reese, and not Richardson, poisoned Richardson's seven children.

Soto, with a space in the middle, misspelled the names Hays, Faison, and Fisher, and in several places confused Richardson with Robinson. "If Lane's [first] book was a *Rush to Judgment*," wrote syndicated "World of Books" reviewer Marion Pinsdorf, then *Arcadia* "is a rush to print with all the roughness ... [and] poor proofreading which that produces. Perhaps Lane will focus more attention on Richardson's case and cause a re-examination. However, Richardson would have been better served by a better book."[30]

Tampa Tribune critic David Clement went even further, suggesting that while Lane was probably right—that the evidence against Richardson had been scant and circumstantial—it was too bad that Lane and not, say, the trusted activist Ralph Nader, had written it.[31] The fact is, people didn't believe Lane. He was the king of manufactured controversies, and though observers knew something was wrong with the Richardson case, Lane wasn't the best person to tell it.

As *Mother Jones* writer Bob Katz observed,

> [Lane] had a style as distinct as a fingerprint on a police blotter: leap like a tiger at a hunch or a tip, call a press conference, make dramatic charges

to illustrate that the issue—be it nuclear proliferation, assassination cover-up or dishonesty in the media—boils down to nothing less than an age-old tussle betwixt good and evil. Then crank up an investigation, borrow and magnify other people's evidence, and, finally, never let up so long as there is a virgin ear unassailed by the accusations.[32]

However, as far as Richardson went, Lane's *Arcadia* thesis wasn't wrong. Seemingly thrilled by the press attention, Cline had raced ahead of Schaub in claiming he had enough evidence to arrest Richardson. When Schaub disagreed and at first refused to charge the father, Cline turned to fellow Arcadian Gordon Hays and his coroner's jury to issue a charge of murder. At that point, Schaub had to take the case because, as Lane alleged, he risked appearing soft on crime if he didn't, but the bulldog prosecutor couldn't put Purvis or Reese on the stand, Purvis because Richardson didn't have insurance and he could prove it and Reese because she may have committed the crime. In *Arcadia,* Lane actually interviewed Reese, calling unannounced at her new home in Nocatee, the site of the Gulf Naval Stores factory just south of Arcadia in DeSoto County. He wrote,

> I stopped at the post office there and inquired about her. The old man behind the counter said, "I don't know where she lives. She's a n****r lady." I asked how I might go about finding her. "Oh, just ask any of them burr heads." I said, "Excuse me?" He laughed and said, "I mean n****rs. They all stick together. Ask any of them where so-and-so lives, and they say they don't know. But tell them you got a check, and they tell you exactly how to get there."[33]

With that, Lane drove to the area's small Black district, where a man directed him to Reese's home. She wasn't there, but in time a woman in dungarees approached and Lane introduced himself. Reese was "huge," he remembered, and at first he thought she was a man. She didn't want to talk, but as Lane theorized, "uneducated negroes" in DeSoto County did "not ask whites, even offensive ones, to leave their homes," so she let him in.[34]

Standing in Reese's house, Lane asked her about Cline, about his relationship with her daughter, and about how she and Charlie Smith had found the bag. Reese didn't say much, being wary of the strange white man who'd just appeared at her doorstep, but when asked about the day the children died, she answered,

> They were in the yard in the morning. Some were in school, some was playing round the house. The older girl, I forget her name, asked me to divide the rice. I go in the kitchen and fix the food for them.... [No,] I didn't fix the food. That was wrong. I divide it up in seven parts. Then I left before they ate. I just get right out of there before they eat.[35]

That's when Lane asked about the smell. How could she serve the food if it reeked of parathion? "I just ... didn't smell it," she replied. "That's all. I don't have to say no more. I talked to the sheriff and the lawyers for the state and I don't have to say no more except I didn't smell nothing."[36]

Back in Arcadia, Lane's investigation turned up no new evidence, at least no credible evidence, nothing that would have freed Richardson or resulted in a new trial. He did find a convicted moonshiner and chronic check kiter named Robert Stancel, who claimed that fellow former inmate Spot Weaver had lied. They'd served time together at the Manatee County jail, where Stancel said Weaver had admitted, "James didn't do the killing." He said Cline told Weaver what to say and what not to say at trial.[37]

But Stancel wasn't credible, for not only was he a felon who'd been in Raiford, he'd also been given immunity by the state to cover any and all crimes committed before August 1968 in exchange for testimony against Henry Trafficante, the brother of Tampa mafia don Santo Trafficante Jr. Stancel claimed that Trafficante "had made him a narcotics traffic offer," but the man he pointed to under oath differed physically from the man he told authorities about.[38]

Lane's other new witness was a Daytona Beach resident named Bobby Woods, whom Robinson had inexplicably subpoenaed as a character witness for Richardson. Woods traveled to Fort Myers, where Robinson learned he hardly knew Richardson at all. Why Woods came is a mystery, but Woods insisted he had met Spot Weaver while applying for travel expenses at the courthouse where Weaver, a complete stranger, had told him that both he and fellow snitch Earnell Washington had lied. It just wasn't believable, Weaver admitting to perjury to a man he didn't know. Perjury was a felony.

But then came the kicker, a scene oddly reminiscent of—and perhaps even drawn from—the 1967 racially charged murder-mystery *In the Heat of the Night*. Woods, Lane wrote, had driven back to Daytona through Arcadia. He hadn't testified and hadn't played a role in the case; indeed, no one knew who he was. But outside the city limits, declared Woods, "a red car filled with white men came charging up on me . . . [and] forced me off the road and into a ditch. I got back onto the road, sped up, and just did get away."[39]

Perhaps Lane's most telling interviews were with Arcadia police lieutenant Joseph Minoughan and Minoughan's boss, Chief Richard Barnard. The two men ran a tiny municipal police department, which was separate from the DeSoto County Sheriff's Office. Their jurisdictions overlapped, with Cline handling all felonies in the county, including those in the city, which is why Cline, and not Barnard or Minoughan, investigated the Richardson case. Still, Minoughan had been the first officer on the scene, both at the house and at the hospital, and he and Barnard had interviewed Betsy Reese.

"Reese told me she warmed up the food," explained Barnard, and that she'd "prepared it and dished it out to the kids."[40] Therefore, he contended that "if there was going to be any case at all, she would be the most important witness."[41] But Cline "kept us out of the investigation. I don't mean . . . [he] was trying hide something" or cover anything up. He just wanted to "keep the publicity to himself."[42]

Barnard then scoffed at Cline's award, a framed meritorious service citation that the pulpy true-crime magazine *Official Detective* gave to the DeSoto County Sheriff's Office for its work on the Richardson case. Cline was proud of it, so proud, in fact, that he allowed Lane to take a picture of him holding it, though *Official Detective* pitched real-life stories as dark erotica and featured headlines that read, "Nervy Rape Victim Fingers a Killer!" and "Sex Crime with a Happy Ending!" Barnard thought it ridiculous.

"That's a great award," he scoffed. "One day I opened a big envelope in the mail addressed to me and discovered that I had one too—for my work on the Richardson case. Can you believe that? There it is, right there. An award for me, and I don't even think there is a case."[43]

EIGHT

A FLORIDA ENIGMA

As expected, Lane's depiction of Cline was a doozy, with Lane seeming to portray the sheriff as part Eugene "Bull" Conner and part Barney Fife. For it's in Lane's interview with Cline that the activist-lawyer quoted the sheriff as saying, "Well, we don't have the problems here, I mean with the colored, that you have in the big cities.... What we have is control. We just control the situation."[1] On that point, Cline sounded like Conner, the infamous commissioner of public safety in Birmingham, Alabama, who'd once used police dogs and fire hoses on peaceful Black children.

At other times, though, Cline seemed like Barney Fife, the fictional deputy-doofus from TV's *Andy Griffith Show*, because, in spite of ostensibly solving the Richardson case and appearing in the press, in 1968 Cline had been reelected sheriff by just eighty votes, a full sixty votes fewer than last time. In 1969 Cline broke his foot playing prisoner in a simulated jail escape but, as Lane remarked, ineptly allowed an inmate to dig his way out of lockup with a spoon.[2] He was, as Lane described him, both devious and simple, a small-town lawman bigoted toward Blacks, who delighted in showing Lane his German shepherd "ketch dog" and his huge collection of guns.[3]

But what angered white Arcadians wasn't Lane's depiction of Cline per se, but his achromatic and unforgiving portrait of the town. They hated it, and no one hated it more than the *Arcadian* editor Bill Hackney. A native of Washington, North Carolina, Hackney was a decorated navigator in a B-24 bombardment group during World War II, before graduating with a journalism degree from the University of North Carolina at Chapel Hill and entering the newspaper business.

In 1952 he bought the *Sun Herald,* a weekly paper in Winter Park, Florida, near Orlando, and sold it before purchasing the *Arcadian* in 1964. He wasn't a native but was active in local politics and civic organizations, and he had a vested business interest in defending Arcadia. When Lane wrote his letter to *Playboy,* for example, Hackney pilloried the lawyer, author, and activist for his "non-concern with the facts" and for failing to tell *Playboy* that Richardson "could have been led to believe" he had insurance.[4]

Then, as if to bolster his point, Hackney reprinted a year-old syndicated column by a right-wing Methodist minister named Donald Wildmon, who in that week's missive just happened to mention *Playboy*. Wildmon opined, "If a fellow is reading *Playboy* he is sophisticated. But, if what he is reading is just a two-bit girlie book, he is crude and coarse. Really, I can't see where lust is any better if it is dressed up a little or just in a cheap form. And I don't think the Creator does, either."[5]

When Lane's book came out, Hackney went into overdrive, printing a long personal rebuttal plus scathing reviews of *Arcadia* by the *Sarasota Herald-Tribune* and the Fort Worth *Star-Telegram*. He then shared a letter that former Arcadia resident and prominent Florida clothing merchant Nat Schlossberg had written to the *Daytona Beach News-Journal*.

Schlossberg, who lived in Daytona Beach but still owned a store in Arcadia, had been angered by a *News-Journal* editorial that praised Lane's book as "a compelling... account" of the "heroic effort of Daytona Beach lawyer John Spencer Robinson to thwart the [attempts] of a reactionary community... to treat Richardson as a 'n****r.'"[6] It was dramatic stuff and prompted Schlossberg to respond.

> Dear Sunday Editor, Your editorial... was quite offensive to me. I was reared in Arcadia and received my grammar and high school education there. Since 1942, I have been making trips there twice a month to operate a business. With this background, I feel I know more about the people of Arcadia than you or the author quoted. I have not heard Black people in Arcadia called "n****r" since I was a child.... [The editorial includes] several "quotes" from this book that I disagree with. The people of Arcadia had nothing to do with the outcome of the trial. This was determined by a court of law with a jury in Fort Myers. In Arcadia, I have seen no racism in many years. In fact, integration in schools

works much better than in most cities much larger in size.... Arcadia is not as you pictured it in your editorial.[7]

Schlossberg was at least partially right. School integration had gone better in Arcadia than in many Florida cities, including, most notably, St. Petersburg, where a year earlier Black and white students had rioted.[8]

Yet Arcadia had issues, even if Schlossberg didn't see them. There were frequent cross burnings in Arcadia, including three in May 1970 alone.[9] In spite of the 1964 Civil Rights Act, which made discrimination in restaurants illegal, Black Arcadia residents still didn't eat in restaurants where white residents did. Lane, in his investigation, even asked William Burton, the local head of the NAACP, about it.

"I'll give it to you like this," explained Burton. Arcadia's "not fully integrated but we [African Americans] aren't putting forth no efforts to make it integrated. Arcadia is not so big a place. It could be integrated overnight.... [But] I don't try to force my people to go no farther than they want to go."[10] When asked if African Americans were employed at downtown businesses, say, at the DeSoto National Bank or at clothing stores like Schlossberg's, Burton replied, "Well, not as cashiers or bookkeepers, if that's what you mean, but several places have them as janitors."[11]

Roosevelt Johnson, an African American educator who came to Arcadia in 1967, was at first the lone Black teacher at the town's mostly white Memorial Elementary School. The reason was that as DeSoto County integrated, he, like every other Black teacher, had to transition out of Smith-Brown School because so few white students would go there that it failed to meet federal desegregation regulations and therefore had to close.[12]

Its students and teachers trickled out to new schools between 1967 and 1969 before Smith-Brown shut its doors in 1970. "I don't exactly know why I was chosen," said Johnson, who later earned his doctorate in education, "but that first day I had several parents ... [who] talked to me about their daughters and concerns that they had," and later, two of those parents withdrew their students from the school. "There was no reason given at the time," explained Johnson. "I assumed ... it was because I was a Black teacher and this was their first experience [with one]."[13]

The kids liked Johnson but struggled at times with the difficult racial implications of having a Black teacher in what had been a whites-only school. Johnson recalled how once, without a drop of rancor, a first-grade boy asked him if he was a n****r. Startled but not angry, Johnson inquired why the boy would ask that. The boy said he'd been telling his father how much he liked Johnson, and the father replied, brusquely, that if the boy liked a Black man so much, then he must be a "n****r lover." The boy just didn't understand. He'd been taught that n****rs were bad, that being Black was bad, but Mr. Johnson was nice.

"I see students . . . that way all the time," said Johnson. "They look at me and they talk to me and they don't see me as Black. . . . They only see me as Black . . . when their parents tell them [I'm Black]." The problem, Johnson believed, was that whites in Arcadia were pressured to hate African Americans at an early age. Not all were, of course, but "once you're reared a certain way," he explained, "no matter how hard you attempt to get away from it, deep within it's there. It may not surface always, but . . . it's there."[14]

The family of Marcille Wallis, the white daughter of a DeSoto grove manager, moved to a house in Arcadia, near the Quarters, in the early 1960s. In a 2022 interview, Wallis explained,

> I'd never heard the N-word at home. Maybe I was sheltered, but my parents never used it, and my mother got angry at anyone who did. But when we moved into that house, I heard a neighbor girl call someone a "n****r." I asked her, "What's that?" And she said "Black people are n****rs. Your nanny is a n****r." I was floored. I assumed a n****r was a bad thing. I didn't know. But Ms. Mae, a n****r? I ran home in tears and told my mother what the girl had said. She was angry, not at me, but at Arcadia in general. She said, "We do not say that word in this house."[15]

As a ninth grader at DeSoto High School, Wallis experienced the first, somewhat disruptive days of integration. Wallis remembered a fight in her gym class in which a white country girl from Nocatee with a penchant for fighting suddenly attacked a Black classmate. "I don't think they really even knew each other," Wallis said. "And if they did, the Black girl hadn't done anything wrong. But the white girl was in a rage. That's when I remember thinking, 'How can someone dislike another person *that* much?' I've never disliked someone that much in my entire life."[16]

In April 1970 the fighting at DeSoto High School nearly spun out of control when a tiff between Black and white students spilled onto an adjacent street and attracted about a hundred students. Before a riot could erupt, Arcadia police and DeSoto sheriff's deputies herded the crowd back into the high school, but the intensity of the event left school superintendent Charles Weaver shaken. "It was bad," he admitted. "You're sitting on a powder keg all the time, walking on egg shells. It might break again five minutes from now. You don't really know [what'll happen next]."[17]

What happened next was a March 1971 boycott, in which DeSoto's African American students vowed to stay out of county schools until the school board sent an additional bus to the Quarters. As it stood, the Black community's lone school bus had a maximum capacity of 66 students. But each day, as many as 120 to 140 students were stuffed on board. "This creates a hazard to the lives of our children," said Eugene Hickson, who would soon declare his candidacy for a seat on Arcadia's city council. Until the overcrowding was fixed, he said, "we will continue to keep our children out of school."[18]

Although unconfirmed, Hickson reported, too, that on rural routes, white bus drivers would purposely ignore lone Black children standing on the side of the road.[19] The unfairness of the thing was infuriating, but before Hickson could press for even more demands—that, for example, DeSoto schools hire more Black cooks or more Black bus drivers—the superintendent sent additional buses to the Quarters. The boycott, which lasted two days and involved some 600 of DeSoto's 725 Black students, made headlines in several regional newspapers.[20]

According to Reverend C. S. Felder, whom Lane in his haste called Reverend C. S. "Elder," there were problems with racism, both in Arcadia and in its schools, but over the previous few years there'd been "some improvement." That remark seemed lost on Lane, who depicted the town as existing in a kind of antebellum stasis in which rich white folks lived in "gracious ... pillared homes" canopied by "huge live oaks" with Spanish moss swaying "gently in the southern breeze." Meanwhile, younger white Arcadians played tennis on "clean, white, municipal courts," while white retirees played "shuffleboard in the sun."[21]

It sounded idyllic, almost *Stepford* in its simplicity, but Lane's white Arcadia stood in marked contrast to what he dubbed the "degeneracy" of the Quarters. What Lane missed, however, was that almost all of Arcadia was poor, not just the Quarters. In 1977 *Tampa Times* travel writer Karen Lachenauer observed that in Arcadia "the other side of the tracks" was in actuality "both sides of the tracks," and that even the town's mansions were crumbling.[22]

Indeed, while the cities of Southwest Florida boomed during the 1960s, tiny Arcadia did not. Between 1960 and 1970, nearby Fort Myers grew 21.4 percent, Punta Gorda 22.9 percent, and Sarasota 18.1 percent, but over that same period, Arcadia shrank by nearly 4 percent, from 5,889 residents to 5,658. DeSoto County grew by almost 12 percent, to 13,060, but even that increase paled in comparison to the explosive growth of the coast, where the population of Lee County, for example, jumped 92.9 percent, to 105,216; Charlotte 118.8 percent, to 27,559; and Collier a white-hot 141.5 percent, to 38,040.

Most of the move-ins were northerners, often retirees drawn to planned communities like Cape Coral, Port Charlotte, North Port, and Lehigh Acres that for easy-to-pay installments offered 80' x 125' homesites and a piece of the Florida dream. By 1970, Lee, Collier, Charlotte, and Sarasota Counties each had a surfeit of homesites; there were a half million of them, most empty, with bridges and roads and boulevards leading to nowhere.

"The scary thing is that there are enough platted lots to move the entire state of Nebraska here tomorrow," said Charlotte County planning director Terry Hixson in 1982. "We never know from day to day when the next permits will be taken out. We build a new school and a year after it's opened, it's overcrowded."[23] By contrast, inland DeSoto County had no big housing developments. People wanted to live near the water, and Arcadia was some fifty mostly desolate miles from the nearest white sand beach. Plus, roads to and from the beach were treacherous, State Roads 70 and 72, toward Bradenton and Sarasota, and US Route 17 toward Punta Gorda.

By all accounts, US 17 was the worst. It ran north and south along the Peace River to Arcadia, then into rural Hardee County and on into Florida's orange country, where in 1977 the accident rate was eight times the state average.[24] "It's one of the most dangerous roads in Florida," explained the head of the Hardee County Farm Bureau, whose members begged the state for years to have the only major north-south thoroughfare in DeSoto and Hardee Counties widened from two lanes to four.[25]

Those counties depend on US 17, wrote a *Tampa Tribune* reporter. "Northerners who winter at trailer parks have no choice but to use it when they arrive, depart, and go shopping, . . . [and] citrus trucks use it to reach processing plants in Polk County. Whether it's recreational vehicles or tractor trailers, all wide vehicles have trouble with the steady stream of undivided traffic."[26] If a semi truck or a school bus stopped to take a left turn at rush hour, the line of cars could be a mile long. During orange season, slow-moving farm tractors hauling trailers laden with fruit drove in convoys, often bringing traffic to a standstill. Cars darted in and out and tried to pass on 17, where there were so many gruesome wrecks through the years locals called it the "killer highway."[27]

There were fatal wrecks on 17 north and south of Arcadia, within, say, twenty miles of the city, on at least eight different occasions between 1960 and 1970. Another, in 1975, was the most gruesome wreck of all, when a car driven by an eighteen-year-old crossed the center line and hit a car containing an Arcadia family head-on. Six perished, including the drivers of both cars, and the family's five-year-old son was the only person to survive.[28] Truck drivers avoided 17 if they could—"it's two-laned and there's no place to go if you're in trouble," explained one—and tourists did as well.

When driving from Orlando to Sarasota and the beach, for example, northern visitors would instead take Interstate 4 into Tampa, then go south on the Tamiami Trail.[29] "Tourists stay away from the area because it's a bottleneck," said one local leader in the 1980s. "And when tourists won't come, neither will nationally franchised motels or restaurants."[30] The solution was to be on or near Interstate 75, which had been completed, for the most part, from the border of Georgia to Tampa by 1970.

However, through the 1960s, the section below Tampa, which would traverse Southwest Florida and follow the coast, was under review. Where would it go? Which counties and towns would be lucky enough to have it? For years, even before there was an I-75, elected officials and businessmen in DeSoto, Glades, and Hendry Counties had been asking for an inland route, a federal highway designation that would move traffic from the southern end of the Sunshine Skyway Bridge, near Bradenton, through Arcadia, LaBelle, and Immokalee before crossing the Everglades at Carnestown, east of Naples. Based in part on existing routes, the plan wasn't workable.

Tourists were going to the coast, not to ranches, so papers like the *Fort Myers News-Press* scoffed. "The desire of inland towns like Arcadia, LaBelle, and Immokalee to share in some of the tourist traffic which they see cities along the Tamiami Trail enjoying is a natural one," opined an editor at the paper in 1954. "But if they're not located on a tourist route then they're not, and no federal highway number that might be given to the roads that reach them can change the geography."[31]

In 1969 the Florida road department proposed for I-75 a series of coastal routes, the most eastern of which (and the one that eventually won) ran twenty-five miles to the south and west of Arcadia. Although not in DeSoto County, the interstate's closest two exits would in time increase traffic to the interior, but large housing developments, the kind that brought thousands of new residents and millions in tax revenue to neighboring counties, failed to materialize.

Southwest Florida grew and grew and grew, joining other places in the Sun Belt, but rural DeSoto County stayed insular and poor. It wasn't until 1984 that for the first time ever the county ordered that people living on rural routes have house numbers and street addresses for their homes. Most had a route number and a mailbox, good enough for the post office, but bad for emergency workers who had no idea how to get to their property. "If somebody tells you to turn at the first road past the Johnsons," said one deputy, "and you don't know where the Johnsons live, you're in trouble."[32]

The truth is, even before the Richardson case, observant journalists like Rosemary Farley of the *New York Times* viewed Arcadia as a "Florida enigma," a place that in spite of the state's post–World War II population boom had changed hardly at all. "There are families there," she marveled in 1960, "who, for five generations, have never set foot outside of DeSoto County."[33] It seemed impossible that Arcadia could be this way, but twenty-two years later, after Florida had added another 5.5 million people, the equivalent of Delaware and Wisconsin combined, a *Fort Myers News-Press* reporter wrote, "It's almost as though the little community of Arcadia has been hidden in an attic somewhere. It's past preserved like an old prom corsage, it offers a . . . glimpse of the old South. Old buildings, towering trees . . . [and] slow-talking folks who are openly apprehensive of strangers."[34]

There was a point, though, when Arcadia and DeSoto County could have changed. In late 1971 a deep-pocketed land development company from Punta Gorda, Punta Gorda Isles Inc. (PGI), bought the 52,000-acre Montgomery Ranch in far eastern Charlotte and DeSoto Counties and southern Highlands County for $15.5 million.[35] PGI planned to develop the Charlotte and DeSoto County portions of the ranch into a community called Deer Run, but for that it needed the permission of both county commissions, Charlotte for the platting of lots in a single 16,000-acre section, DeSoto for lots in three sections totaling 31,000 acres. It was a massive undertaking, a two-county planned community of 70,000 people.

But PGI had to hurry because in July 1973, Florida's new Environmental Land and Water Management Act took effect, requiring any large development affecting more than just one county to submit reports regarding its impact. Water, sewer, housing, transportation, environment—the reports were time-consuming and costly, but what PGI feared was that one of the state's new regional planning councils, which the act empowered, would nix the project altogether unless it platted the development before July 1973.

Therefore, PGI submitted its Charlotte plats to the Charlotte County Board of Commissioners on June 19, 1973, then its DeSoto plats to the DeSoto County Board of Commissioners a week later. Charlotte said yes, for it was so pro-growth that commissioners there allowed a member of the county's own zoning board, who at the same time worked for PGI, to make the presentation.[36] DeSoto commissioners, however, said, uh, maybe. Fearing a quick influx of outsiders and increased expenditures for schools and other infrastructure, they wanted to study the project before proceeding.[37]

The DeSoto commissioners weren't being intransigent, just careful. But they missed the July deadline and wouldn't approve the plats until September. Then, it took nearly a year for the state's regional planning council to review the project, which it rejected for being premature. With 150,000 lots in Charlotte County still empty, why did Deer Run need even more? It didn't, but DeSoto County officials had done the math. They'd seen the dollar signs and knew that by 1994, Deer Run would involve more than $500 million in investments and jobs for 13,000 people.[38] While the average DeSoto County resident might have loathed change, most saw the Deer Run opportunity as too good to miss.

"Look, all you have is one road leading east to west in that end of the county," explained one resident. "This development could mean a whole lot of industry, jobs, new people, and money coming into the county. I'm all for it, and any grocer, repairman, the telephone company, or commercial businessman would be a fool to say that they are not welcome."[39] The question was who'd pay for the infrastructure. DeSoto couldn't; it lacked the resources. So in 1974 the DeSoto County commission jumped at the chance, through the auspices of the state legislature, at creating the Deer Run Improvement District, similar to Disney's Reedy Creek Improvement District, in effect, an independent municipal government responsible for making capital improvements and issuing bonds.[40] Thus, Deer Run wouldn't cost DeSoto or Charlotte County anything.

It was a win-win, development-wise, but by delaying the Deer Run plats in 1973, DeSoto County commissioners had waited too long. The economy went south. In 1973–1974, there was a world oil crisis and a stock market crash; home sales slowed, and in Florida, several big community builders went bankrupt. Somehow, PGI hung on, but in 1975 it sold the Highlands portion of the ranch, then shelved the Deer Run project altogether.[41] For DeSoto, it was a woulda, coulda, shoulda kind of thing, a missed opportunity that would haunt the county for decades. It needed the work, and tens of thousands of new residents would have ended its rural isolation. In 1971 the county lost both the Gulf Naval Stores factory in Nocatee, which closed unexpectedly and threw two hundred people out of work, as well as the Seaboard Coast Line passenger train, which ran daily from Lakeland to Arcadia to Naples.[42]

However, for Arcadia's town boosters at least, there was some good news; in April 1971, in an unsigned but unanimous decision, the Florida Supreme Court upheld James Richardson's murder conviction, refusing to reverse the lower court's ruling or to grant Richardson a new trial. By then, Lane was long gone. He still gave his Kennedy talks but veered sharply into the anti-Vietnam War movement, for which he wrote a book, before representing and touring with the famed activist and actress Jane Fonda. But that was Lane, the lawyer-turned-pamphleteer who would, through the 1970s, defend members of the radical activist American Indian Movement and represent both Jim Jones of Jonestown fame and Martin Luther King assassin James Earl Ray. Yet Lane wouldn't forget Richardson; he and Robinson corresponded frequently with the convicted man who maintained his innocence, but without new and compelling evidence, there was little Lane could do. His book had flopped, so there would be no "Free James Richardson" movement, no celebrity-led protests or nonprofits formed to get Richardson out of prison.

The convicted man stewed, spending the first nine years of his imprisonment in a cell alone. He entered the prison's general population eventually and had his sentence commuted to life when in 1972 the US Supreme Court ruled that, as administered, death sentences violated the Eighth Amendment as cruel and unusual punishment. Richardson preached, learned to read, and sang in the prison choir with convicted murderer and jewel thief Jack "Murph the Surf" Murphy, who'd once stolen the "Star of India" sapphire from a museum in New York.

In 1977 the *Tampa Tribune* reported that Richardson had gone somewhat kooky; his sermons were unintelligible and prisoners laughed, but no one fought or molested the man, nor was he attacked by what he called "homosessions." He dreamed of getting out and starting a church. Just not in Arcadia. "There ain't no way," he said. "I don't know why people [there] treat me like they did. I wants to hate them for what they did to me. I wants to hate them for that.... [But] that's all in the past... [even if] I can't forget."[43]

Meanwhile, tiny Arcadia stayed poor and agricultural. The average annual household income in DeSoto County ($14,387) was $5,000 to $6,000 less in 1979 than that of neighboring counties Sarasota ($19,152), Charlotte ($20,271), and Lee ($19,397). For what few jobs it did have, Arcadia struggled to find skilled workers, and teacher turnover there sometimes hit 17 percent, among the highest rates in the state. "I'm single and I'm in my early twenties," said special needs teacher Cheryl Beverly, "and this is a very small city and there's not much recreation for me.... I want to go back to college and there's no place to go here, and the pay is very low."[44]

Few Arcadia residents went to college. For the class of 1982, the Florida Department of Education reported that just 15.3 percent of graduating seniors in DeSoto County went on to two- and four-year colleges, which made it dead last among sixty-seven counties in the state. DeSoto school officials refuted the department's claims, insisting the correct figure was 30 percent, better but still far below urban counties such as Broward (59 percent) and Dade (60 percent).⁴⁵

As usual, Arcadia's economic development was almost nonexistent, though in 1981 the Tampa-based citrus conglomerate American Agronomics announced it was moving its headquarters there, and in 1982, the Miami-based General Development Corporation, which had built the sprawling communities of North Port and Port Charlotte, among others, declared that it wanted some 8,000 acres in southwest DeSoto County rezoned from agricultural use to planned-unit development in order to build some 17,000 homes.

However, in January 1982, after a single cold night, American Agronomics lost $20 million in fruit and thus scuttled its plans, while the General Development Corporation's Villages of DeSoto never materialized.⁴⁶ "I'm sure . . . [those two projects would] have used quite a bit of local labor," bemoaned DeSoto Chamber of Commerce president George Lane Jr. "It would've been nice to have those jobs, and . . . [that] construction money would've been spent right here in DeSoto County."⁴⁷

At least DeSoto County wasn't losing jobs, due in part to its mega-employer G. Pierce Wood, the mental hospital, though news reports warned that the state, in moving to deinstitutionalize mental patients, could close the facility at any time. G. Pierce Wood had a $20 million budget, which included a badly needed $14.5 million annual payroll, but was a constant source of bad news, sometimes even ugly news, that served to stigmatize Arcadia in the press. In 1979–1980, for instance, the facility's patient death rate, 167 out of 1,103, was 300 percent higher than at Florida's flagship mental institution at Chattahoochee. The *Orlando Sentinel* reported, "In raw numbers, Arcadia had more than twice as many deaths as Chattahoochee though only half the population. On the average, one patient dies every other day at Arcadia."⁴⁸

It wasn't the town's fault, as G. Pierce Wood was a state facility run by the Department of Health and Rehabilitative Services, but the stories there were horrific. In 1979, three eighteen-year-old male patients and a fourteen-year-old female patient escaped the open-grounds facility and went on a home-invasion spree. At a house nearby, they found several rifles and a pistol, killed a cow, and shot at passing airplanes before giving up.⁴⁹ Four months later, a thirty-one-year-old female patient escaped, then committed suicide by jumping under a semi truck, and in 1983, a DeSoto County sheriff's deputy investigating an accidental choking death at the facility was knocked unconscious by a patient and nearly killed at the facility's behavior modification ward.[50]

"I'm not callous or cavalier about this," a G. Pierce Wood administrator said in 1995, but "these kinds of things happen at all psychiatric hospitals. . . . When you put [that many] people in one place, all of whom are declared to be a danger to themselves or others, things are going to happen."[51] The same could be said for the DeSoto Correctional Institution (DCI), Arcadia's other big employer. DCI had space for maybe 560 men, but housed in its cramped, aging, air conditioned-less dormitories were upward of 740 men, who in July 1981 rioted. There wasn't a clear reason, officials said, but on duty that night were just nineteen guards. "If you have a lack of correctional officers," explained first-degree murderer and DCI inmate Donald Halpin, then the prisoners "are going to run rampant. . . . [DCI staffing] is a joke."[52] As Halpin could attest, there were fights, assaults, rapes, robberies, murders, and sometimes even escapes, a startling seven between 1975 and 1985. Residents came to expect them.

"When we hear of a prisoner escaping," explained an eighty-year-old grandmother named Marguerite Dow, "we have to keep our windows closed and our doors locked. But I have a gun and if they walk in, they might not walk out. I'm not afraid to use it."[53] For Arcadians, the payoff was the payroll: $4.5 million in 1982 for 242 employees. And some of the short-term prisoners did community service such as building a children's wing at the Arcadia library, helping to maintain the rodeo arena, and mowing lawns at G. Pierce Wood. The prison really "helps balance agriculture and other businesses' ups and downs," said one resident. "You can count on it just like sunshine."[54] Tell that to the prison's correctional officers, who in the late 1970s made as a starting salary just $8,600 a year, which meant they could file for food stamps if they had a spouse and two children.

All that for working in a barracks-like facility in which 60 percent of inmates who lived in dormitories, not cells, and who could walk the premises freely, were serving time for violent crimes.[55] Naturally, turnover was high; in 1979 the state prison at Raiford reported a beginning-guard replacement rate of 92 percent and a prison in Hillsborough County 93 percent.[56] The reason, apart from low pay and dangerous working conditions, was that law enforcement jobs paid more, about $2,000 more annually, so correctional officers who qualified left when positions came open.[57] But, for hardworking Arcadia residents like Clifford Ray, a white, married father of four who didn't have a high school diploma, there wasn't much else he could do. He needed the work because his three young boys, Ricky, Robert, and Randy, were not only HIV-positive but stricken with hemophilia.

NINE

FACTOR VIII

A genetic disorder in which a person's blood lacks the necessary plasma proteins with which to clot, in the 1980s hemophilia affected some 20,000 American males. It affected males for the most part because the flawed gene that caused it was located on the X chromosome, passed from mother to son, and since males had only one X chromosome and females two, females could neutralize the defective gene while males could not.[1] The result was that males with hemophilia, known as "bleeders," often bled continuously and internally after even the smallest of bruises.

A toddler in Illinois, for example, required sixteen blood plasma transfusions and a ten-day stay in the hospital after bumping his head on the family's sofa.[2] A three-year-old boy in Toronto suffered a brain hemorrhage when he stopped suddenly at a crosswalk, giving himself whiplash, while a seven-year-old-boy in Ohio bled uncontrollably and had to be hospitalized after losing a baby tooth.[3]

"Hemophiliacs don't bleed faster than anyone else," explained the head of a hemophilia program at a hospital in Pennsylvania. "They bleed longer. And the internal bleeding is the most severe.... They can bleed in their joints, just from walking or playing this can be very painful and can cause crippling. This is why many of our older hemophiliacs are crippled."[4] Through much of human history, people with hemophilia seldom lived into adulthood. Most expected to die, isolated and in pain, sometime before their twentieth birthday.

However, beginning in the early post–World War II period, research into blood coagulants led to a commercially available clotting concentrate derived from the plasma of donors that could be injected into hemophilia patients immediately after a bleed. The concentrate was of a protein called factor VIII that the livers of hemophilia sufferers failed to produce. By injecting factor VIII, which beginning in 1966 came freeze-dried in tiny two-inch bottles, those cursed with the disease could live relatively normal lives.

"It's been revolutionary," said the father of a nine-year-old hemophilia patient in 1974. "Peter can now be a regular member of the family. Thank God. No more midnight trips to the hospital," where, prior to concentrate, he needed massive amounts of plasma.[5] As one doctor put it, "You'd either be stretched out on a hard table in an emergency room or more often than not, admitted to the hospital. . . . [But] with these concentrates, high levels of clotting activity could be obtained in minutes instead of hours."[6]

That meant formerly homebound hemophilia sufferers could go to school, hold jobs, take trips, and even have families of their own. In 1979 the *Richmond Times-Dispatch* reported that a boy with hemophilia was the number one–ranked ten-and-under tennis player in Virginia, a feat of hemophilia-patient athleticism utterly unimaginable in the past.[7] The advent of injectable coagulants also meant that the average person with hemophilia could finally have surgeries, with the first hip replacement occurring in 1968, the first open-heart surgery in 1971, and the first coronary bypass in 1977.[8]

There was, unfortunately, a drawback. The companies that manufactured factor VIII gathered the protein from pooled plasma, that is, plasma taken from thousands of donors at commercial blood centers, called plasmapheresis centers, worldwide, where the going rate in the 1970s was five dollars a pint. Companies paid for the blood because there weren't enough volunteer donors to go around; by one count, only 4 percent of Americans ages 18 to 65 donated, so they set up shop in developing countries like Haiti and Lesotho or in prisons or in impoverished urban areas in the United States such as Los Angeles's Skid Row.[9]

The result was that commercial donors often had hepatitis, a virus common among intravenous drug users and alcoholics that can cause severe liver damage, cirrhosis, and sometimes death. Testing for hepatitis was, at the time, in its infancy, so hemophilia patients contracted the virus in droves; in fact, more than 50 percent did by 1976.[10] "Hemophiliacs were willing to exchange the risk of crippling and probable death from massive hemorrhage for the risk of possible death from liver disease," wrote Elaine DePrince, a longtime hemophilia activist and mother of three sick kids. "But they were unaware of the risk of certain transmission. Warning labels on early factor-concentrate packages understated the risks, and physicians minimized the seriousness of multiple hepatitis exposures."[11]

Such lack of information bordered on the criminal, as doctors and pharmaceutical companies had long known that mixing plasma in vats, from thousands of donors, created an intolerably high risk. They'd known it since World War II, when an Army doctor and captain named Emmanuel M. Rappaport noticed that wounded soldiers who'd served on different battlefields and on different fronts often suffered from jaundice, a sign that hepatitis had damaged the liver. What connected the men, Rappaport realized—and reported in a 1945 issue of the *Journal of the American Medical Association*—was that they'd been given transfusions of plasma. He warned that "until a method is devised for either detecting the agent hepatitis in donors or for rendering [it] innocuous by treating the plasma prior to use, . . . [transfusions would continue to] constitute the largest single cause of acute hepatitis" in the Army.[12]

By the early 1970s, several well-known doctors, including hepatitis expert and professor J. Garrott Allen of the Stanford University medical school, began lobbying the federal government to issue a prohibition on paid blood, as the risk of hepatitis, Allen claimed, was "ten to twenty-five times higher for commercial blood than for voluntary blood."[13] The risk was so great that workers at Baxter Pharmaceutical's Hyland division in Costa Mesa, California, which made the company's clotting-factor concentrates, regularly contracted hepatitis simply by breathing the air where vats were located.

"We were getting plasma from some dubious places," explained Edward Shanbrom, a former director at Hyland labs. But "as bad as the [Skid Row–type] centers were, the prison centers were even worse. We had a huge plasma center at Angola Penitentiary in Louisiana, . . . [where] everyone in the prison was infected, and we bought plasma from Angola and used it to manufacture clotting factor. I raised the issue, but the executives [at Hyland] weren't interested in my concerns."[14]

Shanbrom, who codeveloped factor VIII concentrate in the 1960s, left Hyland in 1974 to invent a solvent detergent process that would remove hepatitis and other viruses from clotting-factor concentrates. It took time, but in 1980, Shanbrom patented a process in which factor VIII concentrates could be cleaned.

Meanwhile, a German manufacturer, Behringwerke AG, developed a pasteurized form of factor VIII that had been heat-treated at 60 degrees Celsius for ten hours. Like Shanbrom's process, it too killed viruses, and beginning in 1981, Behringwerke began selling the product in Europe as "Haemate-P" ("P" meaning "pasteurized").[15] In time, both Shanbrom and Behringwerke would offer to license their processes to each of America's four main factor VIII manufacturers—Alpha, Armour, Baxter, and Bayer—but due to the costs of testing and concerns that the Behringworke method required too much plasma, the manufacturers said no.

But the question wasn't why they said no. The question was why hadn't the manufacturers invented a virus-free factor VIII themselves? They had the technology, and as the former head of Alpha once said, there was "no reason ... [for the company] to not have had pasteurized product on the market by 1980."[16] Put simply, America's concentrate manufacturers were intransigent; they had a product that was profitable, and everyone involved in the process, including doctors and even hemophiliacs themselves, had come to view hepatitis as an "acceptable risk."[17] That's unfortunate because by the time manufacturers began removing viruses from clotting-factor concentrates, thousands of hemophilia patients had contracted the human immunodeficiency virus (HIV), and many of them would die.

It was a terrible drive: the seventy-five-mile trek from Arcadia to St. Petersburg, through ranches and farms, then sprawl, until you came to a causeway leading to the Sunshine Skyway Bridge, a 190-foot high, two-span monstrosity that guarded Tampa Bay like the Eye of Sauron. In May 1980, in a freak storm, a 20-ton shipping vessel barreled into its support beams, and a 1,200-foot piece of the bridge's southbound span, six cars, a truck, and a bus fell into the water. Thirty-five people died. Six years later, in August 1986, the Ray family drove over the northbound span, crossing a bridge people were afraid to cross, en route to All Children's Hospital in St. Petersburg.

There, pediatric hematologist Jerry Barbosa asked the Rays to each take

Clifford and Louise Ray with their sons, 1987. The parents faced the unthinkable: their three boys suffered from hemophilia and had acquired the deadly human immunodeficiency virus through a tainted blood product called factor VIII. Courtesy *Fort Lauderdale News* and *Sun-Sentinel*/TCA.

an HIV test. Their youngest son, in prepping for a surgery at the hospital, had come up positive, so Barbosa wanted to test all of them. The results were what he had feared: sons Ricky (nine), Robert (eight), and Randy (seven) all had the virus, while their parents, Clifford and Louise, and the boys' four-year-old sister, Candy, the nonhemophilia-sufferers of the family, did not. "I was in a state of shock," said Louise, a practical nurse raised in Arcadia. "I kept thinking the first test was a fluke. But the second test also came back positive.... [So] I thought that was it; in two years my boys would all be dead.... I didn't know there were stages [to the disease]."[18]

A pleasant woman with a full, round face, Louise had been a good student in high school when she married Clifford, a tenth-grade dropout, at age seventeen. Her mother had married at fourteen, and Louise had three sons by age twenty-one. She knew hemophilia was a problem; her grandfather had suffered from it, so when the boys inherited the disease, she injected them with factor VIII. "The hemophilia was never really a hindrance," Louise told a *Life* magazine reporter in 1987. "They rode bikes, climbed trees. The only thing I prohibited them from doing was tackle football."[19] Nevertheless, each of the boys had a near-death experience; Ricky as a toddler tore the frenulum in his mouth and almost bled to death, for instance, but the Rays saw hemophilia as a manageable disease.[20]

But HIV? HIV was a death sentence. In 1986 there were no medicines, no FDA-approved treatments or antiretroviral therapies like today, only a grim progression through three stages in which the body's immune system ceased functioning. Stage one seemed like the flu: sore throat, headache, fever, fatigue, on average, a two-week period of simply being under the weather as the virus entered the body and multiplied. That was the beginning. Stage two was longer, not as noticeable, an asymptomatic period of five to ten years in which the virus gradually killed the body's CD4 T "helper" cells, which, oddly, didn't fight viruses themselves but stimulated other cells to formulate an immune response.

When these CD4 T cells dropped below 200 per cubic millimeter of blood, the patient entered stage three, AIDS, acquired immunodeficiency syndrome. This was the last, most advanced stage of HIV, when the body no longer had enough CD4 T cells to stave off infection, and the body succumbed to any number of AIDS-defining illnesses, such as pneumocystis pneumonia, salmonella septicemia, and Kaposi's sarcoma. "At this point, the patient has no defenses and becomes overwhelmed," said a public health nurse in Baltimore. "It's a horrible way to die.... Respiratory failure. Seizures. Total debilitation. There's dementia, there's blindness, ... [and] wasting away."[21]

In terms of communicability, though, HIV wasn't that easily spread. Touching, kissing, eating from the same spoon, or drinking from the same cup did not transmit the disease. It wasn't in saliva, sweat, urine, feces, or tears; it wasn't spread by mosquitos or ticks; and you couldn't get HIV from being sneezed on by an infected person, using the same toilet seat as an infected person, or giving them mouth-to-mouth resuscitation. "It's a very difficult disease to get," explained an official at the Centers for Disease Control (CDC) in 1985. "The likelihood of casual transmission ... is like being struck by lightning."[22]

Unfortunately, one could get HIV through tainted blood transfusions or in the Rays' case, tainted blood factor, or through the sharing of infected needles. Women could pass HIV to babies during pregnancy or childbirth, or through breastfeeding, but most people got it through sex, especially anal sex, because HIV was in semen, and a person's rectal lining could easily tear, which meant bleeding. That's why AIDS was known, at first, as GRID, gay-related infectious disease, because a disproportionate number of gay men had it.

In fact, the first reporting of AIDS in America appeared in the CDC's June 1981 *Morbidity and Mortality Weekly Report,* in an article noting that five gay men in Los Angeles who did not know each other or have partners in common had contracted pneumocystis pneumonia, "an infection almost exclusively limited to severely immunosuppressed patients." The report's editors opined that "the fact that these patients were all homosexuals suggests an association between some aspect of a homosexual lifestyle or disease acquired through sexual contact."[23]

By December 1981 HIV had passed to 180 known victims in 15 states, 92 percent of whom were gay men. Thus, reporters called it the "gay plague," but outbreaks among Haitian immigrants, intravenous heroin users, and hemophilia sufferers led to yet another name, the "4-H disease." "The AIDS virus doesn't know if it's infecting a homosexual," said Dr. Jeffrey Sachs, a Florida state epidemiologist. "Those who dismiss the disease as affecting only homosexuals miss the point."[24]

Indeed, HIV evolved in Africa, scientists have theorized, sometime between the 1880s and 1920s, most likely in Leopoldville, today's Kinshasa, the bustling capital of what was then the Belgian Congo.[25] Through a process known as "zoonosis," the virus jumped at some point from chimpanzees to humans through the butchering and eating of bush meat. It passed person to person, receiving a boost from Leopoldville's booming sex trade, then across Africa due to millions of botched vaccinations in which colonial governments, in fighting syphilis, smallpox, and polio, among other diseases, commonly reused needles.[26]

Now add global shipping and travel networks, and it's safe to assume AIDS had passed to Europe by the 1960s. This isn't conjecture. In 1976 a twenty-nine-year-old Norwegian sailor and truck driver named Arne Røed died a horrible death from a host of AIDS-defining illnesses. Røed, who had visited ports in Africa as a teenager in 1961–1962, was known to have frequented prostitutes and to have passed HIV on to his wife and, through a pregnancy, his daughter in the latter half of the 1960s. In 1986 the Røed family's serum samples tested positive, postmortem, for HIV.[27]

In America, the first confirmed HIV cases were the five gay men mentioned in the *Morbidity and Mortality Weekly Report* in June 1981. But there is speculation and some tantalizing evidence that a sixteen-year-old African American male named Robert Lee Rayford died of AIDS in 1969. Rayford, who'd never left the United States or traveled beyond St. Louis, had clearly been sexually abused, perhaps as a prostitute; he had chlamydia in his blood and lesions on his thighs, rectum, and anus caused by Kaposi's sarcoma, a cancer typically occurring in patients ages fifty to seventy but rare among youths. Doctors at the time had no idea why Rayford was so immunosuppressed. Therefore, they took tissue samples, which in the early years of HIV testing, came up both positive and negative for the disease, then were lost forever during Hurricane Katrina in 2005.[28]

In 2016 researchers conclusively determined—through the same technique used to reconstruct the ancient Neanderthal genome—that blood collected by researchers in New York and San Francisco in 1978 and 1979 was infected with HIV. Then, by tracing the specific strain of HIV back to Africa, they came up with some pretty specific dates: AIDS had traveled from Kinshasa to Haiti sometime around 1967, most likely in Haitian men employed by the United Nations as civil servants in Africa during decolonization.

From Haiti the virus moved to New York circa 1971, either through Haitian immigrants or gay American men who had vacationed in Haiti or through plasma collected in Port-au-Prince through the private American-owned company Hemo Caribbean, which then sold plasma in quantities of 5,000 to 6,000 liters a month to factor VIII manufacturers in the United States.[29] It is unclear exactly when tainted blood first reached hemophilia patients in the United States, but in July 1982 the CDC reported that three adults with hemophilia had been hospitalized, in Ohio, Colorado, and Florida, with pneumocystis pneumonia. Two died, and though none was homosexual or had a history of intravenous drug use, each had tested positive for an immune deficiency.

An article in the CDC's weekly report in July 1982 noted,

The clinical and immunologic features these three patients share are strikingly similar to those recently observed among... homosexual males, heterosexuals who abuse IV drugs, and Haitians who recently entered the United States. Although the cause of severe immune dysfunction is unknown, the occurrence among the three hemophiliac cases suggests the possible transmission... through blood products.[30]

Realizing the seriousness of the situation, that same month, the CDC sought to warn hemophilia patients of factor VIII's possible immunodeficiency risk by contacting the not-for-profit National Hemophilia Foundation in New York. However, as lawyer Eric Weinberg and investigative reporter Donna Shaw wrote in their 2017 book, *Blood on Their Hands: How Greedy Companies, Inept Bureaucracy, and Bad Science Killed Thousands of Hemophiliacs*, the foundation "seemed blatantly influenced" by industry ties.[31]

In 1982, for example, the National Hemophilia Foundation received almost 23 percent of its funding from factor VIII manufacturers, which on occasion threatened to withhold payment if foundation officials took a position they didn't agree with. Factor VIII manufacturers also paid doctors serving on the foundation's medical advisory board to consult for them and conduct clinical trials and once drew up a resolution (that the board accepted and distributed) advising members not to sue manufacturers in a class-action lawsuit.[32] Incestuous, symbiotic, the relationship between the two—a nonprofit patient advocacy group on the one hand and a for-profit pharmaceutical industry on the other—left ordinary hemophilia patients in the cold.

Dr. Louis Aledort, then the medical director of the National Hemophilia Foundation, would claim there wasn't enough evidence in July 1982 to say that AIDS was blood-borne. So, not wanting to incite a panic among people with hemophilia who needed factor VIII, Aledort took a wait-and-see approach regarding AIDS. "They expected me to say, 'Recall all factor," he explained in a 1993 *Orlando Sentinel* article. "They wanted me to say things I disagreed with, and I wouldn't do it.... We were wrong. We didn't think it was a virus, and we didn't know it was 100 percent lethal. There were uncertainties."[33] But as evidence mounted through 1982 that HIV was a blood-borne pathogen, the foundation dragged its feet. So did the factor VIII manufacturers and, most significantly, the Food and Drug Administration, which oversaw America's blood supply.

All the while, the CDC kept publishing its reports, including one in December 1982 that examined the death of a baby who received blood transfusions from nineteen different donors, one of whom had AIDS. The infected man donated the blood on March 10, 1981. The baby received the blood the next day and within seven months had developed "a host of viral and bacterial infections" due to a bad immune system.[34] The CDC suspected blood-borne HIV and held an emergency meeting on the matter in January 1983 with, among others, the FDA, the National Hemophilia Foundation, the Red Cross, commercial blood banks, representatives of gay rights groups, and officials from the four main concentrate manufacturers.

They couldn't agree on anything, from excluding gays from making blood donations to even testing donations for hepatitis, which some 80 percent of AIDS patients had. "I had worked around the world in a variety of governmental settings," exclaimed CDC epidemiologist Donald Francis, "including dictatorships and military regimes, and I had never seen the sort of repression of the truth that I was dealing with then. We told them what the danger was. We told them what to do about it. And they ignored us."[35]

The result was more than a year of inactivity, with hemophilia patients using tainted blood factor without appropriate warnings from either drug companies or the FDA or the National Hemophilia Foundation itself. In fact, the foundation continued to downplay the factor VIII AIDS risk even after concentrate manufacturers began issuing recalls beginning in 1983, when on the very rare occasion a full-blown AIDS sufferer was discovered to have donated blood. Foundation president Nathan Smith argued in 1983 that the risks of not treating hemophilia with factor VIII are just as great as or probably greater than those of using factor VIII and contracting AIDS.[36]

What data he used is unknown, but well into 1985, when scientists finally developed an HIV screening test and concentrate manufacturers began marketing a pasteurized factor VIII, America's hemophilia patients contracted HIV. By some estimates, a full 50 percent did, which led victims and their families to describe it as a holocaust. "I struggle with [what's happened] every day of my life," said a Los Angeles mother whose seven-year-old son died in 1989. "What makes you angry is you put your trust in these people. They did nothing but lie to me. Nobody told me death was a side effect of this concentrate. Yes, it was a wonderful product. Yes, he needed it. But they helped me murder my son."[37]

TEN

THE COWARD'S WAY OUT

Adding insult to injury was America's irrational fear of AIDS. In 1986, followers of right-wing politician Lyndon LaRouche collected a whopping 683,000 signatures for an AIDS-quarantine initiative on California's November ballot. An extreme conspiracy theorist who claimed that scientists in Russia had engineered HIV in order to kill Americans, LaRouche pushed Proposition 64, which, if passed, would have declared AIDS "an infectious, contagious, and communicable disease" like tuberculosis.

There was no mention of a quarantine in LaRouche's proposition, but that was the intent. If passed, California's health codes allowed for the isolation of people with infectious diseases, which meant, at least in theory, that California's AIDS patients and even those with HIV could have been put into camps.[1] The proposition failed, but nearly two million Californians, driven to a frenzy by the fear-mongering of LaRouche's Prevent AIDS Now Initiative Committee, PANIC, voted for it to pass.

Likewise in 1986, politicians backed state-level AIDS-quarantine initiatives in Washington, Colorado, Ohio, Texas, Florida, Maryland, and North Carolina, and in June 1986, the US Department of Justice issued an opinion, even then legally suspect, that employers who took federal funds could fire employees with AIDS due to their "real or perceived" ability to spread the disease.

In other words, an employer couldn't fire a person for having AIDS; that would be discriminatory. But they could fire a person if they *thought* he could give you AIDS. Needless to say, the opinion was a bad one. The Department of Health and Human Services, the Centers for Disease Control, and others had been trying to tell people that AIDS wasn't the flu, that it couldn't be spread through casual contact. But in poll after poll, Americans were shown to have had some pretty big misconceptions regarding the disease.

In a 1987 Ohio Department of Health study, a full 33 percent of respondents thought they could get AIDS by sharing a drinking glass. Twenty percent thought mosquitos could spread the disease, and 19 percent said food servers and kitchen workers could as well.[2] That same year, Gallup found that 18 percent of respondents feared catching AIDS from toilet seats, 11 percent from coworkers, and 8 percent from being kissed on the cheek. Another 5 percent thought they could get the disease by shaking hands.[3] "This is absolutely horrendous," bemoaned the director of an AIDS agency in Los Angeles. "Even with all the media attention, the public still doesn't understand how the disease is transmitted."[4]

Indeed, Americans' lack of understanding about AIDS had real-world implications. In 1987 in the tiny coal town of Williamson, West Virginia, townsfolk ostracized and even threatened the life of a gay AIDS patient whom officials banned from using the town's swimming pool. When rumors spread that he was "spitting into salad bars and licking salt and pepper shakers in restaurants," which he wasn't, Williamson's on-the-spot police chief stoked fears by saying, "I don't know this person. . . . He might be the type if he knows he's going [to die], he might want to take some of us with him." At wit's end and considering suicide, the man found help not through locals but through a statewide AIDS-support network that moved him to a different city.[5]

Meanwhile, firefighters assisting an emergency medical team near Port St. Lucie, Florida, came under fire for refusing to transport a forty-year-old AIDS patient to the hospital. "The risk is just not worth it to me," said one. "I'm a fearless guy. I'm a pilot. I'm a scuba diver. It's not like I'm a coward or a pantywaist. . . . [But AIDS] scares me."[6] Policemen, even hardened cops from Chicago's Town Hall District, were scared too. According to an April 1987 *Chicago Tribune* report, police there refused to arrest or have any contact with prostitutes who had HIV. They even displayed mugshots of known carriers on a bulletin board that read, "HAS AIDS."[7] That same year, in Elgin, Illinois, a nearby suburb, police panicked after realizing a man they'd arrested on a DUI charge had the disease, so they stashed him in the department lobby, unattended, while scrubbing down places he'd touched with bleach. The cop who arrested him said he went home, showered, and washed his face at least thirty times.[8]

In hospitals nationwide, a small but still disconcerting number of doctors and nurses refused to treat patients with AIDS. In the summer of 1987, a Washington, DC, man named Rod Miller cut his foot on a rock during a visit to a Delaware beach. Miller went to the hospital, but the orthopedic surgeon there decided Miller and his friends were too effeminate, so he told Miller he wouldn't operate on him without giving him an HIV test. "Two of Rod's friends were there," said Miller's attorney. "One was wearing a Key West t-shirt and the other was wearing a t-shirt that read 'Gentleman Prefer Blondes' and he happened to be blond. The doctor told Rod that was the reason he suspected that he ... [had] AIDS."[9]

In the 1980s, undue fear of the disease struck even funeral homes, which, on occasion, refused to embalm or even receive bodies with AIDS or allow families with loved ones who had died of AIDS to hold services with open caskets. Judges blocked visitation rights to divorced parents with AIDS, diners boycotted restaurants who had cooks or servers who had AIDS, and dentists refused to clean infected people's teeth.

"Without question we are witnessing the phenomenon of AIDS hysteria," commented Rutgers University historian Robert Gottfried, who authored a book on Europe's Black Death. "People are afraid to kiss, drink from a common cup or sit on an unfamiliar toilet seat.... These kinds of reactions are unreasonable and undeserved," he wrote. "I would be shocked if, in a population of 220 million Americans, you could even statistically measure the mortalities from AIDS."[10] What Gottfried meant was that for a country with such a large population, AIDS had killed a relatively small number of people, an estimated 100,777 between June 1981 and December 1990.

The numbers were bad, of course, even horrific, but more Americans died of heart disease, car wrecks, homicides, suicides, diabetes, cirrhosis of the liver, or pneumonia through the 1980s than of AIDS. Yet somehow fear was growing. In 1985 a Media General/Associated Press poll found that when Americans were asked which diseases they feared the most, 78 percent said cancer and just 23 percent said AIDS. Yet less than two years later, that same poll found that 47 percent said cancer, and an incredible 48 percent said AIDS.[11] Health officials called the phenomenon "AFRAIDS," an irrational fear of AIDS that through the mid-1980s occasionally appeared in schools.

The stories were achingly similar: a child had acquired AIDS through tainted blood factor taken for hemophilia or through an HIV-positive mother while in the womb. News would leak that the child was infected, and parents and school officials would panic. There'd be meetings, nasty slurs and even death threats, then calls for a boycott, and officials would respond by ignoring or even questioning expert medical advice and banning the child from school.

In Florida, the state's first AIDS-in-school case erupted in September 1984 in Miami when the father of three HIV-positive triplets attempted to enroll the girls in kindergarten in an elementary school in Little Haiti. Since neither the Florida Department of Health and Rehabilitation nor the Florida Department of Education had policies for children with HIV or AIDS, Dade County school administrators decided to keep the girls out of class. "We put them on hospital-homebound," said Bob Adams, who handled health issues for Dade County schools, "which means we'll send a teacher out [to their home]. It may have been the coward's way out, but that's how we handled the situation."[12]

The only problem was that doing so was illegal. No court had decided it yet, specifically, but in a similar case in 1979, federal judge John R. Bartels ruled that the New York City Board of Education had violated the rights of forty-eight special-needs students who were carriers of hepatitis B by placing them in separate classrooms. Like AIDS, hepatitis B was a blood- and semen-borne disease and thus nearly impossible to acquire at school. It had "limited communicability," ruled Bartels, and since the New York board "had been unable to show a single case of transmission" in school, restricting the kids' access to regular classrooms ran counter to the "the least restrictive environment" provisions of the federal Education for All Handicapped Children Act of 1975.[13]

That was the law. But until the girls' father sued in the Miami case— the mother died of AIDS in 1985—they'd attend school in a tiny room at a Catholic Haitian center that the school board had rented for the year for $3,276. It also paid $330 for meals and $22,192 for a teacher, who drove the girls to and from school for an additional $1,110.[14] All that for a quarantine that clearly wasn't legal. Dade County school officials claimed that they were erring on the side of caution, that they were being safe, but what they really feared was a boycott.

In September 1985, parents of more than 11,000 New York City school kids, angered that the board of education there had allowed an anonymous AIDS-infected student to attend class at an undisclosed school in the city, staged a sit-out. At an elementary school in Queens, parents demonstrated, holding up signs that read, "Teacher's Aides, yes! Student AIDS, no!" and chanting "Two. Four. Six. Eight. No AIDS in any grade!"[15] A picketer said, "Look, we're not talking about a kid who has to take two aspirin every few hours. We're talking about AIDS ... and it's scary as hell. Kids share a lot of things, and I just don't want a kid with AIDS asking my kid if she wants to suck on a lollipop. God forbid something like that should happen."[16]

Next door in New Jersey, things got even crazier when a healthy, non-HIV-positive boy attempted to enroll in fourth grade at an elementary school in rural Warren County. The nine-year-old boy and his five-year-old sister had been adopted recently, and the sister had AIDS. She wasn't even in school, but when news spread, parents flipped, forming a group called Save Our Students, SOS, and keeping more than 60 percent of them out of school.[17] "We tried to educate people that this was a healthy child and there was no legal basis, in fact there was no basis, to keep this child out of school," said an attorney for the borough board. "Parents did not react well to the news."[18]

At roughly the same time, parents in Kokomo, Indiana, went ballistic when thirteen-year-old Ryan White attempted to reenroll in school. He stayed home through the spring but was barred from attending Western Middle School in the suburb of Russiaville that fall. "With all the things we do and don't know about AIDS," said local school superintendent James O. Smith, "I decided not to [enroll Ryan]. There are a lot of unknowns and uncertainties, and then you have the inherent fear that would generate among classmates."[19]

Ryan's mother, Jeanne White, sued, claiming in federal court that her son's civil rights had been violated. They had, of course, but as Ryan's case wound its way through the court system and Jeanne White appealed to the press, the residents of Russiaville and Kokomo seethed. They signed a petition a thousand strong supporting the school board, formed a protest group called Concerned Citizens and Parents of Western Middle School, and raised $12,000 in grassroots solicitations to pay for their campaign.

In the meantime, Ryan attended school from home through a speaker phone, read comic books and played video games, and worked a newspaper route. "He's an exceptionally mature child for his age," said Ryan's pediatric physician. "Emotionally, he's been very stable and not depressed about it."[20] However, his mother knew that damage to the boy's psyche was severe. People dumped trash in their yard; kids on bikes yelled "FAG!!!!" and other epithets, and frightened worshippers refused to sit near the teenager in church. Folks "would back away from me on the street," Ryan recalled. "They'd run from me. Maybe I would have been afraid of AIDS, too, but I wouldn't have been mean about it."[21]

As Ryan's story spread, he became a hero of sorts, a kind of AIDS celebrity who in April 1986 attended a New York City fundraiser with movie stars Elizabeth Taylor and Brooke Shields. He also appeared on *Good Morning America* and was the personal guest of Olympic diver Greg Louganis at the US Indoor Diving Championships in Indianapolis, where Louganis gave him a medal.[22] Americans were also appalled by Kokomo, whose residents, in turn, despised being told what to do.

"It's disgusting that we should apologize to anyone and especially out-of-staters," read a letter to the *Kokomo Tribune*, "for the fact that we have decent parents who will do anything possible to protect their children from an incurable, life-taking, communicable disease."[23] If that meant ostracizing the Whites and spreading rumors about Jeanne White, then so be it. She didn't care about other people's kids, they said. She didn't care about her own kids. She just wanted money. "Dear Mrs. White," read a letter sent to her home, "You are such a puke. I'm sick of seeing your fat, ugly face on TV.... You do not love your son."[24]

Yet, many Kokomo residents supported the Whites. The editors at the *Kokomo Tribune* did, receiving death threats for their trouble, as did a group that wore buttons that read FOR, meaning "Friends of Ryan." But in February 1986, when Ryan returned to school following a judge's order, roughly 150 of the 361 students at Western Middle School were absent. It was good to be back, said Ryan; however, that same day, a different judge, upon receiving a petition from the Concerned Citizens and Parents group, issued a temporary restraining order that again barred Ryan from school.

It wasn't fair, but in news footage shown on national TV that night, members of the group gloated. They smiled and gave thumbs-up signs for the cameras, but viewers saw them as bullies—small-minded, uneducated bullies.

They looked "like a bunch of country bumpkins," admitted Western school principal Ronald Colby, a Ryan White supporter who, to placate parents, had ordered the teen to use a separate bathroom and to eat from disposable trays.[25] Colby also held two AIDS information sessions for students, with the entire student body assembled in the gym. There, he carefully reviewed how doctors said people could or couldn't get AIDS and how students should treat Ryan when he returned to school.

"You explain the situation in as logical terms as they can understand," remarked Colby, "so when they go home they can get part of it straight and their parents will maybe listen to [them]."[26] Many did, but when Ryan returned to school in April 1986 after a different judge's order, dozens of panicked parents raced to school to get their children out. They then formed the Russiaville Home Study School in an old American Legion hall, where twenty-one middle-schoolers, two teachers, and a volunteer worked in an AIDS-free bubble devoid of Ryan White. Colby felt sorry for them. They were angry, distrustful of medical advice, and afraid. "I can't change the parents' minds," he said. "The Pope can't change their minds. There's nothing I can do."[27]

The Ryan White case blew up nationally in the spring of 1986. Soon there'd be a Ryan White made-for-TV movie, and the teen, now a celebrity, would grace the cover of *People* magazine. In the meantime, Kokomo was skewered in the press, and teachers and administrators throughout the United States began pushing their local school boards and state departments of education to develop policies for students with AIDS. If they didn't have policies, they risked becoming another Kokomo, another flashpoint in the war between demanding, hysterical parents and students' civil rights.

Most districts favored inclusion but adopted a case-by-case approach, requiring officials to confer with doctors or health department officials before letting a student in. But no matter what school officials did, they found it difficult to combat paranoia. Belle Glade, Florida, was a case in point. A poverty-stricken agricultural community in Palm Beach County similar to Arcadia, Belle Glade had a large Haitian immigrant population and early on the highest per capita AIDS rate in the United States.

When news spread, athletes from neighboring sports teams refused to play there; members of marching bands did too, as if standing on the field and playing an instrument in Belle Glade exposed them to AIDS. At away games, Belle Glade football players were subjected to verbal abuse. Fans held signs that read "GLAIDS," while callously chanting, "Give me an A! Give me an I," and so forth.[28] It was beyond appalling. "I'm really offended by the whole situation," said the coach of Glades Day School. The athletic director at Glades Central High School said, "It's basically parents who read only the headlines and who don't read the meat of the information. The kids joke about it, but ... when it affects the way people look at you and treat you, it isn't a joke anymore."[29]

The fact is, people stigmatized people with AIDS. They fired them from jobs, forced them from schools, and in Belle Glade's case, made pariahs out of entire towns. So it isn't a surprise, then, that as the Ray boys were diagnosed as being HIV-positive, Dr. Barbosa told the family not to say anything to anyone. They should have listened, but in September 1986, they told a pastor at their church. That's when Arcadia heard the news.

ELEVEN

WE TREATED THEM YOUNG 'UNS WRONG

In 1986 Arcadia had fifteen Baptist churches. Most were of the fire-and-brimstone variety, the Southern Baptist Convention variety, whose members believed that the King James Version of the Bible, published in English in 1611, was the literal word of God. They did not have female pastors; they viewed homosexuality as sinful; and most, including the pastor of the Ray family's Central Missionary Baptist Church, believed AIDS to be "a punishment from God for the lifestyles and immorality of modern society."[1] In Arcadia, Baptist ministers said prayers before football games and government meetings and held services, live, on the radio station WAPG, whose call letters meant "W—Arcadia Praising God."[2]

The Rays were believers. Louise had grown up in the church, which had maybe fifty members who attended services in a small cinderblock building east of the downtown. There, after receiving the news that the boys were HIV positive, in September 1986 Clifford and Louise met with pastor Carl Fuentes in his office. Fuentes had only recently been hired. He'd been valedictorian of his class at Florida Baptist College in Lakeland, but nothing in his background had prepared him for a congregant, let alone three congregants, with AIDS.

Therefore, Fuentes asked the church's former pastor for help because "a wise man taketh counsel," he said, and together they informed the congregation. "We simply felt that the church was entitled to know," explained Raul Gamiotea, the former pastor. People wept and prayed and gave $250 as a love offering and asked Fuentes and Gamiotea to give it to them.[3] But here the story diverges. According to the Rays, the two pastors paid a visit to their home. "They both looked real serious," remembered Clifford. "They asked us if they could come in to talk, and then they asked us to send the kids outside." Fuentes and Gamiotea then gave the family the $250, but—the Rays claimed—asked them *not* to come back to the church.

"They told us that they were afraid that there'd be a panic," maintained Louise. "They said they thought they would get phone calls and threats from other people in the church if we brought our children around."[4] The Rays were heartbroken, they said, and their oldest boy, Ricky, cried. "What are we going to do if no church takes us back?" he asked. "How are we going to worship God?" Clifford said they'd do the best they could at home, but he wondered to himself, "Where is the Christian atmosphere where we are all supposed to help each other?"[5]

When the Rays went to the next service in a show of defiance, "the look on people's faces was total shock," recalled Louise. "Nobody said anything ... [but they gave] the cold shoulder. Some people walked around to the other side of the church to keep from going near us."[6] For their part, both Fuentes and Gamiotea claimed that wasn't true, that the Rays were not shunned, at least not officially, and that as pastors they "wouldn't hesitate to baptize any one of those children" if they came back.[7] But the Rays didn't go back. Word spread, and soon tiny, luckless Arcadia became Kokomo, Indiana, part two.

It began two days into the 1986–1987 school year, when DeSoto County school superintendent Larry Browning opted to pull all four Ray kids, including non-HIV-positive Candy, from school. Candy returned two weeks later, but the boys, decided Browning, would enter a homebound tutoring program where they'd receive just nine hours of face-to-face instruction per week. In the interim, the school board would formulate a policy, insisted Browning, which it did in private meetings, most likely against state sunshine laws, in September and October 1986.[8]

However, the policy the board created was for communicable diseases in general, not AIDS, and it allowed the superintendent to decide which kids could go to school in person on a case-by-case basis. The Rays thought home school was temporary, but now Browning said it wasn't. Browning defended the boys' nine-hour-a-week curriculum, calling it "highly concentrated," and "comparable to what only wealthy children got back before there were no public schools."[9]

The Rays disagreed. For them, the board's homebound program was exhausting. Louise worked nights, and someone had to watch the kids when the teacher wasn't there. But their friends had abandoned them, they no longer went to church, and neighbors had stopped coming around. "We used to have some friends down the street," said son Robert. "When we asked them why they didn't play with us anymore, they said because their momma told them we had the AIDS."[10] At one point, even the boys' barber refused to serve them, weirdly fearing loose hair would transmit the disease.[11]

At work, Clifford and Louise faced uneasy situations. People stared, and every word uttered by a boss or a coworker seemed like an insinuation. They grew paranoid, and Clifford, who for years had guarded prisoners for a living, turned nervous. They needed a change, so in March 1987 they moved the family to Bay Minette, Alabama, a town close to Mobile where Louise's mother lived. They had nothing and slept for a time in an old school bus while Louise worked at a hospital and Clifford searched for work.

The kids, though, were happy. They made friends and attended school for two weeks without telling the Bay Minette school board of their condition. "Looking back, I realize we were just running," said Louise. "The boys went to school about two weeks and then we started getting calls from the school asking why they were so behind. I asked if they had gotten the records from Arcadia yet and they said no. Well, when they came, they had the recommendation for homebound and why. They said that Candy could stay but the boys couldn't."[12]

Discriminated against again, in April 1987, the Rays returned to Arcadia, where, broke and unemployed and facing an intransigent school board, they decided to fight. They found an attorney in St. Petersburg through their pediatric hematologist, Dr. Barbosa, but when the story hit the press, the attorney resigned. He feared the attention, presumably, which blew up with an April 12 *Tampa Tribune* article with the headline "Fear, Ignorance Force Family to Flee." Reporter Bettinita Harris wrote, "Clifford and Louise Hudson Ray and their four children were run out of their hometown by ignorance and fear, and it may happen ... again."[13]

Harris, a twenty-something African American journalist who'd been a health and social sciences reporter at the St. Petersburg *Evening Independent,* heard of the Rays through Barbosa. Harris was at the *Tampa Tribune* now, covering higher education, but knew a gut-wrenching story when she heard one. Therefore, she raced to Arcadia to meet the Rays but had trouble at the *Tribune* finding a photographer; most were so afraid of AIDS, she remembered, that they wouldn't go. But Harris found one in Mark Guss, a longtime Tampa Bay–area photographer, who captured the Rays at home, at the dinner table, Clifford in a Confederate-flag trucker's hat on one side, brooding, with four bright-eyed children in the middle and an attentive Louise on the other.

They were the very portrait of rural Florida's white working poor, but now they were the other, the outcasts, and Harris told their story. She explained in a 2023 interview,

> You know, as an African American reporter, you develop a kind of sixth sense around white people in which you can tell if they are uneasy sitting in front of you. But I never got that from the Rays. They just wanted to live their lives and raise their kids. There wasn't anything complicated about them. And I remember, as we were getting ready to leave, Louise asked, "If you were us, what would you do?" And I said, "I'd stay and fight." That always bothered me. I wouldn't say the Rays did anything because of me, specifically. But I was naïve. I always thought you fought injustice, that right was right and wrong was wrong, but I had no idea what would happen.[14]

What happened first was a hearing before the DeSoto County School Board, for which the Rays hired a second attorney, Judith Kavanaugh. A "diminutive woman with a cherub's face," wrote one journalist, Kavanaugh was a thirty-nine-year-old environmental attorney from Sarasota who could "spit venom with the best of them."[15] She'd come to environmental law almost by accident when in 1977, as a newly minted attorney fresh from Texas, she helped the conservationist Izaak Walton League in its attempts to stop the building of an oil refinery at Port Manatee. The league lost when circuit court Judge Frank Schaub dismissed the case, but Kavanaugh proved so proficient at navigating Florida's environmental laws that in 1978 State Attorney James Gardner hired her as an environmental prosecutor, the first such prosecutor in the region.

She focused on pollution, taking on Tropicana for dumping bad orange juice into a river and Manatee County for failing to meet air-quality standards by refusing to pave its roads. "I believe firmly in the law," said Kavanaugh. "My friends say I have an overdeveloped sense of justice. I can be hardheaded, but you've got to stick to your position. I feel people either really like me or really dislike me ... [and] don't always approve of what I do."[16] Kavanaugh was a good lawyer. In 1980 she returned to private practice, where she built a career as a work-obsessed, environmental law specialist who advised ranchers, land developers, phosphate companies, and local government officials alike. She had five kids, too, and was home, on a badly needed sabbatical, when she saw the Rays' story in the *Tampa Tribune*.

> This was in 1987. I was at home with my husband and saw the boys in the paper. They were just so sad, and all they wanted was to go to school. They were my kids' age, which sort of bothered me. So I'm mumbling and grumbling, and my husband, Bill [Earl], who was also an attorney, said, "Well, you've got some time off. Why don't you do something about it?" So, that's what I did.[17]

Kavanaugh called Dr. Barbosa, whose name she read in the paper, and he told her the Rays needed representation. She didn't plan on doing much, she said.

> I thought I'd drive over to Arcadia and meet with the school board and explain it to them. I mean, it was really clear. Keeping the boys at home was a violation of Section 504 [of the federal Rehabilitation Act], which said students with disabilities should be placed in regular classrooms. So we met, and I said, "Look, you're going to lose this. We're going to go into federal court and you are going to lose. And you're going to pay my fees, too, and they're a lot!" But they just scoffed. They said, "We're not putting those boys in school without a court order." So I said, "OK, bring it on."[18]

The school board attorney was a Fort Myers–based barrister named Harry Blair, who should have known better. His client under no circumstances could keep the boys out of school. That was settled law, which the US Supreme Court had ruled upon just a month before, in a decision involving a Florida case in March 1987. The case included a Fernandina Beach schoolteacher who'd contracted tuberculosis (TB) and who'd been fired from her elementary school in 1979. TB is an infectious lung disease caused by bacteria spread person to person through spittle and phlegm. It is deadly, if untreated, but those who take antibiotics for two to three weeks and who self-quarantine aren't contagious anymore. So, when the Nassau County School Board voted to fire the teacher, the teacher sued, claiming her dismissal violated Section 504 of the federal Rehabilitation Act of 1973, which reads as follows: "No otherwise qualified, handicapped individual in the United States shall solely by reason of handicap, be excluded from the participation in, be denied the benefits of, or be subjected to discrimination under any program or activity receiving federal financial assistance."[19]

The question for the court, then, was whether or not having a possibly contagious disease was the same as being disabled. The teacher said yes, and by a 7–2 vote the Supreme Court concurred. It did not, however, address AIDS, only contagious diseases in general, but the implication was clear: AIDS victims were a protected class under the law.[20]

Around the country, employers and school districts took note. In May 1987 in Miami, the Dade County school board agreed to a settlement with the father of the Haitian triplets with AIDS; the family received money and an apology, and the girls were allowed back into school. In addition, the board agreed to provide a community-wide sensitivity training program for teachers, students, and parents regarding AIDS and to train administrators and even custodians as to the handling of students with AIDS.[21] The board had "no choice" but to allow the girls to attend school, admitted board vice chairman Michael Krop, who added, "the disease can't be spread by general contact."[22]

Through the spring of 1987, school districts across the United States as well as the entire state of New Jersey revised their draconian policies to allow AIDS victims to attend regular schools. Great Falls, Montana; Rocky Mount, North Carolina; Plymouth, Connecticut; and Wilmette, Illinois, to name a few, each would craft an AIDS-inclusive policy before lawyers like Judith Kavanaugh did it for them.

However, Arcadia didn't get the memo. Neither did neighboring Bartow, whose school board not only proposed removing its HIV-positive students from classrooms and segregating them but holding mandatory testing for students "suspected" of having AIDS.[23] But Bartow didn't have an HIV-positive student that its officials knew of. DeSoto had three, and its plan, after being confronted by Kavanaugh, was to bring the boys on campus to be educated in a portable classroom separate from other kids. In a proposal written by Blair and passed unanimously by the board, "the children ... would be transported to school, receive regular classroom instruction from a full-time teacher, be served regular school lunches, ... [and be] entitled to use playground facilities and other such amenities," as long as they were alone.[24]

Kavanaugh guffawed. This was separate but equal, she said, referring to the 1954 *Brown v. Board* Supreme Court ruling that maintained segregation by race in schools was unconstitutional, even if the schools were of the same quality. "It's against the law," exclaimed Kavanaugh. "Segregated classes are against the law.... I can't believe the school board is this naïve."[25] It was vicious too, with Blair at one point comparing the Ray boys to Typhoid Mary and insisting that letting them attend regular school was like "playing with a lighted match around gasoline."[26]

Superintendent Browning then said he saw a parallel between isolating and burning orange groves with citrus canker and isolating children with AIDS, and board chairman James Westberry Jr. declared that Clifford and Louise Ray were only in it for the money.[27] Never mind that the school board had opted to pay Blair one hundred dollars an hour for bad advice. On a rumor, the board also paid not one, but two private investigators to follow the Rays, hoping to prove they were living outside of DeSoto County and therefore ineligible to attend local schools. Meanwhile, Clifford took a job hauling fruit part time at $25 a load, but with Louise now out of work, the family lived on welfare. Clifford said he didn't like having to resort to government assistance, "but when you've got kids, you do a lot of things you thought you'd never have to do."[28]

With Kavanaugh to guide them, the Rays gave the school board an ultimatum: enroll the boys in regular summer school by Monday, June 15, 1987, or Kavanaugh would file a lawsuit in federal court. Browning refused, insisting, "I'm morally just in what I'm doing. Some people are saying, 'This is barbaric.' In ten years, it may turn out we were totally wrong. But this is the correct thing to do right now."[29]

Yet, was it? By 1987 the American Medical Association, the American Academy of Pediatrics, the Centers for Disease Control, the US Public Health Service, and Surgeon General C. Everett Koop had all issued statements regarding the transmissibility of AIDS. Koop, in a widely publicized speech in April 1987, said, "There is absolutely no health reason why children carrying AIDS should not attend school.... [They] must be nurtured, helped to grow and develop, allowed to interact with peers ... and encouraged to participate in all activities of childhood despite shortened lives."[30]

That's what the boys' doctor, Jerry Barbosa, had told the board, repeatedly. He also provided Browning with literature, including a copy of the CDC's AIDS task force guidelines, which stated unequivocally that "casual, person-to-person contact, as would occur among school children, appears to pose no risk. . . . For most infected children, the benefits of an unrestricted setting would outweigh ... the apparent non-existent risk of transmission."[31]

A forty-four-year-old Bolivian immigrant, Barbosa received his medical degree from the University of Madrid in 1971. He completed his training in pediatric hematology and oncology at the Medical College of Virginia in Richmond, and in 1976 he became a professor at the University of Florida medical college in Gainesville before starting the cancer unit at All Children's Hospital in St. Petersburg in 1979.

There, he handled patients from Florida's Gulf Coast in what had to have been the hospital's worst job, telling parents that their children had cancer and that, in many cases, their children were going to die. "You know, there's a lot written about the psychosocial aspects of childhood cancer," Barbosa explained in a 1983 interview. "Everybody's talking about the impact of cancer on the family. . . . But there's ... very little written about the effect the situation has on health care professionals. . . . In pediatric oncology, we see our patients more than adult oncologists [do]. You see these patients for many months, many years—like friends. And your friends keep dying. It gets to you."[32]

In response, Barbosa worked feverishly—"if it takes hours, he spends hours," said one nurse—and though busy with his own family, he told anxious parents to call him at home day or night. By one count, he and an associate handled fifty to sixty outpatients at any one time, plus ten in-house patients at All Children's cancer ward. And this was before AIDS, which in 1986 brought Barbosa face to face with the Rays. He also treated another AIDS patient, a seven-year-old Bradenton boy with hemophilia named Chris Case, who had contracted HIV through tainted factor VIII. The *Orlando Sentinel* reported that the child had been outed by a housekeeper who told his teacher, who in turn told his principal, who then instructed the parents to keep the boy out of school.[33]

That was in April 1987, just as the Ray case was heating up. And while both the Case and Ray families worked with attorneys to file paperwork, Barbosa went on the offensive, giving interviews and skewering the Manatee and DeSoto County school boards in the press. He fought doggedly and said,

> When you go to medical school, they say you have to draw a line between your personal feelings and your patients. There is no way you can do that if you care. . . . I don't think my duty was just to treat hemophilia. I think it's part of my obligation to those families to make sure the children grow up to be part of our society and their rights are respected.[34]

At various points, Barbosa offered to address the two boards and to conduct an AIDS workshop in Arcadia at his own expense, but Browning said no. By then, the board had circled the wagons, and Browning openly appealed to the DeSoto County public for support. "You know the silent majority responds only when they are displeased," he said. DeSoto is "homespun America. Rural people, hardworking, interested in providing for their children, with old-fashioned values, . . . [and] we don't want our children to contract anything in school, measles, mumps, or AIDS."[35]

When Barbosa heard that, he exploded. "That's garbage!" he said. "We've been trying for months to get the message across that they don't pose any danger. . . . The thing that's frustrating is that we've given the board all available literature and they still don't want those children. Initially I thought it was ignorance. But not now. Now it's fear, maybe superstition."[36]

The Rays' attorney, Kavanaugh, had a different take, as she explained in 2023.

> Yeah, the board was fearful. But probably less so than average Arcadians were. The townsfolk were hysterical. And a lot of it had to do with critical thinking. Arcadia was poor. Its education level was low. And just like during the Trump era with Covid, when people feel threatened, they absolutely hate being told what to do. And here was this uppity woman lawyer and this big-city doctor telling them what to do. And they didn't like it. I know the board hated my guts.[37]

Things got worse when, beginning with Bettinita Harris's article of April 1987, the story went global, spread first by Associated Press reports, then by Ronald Reagan, the conservative American president, who in his first-ever speech on AIDS, alluded to the Rays. Reagan had been in office since 1981, but his response to AIDS, said the president's former physician, was that "it was [like] measles and it would go away."[38] The president also had several key advisers who viewed AIDS as a "gay disease," and cuts to public health programs in particular were part of his conservative agenda.

Therefore, what the Reagan administration did for AIDS was "very late and not enough," explained immunologist Mathilde Krim, who in the 1980s chaired the AIDS Medical Foundation. "By 1983, it was clear we were dealing with a major problem, . . . [but] a combination of homophobia, stupidity, and lack of imagination" led to the delay in responding.[39] Reagan didn't even say the word "AIDS" in public until September 1985. He told jokes about it, privately, and his wife, Nancy, once raced to see the president's personal physician "in a panic," wrote her biographer, after drinking from the same glass as her gay hairdresser. The physician "tried to reassure her that it was impossible to get AIDS that way," but Nancy wasn't satisfied. "How do you know?" she demanded. "How do you know?"[40]

By 1987 the Reagans did know. They'd lost a dear friend to AIDS in Hollywood star Rock Hudson, and the story of Ryan White had changed how people viewed and feared the disease. So, finally, at a May 1987 meeting of the American Foundation for AIDS Research in Washington, DC, President Reagan spoke up. "I was told of a situation in Florida," he said, in which "three young brothers, ages ten, nine, and eight, were all hemophiliacs carrying the AIDS virus. The pastor asked the entire family not to come back to their church. Ladies and gentlemen, this is old fashioned fear, and it has no place in the home of the brave."[41] Almost unbelievably, the president of the United States had criticized Arcadia, which in 1984 had voted for the Republican candidate by a margin of two to one. Locals were shocked, even dumbfounded. "For him to make a remark like that is uncalled for," said DeSoto County commissioner John E. Johnson, who found it "morally wrong" to brand Arcadia's residents that way.[42]

Reagan would criticize Arcadia in May 1987. However, the Ray story exploded with ABC's "A Town without Pity" report on its *World News Tonight* TV program that June. Airing on Thursday, June 25, introduced by anchor Peter Jennings and narrated by correspondent John Quiñones, who visited there, it began with the Ray boys shown running and laughing and scrambling up a tree. They looked happy. Quiñones declared,

These are the Ray family children. With their boundless energy, they are the picture of good health. Eight-year-old Randy, nine-year-old Robert, and ten-year-old Ricky. It is hard to think of these boys as victims of AIDS, but they are. And because of fear and ignorance about AIDS, the boys have become outcasts, shunned in their own hometown.[43]

The camera then cut to Ricky, a handsome boy with short, tousled hair. "They saw us go by the church," he said in a gravelly voice, and "they turned their heads like we didn't exist." Next, the camera showed Louise injecting the boys with factor VIII at home on the couch, as Quiñones explained that they'd acquired HIV through contaminated blood. They didn't have AIDS yet, he asserted. They had HIV, stage two, but in every other respect were normal boys.

However, Quiñones continued, "many of the residents of this small farming community of Arcadia have not treated the boys normally. The county school district has not allowed the boys to attend classes with other students even though medical experts say the AIDS virus cannot be transmitted through casual contact." The boys had been kicked out of church, shunned at a town fishing tournament, and banned from a barber, stated Quiñones, who spoke with a fireman, a rancher, and the outgoing pastor of the Rays' Baptist church, Raul Gamiotea. Arcadians were "deathly afraid," exclaimed Gamiotea, who, with piercing eyes and wearing a three-piece suit, was the very portrait of an evangelical minister, "and anyone who says he isn't afraid of AIDS is either a fool or a liar or both."

Then came Clifford Ray, wearing a red trucker's hat with a Confederate flag and the slogan "God's Country" emblazoned on the front. He looked exhausted. People here "are gonna look back one day... [and say] 'We treated them young'uns wrong,'" he said. "And there ain't gonna be nothing they can do but hang their head in shame." Next, Quiñones turned to Ricky and asked, "What do you want to do more than anything?" To which Ricky replied, "Go back to school... [so] I can have a good job when I grow up. Sometimes it makes me angry. What they're doing isn't right." With that, he strolled away with his brothers, to the sign-off, "John Quiñones, ABC News, Arcadia, Florida."

TWELVE

HATESVILLE, USA

ABC's June 1987 "Town without Pity" news report was just three and a half minutes long, and at no point did either Peter Jennings or John Quiñones actually say those words. In fact, they appeared only momentarily in a graphic as Jennings intoned, "When we come back, the tragic story of AIDS. One town and three brothers." That was it. But somehow "A Town without Pity," the unspoken title of a Thursday-evening nationally televised news segment, reverberated with the press, which visited the town en masse in the run-up to the Rays' July 1987 hearing before federal judge Elizabeth Kovachevich in Tampa.

Only the second female district judge to serve in the thirty-five-county Middle District of Florida, Kovachevich was a 1961 Stetson law grad known for her controversial views. In 1971, as a member of the Board of Regents of the university system of Florida, Kovachevich shocked observers by calling the state's new co-ed dormitories "taxpayers' whorehouses." A staunch Catholic who lived with her parents, unmarried, into her fifties, Kovachevich was a "workhorse of a judge," whose mission, it seems, was "to attack the backlog of cases that the Middle District was confronted with."[1] Therefore, Kovachevich maintained a "rocket docket," racing through a mind-boggling 767 cases in the year ending July 1987 alone.

That meant marathon court sessions, including four months of 7:30 a.m. to 5:00 p.m. hearings during the 1985 racketeering trial of former baseball great Denny McLain, in which Kovachevich served jurors food in the jury box. Critics complained that Kovachevich's trials were unfairly rushed, and in August 1987, an appeals court threw out McLain's conviction because her "drive to speed up the proceeding denied [the defendant] a fair trial."[2] However, in the Ray case, Kovachevich needed to move quickly.

Kavanaugh filed suit in June, and the boys, if successful, planned to return to school that August. On June 19, 1987, Kovachevich held an emergency hearing in Tampa in which she asked for a brief period to study the AIDS-in-schools issue, with a hearing set for July. On one side were Kavanaugh and the Rays, who had the Supreme Court's March 1987 tuberculosis ruling to gird them as well as testimony from three key physicians: Dr. Barbosa, pediatrician Dr. Samuel Gross from the University of Florida, and most notably, Dr. Robert A. Good, one of the biggest names in the history of American medicine.

Regarded as the founder of modern immunology, Good was an endowed chair at the University of South Florida College of Medicine and a former director of the Sloan-Kettering Institute for Cancer Research in New York. In 1968 Good performed the world's first bone marrow transplant, and in 1973 he appeared on the cover of *Time* magazine. He was a superstar doctor who chaired the Florida Governor's Taskforce on AIDS and who, in a career spanning some 50 books and more than 2,000 authored or coauthored articles, also discovered T cells, whose immunological suppression was the root cause of AIDS.

On the other side were Blair and the DeSoto County School Board, whose experts included Dr. Steven A. Armentrout, head of the hematology and oncology division at the University of California at Irvine, and British biologist A.D.J. Robertson. Armentrout was a respected doctor, but his testimony in this and a second school case in California was, a judge put it, "fringe."[3] Without evidence, Armentrout insisted that AIDS victims should be kept from school because "doctors at some future date would discover currently unknown ways in which AIDS could be transmitted."[4] It was, in philosophical terms, an argument from ignorance, in which Armentrout insisted that his position was true because there was no evidence to refute it. In doing so, he placed the burden of proof on the Rays. But how could they disprove an entirely new mode of AIDS transmission that hadn't been discovered yet? They couldn't, and in front of a discerning judge like Kovachevich, Armentrout's nonargument was moot.

Then there was Robertson, the biologist and president of a minuscule think tank called the Research, Testing, and Development Corporation of Lexington, Georgia, whose claim to fame was a March 1986 article in the far-right *American Spectator* magazine in which he made the absurd claim that AIDS might pass through cows and cow milk as well as bug bites and coughs.⁵ None of that was true. But followers of Lyndon LaRouche loved the article because Robertson favored a draconian Proposition 64–like infectious-disease program for all of America, including mandatory blood tests and the quarantining of people with AIDS.⁶ He'd even written an end-of-days letter to President Ronald Reagan about it, which Kavanaugh showed to the court.

"The only means of preventing... [AIDS'] inexorable spread," Robertson wrote, "is quarantine restrictions similar to those once available for tuberculosis, smallpox, and typhoid.... If we take no immediate, effective action to control the spread, our (civilization) will collapse forever."⁷ How Blair had found Robertson is unknown—from the article, probably—but Robertson and Armentrout were bad witnesses. They did nothing to bolster the case and were out of step with current medical thought, especially when Kovachevich had the CDC guidelines to go by and heard testimony from Barbosa, Gross, and Good.

Barbosa explained that Clifford, Louise, and Candy Ray had all tested negative for AIDS despite living with the boys "all their lives," the idea being that if they hadn't contracted AIDS at home, then kids sitting next to the boys in school wouldn't either. Gross said that though the boys had a deadly disease, they were "otherwise healthy and normal," and thus there was no medical reason to keep them from regular school. And finally, Good told the court that in more than 35,000 known cases of AIDS, he knew of "no instances of transmission by casual contact," not one.⁸

The hearing, understandably, was a big deal, not only for the Rays and the school board but for the public in general, many of whom crowded into a courthouse in Tampa and picketed outside. Carrying placards that read, "Demand Action on AIDS" and "AIDS Hysteria Kills," members of a group called Cure AIDS Now staged an impromptu awareness campaign. "We would like to steer the reaction to AIDS away from far right, fundamentalist views," explained a member, "and toward a humane and realistic strategy to deal with the disease."⁹

But across the street, people jeered the picketers and called them "faggots" and "gays." One of them identified himself to the press as a twenty-five-year-old Wisconsin transplant named Dave Morgan, who'd just recently moved to Florida. "I can understand what these people are doing," he said, "but if these guys would live their lives right, they wouldn't have this problem. We don't have no homos in Wisconsin."[10] Morgan was misinformed. There were gays in Wisconsin, and AIDS wasn't just a gay disease, but the rancor shown to the Rays would explode exponentially when on August 5, 1987, Kovachevich issued her ruling.

The boys could go to school, regular school, and like it or not, the board in Arcadia had to take them. In a thirty-three-page order "sprinkled with phrases underlined for emphasis," Kovachevich declared,

> The reality is the Ray boys have already been dealt a hand not to be envied by anyone. The boys at their young ages are already having to face two potentially life-threatening diseases.... This is more than most people face in their entire adult lives. Denial of the opportunity to lead as normal an educational and social life as possible is adding insult to injury. Unless and until it can be established that these boys pose a real and valid threat to the school population of DeSoto County, they shall be admitted to the normal and regular classroom settings to which they are respectively educationally entitled.[11]

Kovachevich admitted that she understood the community's concern. She herself remembered fearing polio as a child and how images of an iron lung "struck terror into the hearts of parents and children everywhere." But, she cautioned, AIDS wasn't polio. Polio spread through fecal matter and coughs, and such means of transmission, she wrote, were "not supported by the evidence in this case." Therefore, she would not let "community fear, parental pressure, and the possibility of lawsuits" influence her ruling.[12]

The DeSoto County School Board could appeal if it wanted to, but as Blair advised its members, it would lose. A *Tampa Tribune* editorial declared,

> The ignorant and the stubborn were defeated yesterday when a federal judge ruled that three Florida brothers exposed to the virus that causes AIDS can no longer be banned from school. Educators are supposed to be an enlightened bunch. But DeSoto County school officials in west central Florida have acted like imbeciles ... [in clinging] to the notion that ignorance is bliss.... We hope this ends the school system's despi-

cable treatment of the Ray family. These children, and others like them, don't deserve to be blacklisted from school.[13]

The board complied, but the following week, in two long meetings in the auditorium of an Arcadia middle school attended by 300 residents one night and 200 residents the other, members of the public vented their views. When Blair explained that an appeal wasn't winnable, the crowd booed and yelled, "Appeal it! Appeal it!" then cheered loudly when Blair said that personally he resented "remarks by the press that characterized this school board as that of a small, rural community of ignoramuses."[14]

But the board had chosen to fight and lost, and now the town was in a frenzy. People were afraid. "I beg you," pleaded a man named Bob Werner, "I want some guarantee, some assurances our kids aren't going to get AIDS." Werner then accused the judge of making a bad decision and of sentencing his children to death. Next up was Robert Sanders, the father of a four-year-old. Sanders said, defiantly, "I will tell this board, the news media, the Centers for Disease Control, the American Academy of Pediatrics, and the Red Cross, my son is not going to go to school."[15]

A woman named Sharla Padgett told the crowd that when she had tried to explain AIDS to her seven-year-old daughter, the girl cried and said, "Mama, I don't want to go to school if I have to be scared." Then, Pat Bowling, the mother of another seven-year-old, asked coyly, "I want a straight answer from you: will you provide private tutoring for my son in my home?" like the Rays had been given. To which board members replied, no, her son didn't have special needs and didn't qualify. So Bowling said bitterly, "Well then, take me to jail, Joe," because she wouldn't be sending her son to school.[16]

Calls for a boycott excited the crowd, members of whom the following week formed Citizens Against AIDS in Schools, a parents' group headed by former DeSoto County sheriff's deputy Danny Tew. A thin, slow-speaking man in his thirties, Tew had been fired from his job in 1981 by Sheriff Robert Thomas, who, incidentally, had succeeded Frank Cline, for lying to a judge on an affidavit for a search warrant. Tew was acquitted in 1982 when he testified in court that Thomas had told him what to write.[17] He left the force, and in 1987 Tew and his wife owned a beauty salon and tanning parlor in Arcadia that doubled as the headquarters for Citizens Against AIDS in Schools.

Citizens Against AIDS in Schools rally, August 1987. Upward of a thousand people attended the rally at a rodeo arena in Arcadia. Angry at a judge's decision to allow the Ray boys into regular school, the organization's harsh pronouncements earned Arcadia the sobriquet "a town without pity." Courtesy *The Palm Beach Post*/Imagn Images.

Tew said the group had three goals: mandatory, twice-yearly AIDS testing for all students; a requirement that doctors share with officials the results of those tests; and the uncovering of any new evidence regarding the Rays that would keep the boys out of school. These goals were all pie in the sky, of course, because the group's obvious intent was to engage the media, no matter how much Arcadians said they hated the media for its depiction of the town. The more journalists wrote, the more Arcadians spoke, and for a town that already had credibility issues, none of the coverage was good.

At a raucous meeting on Friday, August 21, at Arcadia's rodeo arena, more than a thousand people gathered to hear Tew rail against the government. Insisting that the board's authority had been "usurped by the federal court system," Tew compared Kovachevich's decision in the Rays case to the forced desegregation of schools.[18] Not to be outdone, local Baptist minister Don Yates pontificated on the moral decline of America, and group member and excited mother of two, Beth Staton, berated gays. The government should pass laws banning homosexuality, she said, because if it had "stood up to the gays" in the first place, "we wouldn't be here."[19]

Members of Citizens Against AIDS in Schools were hysterical about gays. They spoke of homosexual conspiracies to suppress the truth, and they passed out pamphlets for the book *The AIDS Epidemic: A Citizens' Guide to Protecting Your Family and Community from the Gay Plague* by Lawrence Lockman, a radical lumber-mill worker in Maine. Lockman wasn't an expert, but his solution to the AIDS crisis was to "stop coddling gay rights activists and their pathetic followers" and "to quarantine all known male homosexuals" by putting them into camps. Ever the conspiracist, Lockman also claimed that gay men were purposely infecting female prostitutes in order to pass the disease to heterosexual Americans, whom he called "straights."[20]

Lockman was bad enough, but another Citizens Against AIDS in Schools favorite was the evangelist Moody Adams, who wrote the 1986 opus *AIDS: You Just Think You're Safe*.[21] In it, Adams excoriated homosexuals for wanting "to hide the facts about where AIDS started," because "the American strain of AIDS came from men who play in other men's rectums; homosexual men who use their genitals and arms, their tongues and toys to frolic in a cesspool of germs. From this vagina of viruses AIDS proliferated. Within this womb of filth it flourished."[22]

To illustrate his point, Adams described in detail "Fourteen Sex Acts That Are Real Killers," including rimming, fisting, ringing, oral-genital sex, and water sports. As for AIDS victims in schools, Adams, who did not have a medical degree, insisted that infected kids should be quarantined because "little children bite, share food and drinks and get careless in the bathroom. Any of these has the potential for communicating AIDS."[23] Yet contrary to Adams's assertions, sharing food and drinks and being messy in the bathroom did not communicate AIDS, and as of 2018, there have only been four recorded instances in the world in which human bites have led to what experts deemed "highly plausible" or "confirmed transmission" of AIDS.[24]

But, for Citizens Against AIDS in Schools, Adams was the expert, not Barbosa, so they invited the Louisiana minister to debate the doctor in Arcadia. Barbosa said no. "He told us he didn't feel safe coming," explained Peggy Sisco, a secretary for the group, which offered to arrange police protection for Barbosa. Barbosa said that was absurd. He didn't need protection. He refused to come to Arcadia because a debate with Adams, an antigay, antiscience, tent-revivalist minister, wouldn't do any good. "How do you educate these people?" exclaimed Barbosa. "How much evidence do they want?"[25]

What they wanted, beyond reason, was a cast-iron guarantee that their kids wouldn't get AIDS, but children had a far higher chance of dying on the way to school in a car accident, about 1 in 5,000 in 1987, than they ever did in the utterly infinitesimal chance, in a classroom setting, of getting AIDS. Arcadia's kids had a better chance of winning the new Florida lottery, which started in 1988, at odds of 1 in 14 million. They had a better chance of dying in a commercial plane crash at 1 in 3 million or being struck by lightning, which, on occasion, killed cows in DeSoto, at odds of about 1 in 1.2 million. The kids who went to school with the Rays were not going to get AIDS, at least not from them. But no matter what legitimate experts said, most townsfolk didn't believe them.

"There isn't anyone who doesn't feel sympathy for the Ray children," said Sue Ellen Smith, an Arcadia schoolteacher and the wife of then-mayor George Smith. "But there are too many unanswered questions about this disease, and if you are intelligent and listen and read about AIDS, you get scared... because you realize all the assurances are not based on solid evidence."[26]

According to news reports, Sue Ellen Smith was working on a master's degree, and her husband was a graduate of the University of Miami. They should have known better or perhaps not been as scared, but they removed their son from DeSoto County schools and sent him to school in another town.[27] The mayor, the superintendent, members of the school board and county commission, numerous preachers and ministers, a well-known Arcadia doctor, the sheriff, and even the football coach all favored the testing, and by extension the quarantining, of students for AIDS.

"There weren't many people in Arcadia who supported the Rays," said their lawyer Judith Kavanaugh. "I'm sure there were some, but I didn't see any, and that parents organization was a hate group."[28] Melody Patton, a twenty-six-year-old DeSoto County mother of two and vice president of Citizens Against AIDS in Schools, said the media depicted the group "as either crazy, lunatic, ignorant or redneck.... The only people who disagree with us is the scum of the community."[29] Patton disliked the Rays personally and said,

"Everybody knows they are low-hygiene-type people." She saved her meanest barbs for Clifford and Louise Ray.[30] They loved the attention, she claimed, and hoped to profit by not only suing the board but by accepting donations and selling the movie rights to Hollywood. As Patton told Steven Petrow,

> I don't care to know where they live. But they talk about people driving by and staring and stuff. I feel that they invited that when they decided to go public.... They're very prominent. We went to McDonald's a couple of weeks ago ... [and] they drove by through there five times in two hours, just doing nothing but cruising town—just so they could be seen. Why would they do that? Really?... I think they have the feeling... "we're somebody special." It's like they're trying to rub it in.[31]

Anger toward the Ray parents was palpable, explained Petrow, who attended the first Citizens Against AIDS in Schools rally, drove around speaking to residents, and sat with regulars at Wheeler's Restaurant, a downtown café where Arcadians came to gossip. He wrote,

> The court ruling had shocked the school board and many of the parents had vowed to keep the Ray boys out of school.... AIDS itself no longer commandeered center stage.... [The talk at Wheeler's now] focused almost entirely on the media "assault" of the town, the "takeover of schools by the federal government," and the endless speculation that the Rays had sold ... story rights for hundreds of thousands of dollars.... A native daughter suggested that killing the Ray boys might not be a bad idea, and the father of a four-year-old [said authorities should] "fix all mothers who might pass AIDS to their babies." At the same time, the press continued to seek out "hot" stories, which meant looking for the worst in Arcadia. Whether because of the close media scrutiny, the intensity of the issue, or the hot Florida summer, many Arcadians seemed to become unhinged, often confirming the worst suspicions and stereotypes.[32]

The evening of the rodeo meeting, Clifford Ray received an anonymous death threat. "Your house will burn," someone said before hanging up. Petrow himself worried "what would happen if word got out in town that I was gay?"[33]

As the opening of school approached, parents planned to boycott, and

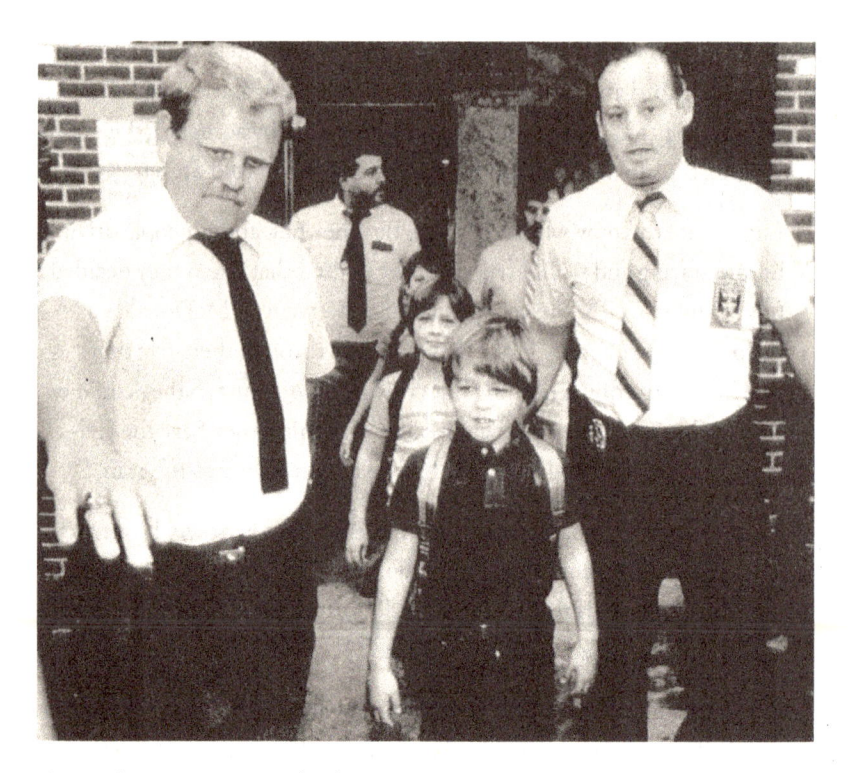

The Ray boys returning to school, August 1987. Facing death threats and a parent-led boycott of nearly half of their classmates, the boys returned to school under armed guard. Courtesy *Tampa Bay Times*/Zuma Press Wire.

many enrolled their kids at an Assembly of God church school in Arcadia called the Sonrise Christian Academy. Sonrise emphasized creationism, wrote an *Arcadian* newspaper reporter, and its texts "resemble those used in the 1940s and '50s, rather than the texts of the 1980s."[34] As in the past, others sent their children to Port Charlotte to the same K-8 Catholic school that richer, white Arcadians used during integration, but most planned to stay and fight.

On Monday, August 24, 1987, in front of a phalanx of print and TV reporters and out-of-town news trucks, the Rays returned to a half-empty school. Of 632 students at Memorial Elementary, only 337 showed up, with the lowest rates of attendance in grades two, four, and five, which the Ray children attended. Countywide, officials expected 3,771 students, but only 2,473, that is, 65.5 percent, showed up, a decline of 1,298 students from the year before. There wasn't any violence, thankfully, owing perhaps to a heavy police presence and ten plainclothes Arcadia police officers and DeSoto County sheriff's deputies guarding the halls inside.

The *Fort Myers News-Press* reported on one incident, though, when an unidentified man stormed into a crowd of reporters and demanded that they leave him alone. When cameramen started filming the man, he backed one into a car, shouting, "You better get that out of my face, or you'll be eating it, clown!"[35] The angry man stood in sharp contrast to the photogenic Ray boys, who, when school ended, jumped laughing and waving into the bed of their father's enclosed pickup truck and headed home. They had a good day, they said, and though students in Robert's class kept calling him "the AIDS kid," by recess they'd all gathered around the monkey bars "asking him about being in court and how he felt about being famous."[36] The boys' classmates weren't afraid; the adults were. As attendance picked up from 337 on Monday to 380 on Tuesday to 410 on Wednesday, bomb threats began rolling in.

There were three in two days, including one to a local radio station in

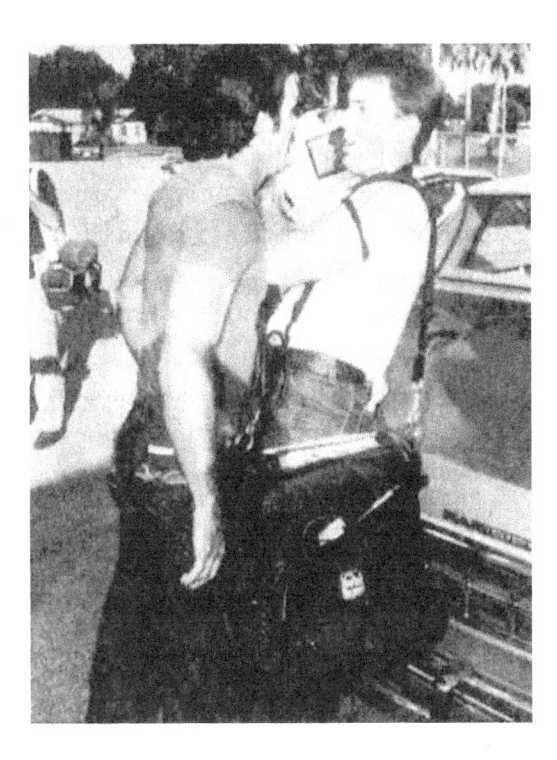

Anger at the press in Arcadia, August 1987. On the Ray boys' first day back to school, an angry man confronts a news cameraman outside of Memorial Elementary. Courtesy *Orlando Sentinel*/TCA.

which a man said, "I broke into Memorial Elementary last night. I placed two bombs in the air conditioning ducts. They're going to explode."[37] Authorities searched the school prodigiously, finding nothing, and there was a sense that in spite of the threats, Arcadia was returning to normal. By Friday, attendance had grown to 461, the majority of journalists had left, and a confident Clifford told Louise, "We've got this thing beat."[38] However, that night, the family stayed at a relative's house in Nocatee, with plans to visit the family of an HIV-positive child in Okeechobee that weekend. They didn't make it because on the evening of Friday, August 28, 1987, someone poured a flammable substance onto a pile of toys in the laundry room of their house and burned it to the ground.

Clifford's brother, twenty-seven-year-old Andy Ray, had been home at the time. He'd fallen asleep watching TV, he said, and awoke to find smoke billowing through the house. According to press reports, Andy suffered from seizures and said he may have had one that night. He'd also downed a valium and a beer and was disoriented but had the presence of mind to throw a barbell through a bedroom window to escape. He was outside battling the flames with a garden hose when twenty-eight-year-old friend and neighbor Jimmy Smithers came to help.

Smithers arrived at about 10 p.m. with plans to accompany Andy to the Reef & Beef. But, faced with a burning building, the two men went back inside, reportedly to salvage a fan and a color TV, when Andy, overcome by smoke inhalation, collapsed to the kitchen floor. Smithers picked him up and carried him over his shoulder through the front door, whereupon the two men fell into a ditch, exhausted, and lay there until help arrived.[39] At least, that was their story.

Andy hadn't seen anyone enter the house, nor could he explain how a flammable substance had been set alight in not just the laundry room, investigators claimed, but in two or three other places in the house. Did someone walk in while Andy was sleeping? Or did Andy do it? And what about Smithers? In January 1987, Smithers, an ardent Ray supporter, had been sentenced to eighteen months' probation for breaking into a sheriff's office patrol car and stealing a uniform jacket.

Why? Who knows? But Smithers had two drunk-driving arrests on his record and liked to do things "his own way," explained his mother, "whether

The Ray family's burned-out house, 1987. On Friday evening of the Ray boys' first week back in school, someone started a fire inside the Ray residence. An uncle of the boys had been home at the time, but when the Rays fled to Sarasota, the press severely criticized the town. Courtesy Peter B. Gallagher.

she liked it or not."[40] Could he have started the fire? And to what end? To garner sympathy for the Rays? Or had Clifford and Louise done it? That's what many suspected, that the Rays had ordered Andy and/or Smithers to burn the home in hopes of receiving donations. "Yeah, that was the rumor," said Kavanaugh, "and for a while there were people out there whispering that I'd done it, that somehow I wanted the money and had cooked up this big plan. But all I know is the Rays were terrified."[41]

They'd lost everything, even Louise's wedding dress, and hid out in an undisclosed Sarasota-area motel but moved to a duplex after the motel owners, fearing AIDS, asked them to leave. The press had a field day, and the same TV crews and news trucks that had left town after a slow week of classes, raced to get back in. "Do you know how many cars there have been?" asked a sixty-five-year-old neighbor. "I expect Pope John Paul II to be here at any time."[42]

DeSoto County Sheriff Joe Varnadore came to the scene, as did investigators from the state fire marshal's office, but other than proving arson, they had no idea who'd done it. Without saying why, Varnadore would clear Clifford,

Louise, and Andy Ray to focus on Smithers, but Smithers's lie-detector test was inconclusive, and the investigation died. "All they got is circumstantial evidence," said Smithers. "It'll be an electrical fire or else they'll find some poor guy on the road with a bad record and pin it on him. I was at one time proud to be from this town." But when he got off probation, he said, "I'm a gone cookie. They can kiss it."[43]

The Rays also quit town, permanently. Early the next week Louise Ray appeared on ABC's *Nightline* and NBC's *Today* show, and donations began rolling in. At St. Paul's Catholic Church in Arcadia, where Reverend Michael Hickey had sermonized in support of the Rays, the telephones rang nonstop, with a priest handling more than a hundred phone calls in a day.[44] Concerned viewers from California to New York and even Europe and Australia began mailing checks of upward of $50 apiece, some $50,000 in all. There were so many checks that Kavanaugh established a Ray Family Relief Fund to keep track of it all. Everything was above board, but the scope of the Rays' fame—and conversely, Arcadia's infamy—was amazing.

The family did *Donahue* on a Thursday, testified before a US Senate committee that Friday, and took a personal phone call from Jeanne White, the now-celebrity mother of famed AIDS victim Ryan White. As fate would have it, in the summer of 1987, the Whites had relocated thirty miles to the south, from Russiaville, Indiana, to the Indianapolis suburb of Cicero. Ryan's new high school, ironically, was in a town called Arcadia, Indiana, where members of the student government ushered the teen to his first-period class, and kids greeted Ryan with handshakes and hellos.

"There was a lot of trouble at Ryan's other school," remarked a student named Billy Beechler. "We didn't need that here. We want to accept him. Why cause him any problems when he's had so many in the past?"[45] There it was: Arcadia, Indiana, schoolkids treating AIDS victims better than adults in Arcadia, Florida, did. Just two of Ryan White's classmates boycotted. There were no bomb threats, no parents arguing with cameramen, and no bigoted comments in the press.

"That's not to say we don't have some opposition," said Arcadia, Indiana, school superintendent Bob Carnal. "On any issue like this you'll have some mixed feelings and concerns. But what appears to be happening is our efforts in educating the kids are paying off. They're telling their moms and dads:

'This is okay.'"[46] Naturally, the national news media linked the two stories almost immediately, with headlines such as "Two Towns Called Arcadia" (*Chicago Tribune*), "Two Arcadias, Two Responses to AIDS in Schools" (*Arizona Daily Star*), and perhaps the most bitter, "Tale of Two Arcadias: One without Pity, the Other with a Hug for a Dying Boy" (*Fort Lauderdale News*).[47] What with the arson and several erroneous reports that the Rays had been firebombed—in other words, chased out of their home by crazed residents wielding Molotov cocktails, which didn't happen—for a time, Arcadia, Florida, became the most despised town in the United States.

"They're calling us Hatesville, USA!" complained school board employee and Citizens Against AIDS in Schools member Bob Werner. "You wouldn't believe the phone calls we're getting."[48] Group vice president Melody Patton, who'd been vocal in the press and who, in opposition to Louise Ray, had appeared on ABC's *Nightline,* received prank calls at home and even death threats from people supporting the Rays. "Every queer in California has called me," Patton said, but "they don't scare me in the least. What they do is make me mad."[49]

Arcadians were mad—not at what their treatment of the Rays had done to the town but at the town's portrayal in the press. Arcadian John Riley was a truck driver and had stopped at a filling station in California after news broke of the fire. He was chatting with other drivers when one of them asked where he was from. "Arcadia, Florida," he said, to which the driver responded, "Oh. We've heard about you people."[50]

Letters to the editor and opinion columns critical of Arcadia appeared in newspapers throughout the United States. Many resembled this angry missive to the *Miami Herald:* "The residents of Arcadia should hang their collective pea-brained heads in shame. Small town. Small minds. . . . Truly a town without pity."[51] Syndicated columnist Chuck Stone, a senior editor at the *Philadelphia Daily News* and a World War II Tuskegee Airman, unleashed his own critique, insisting that in Arcadia, "rednecks had declared communal war on three AIDS-infected brothers," while demonstrating the same "separate but equal mentality" parents all over the South had clung to just a generation before. Arcadians, he wrote, were "like refugees from a Faulkner novel," whose willingness to exclude children, this time due to AIDS instead of skin color, was a "sickening déjà vu."[52]

The connection between AIDS and race wasn't lost on Arcadians, either. A letter to the editor by African American teacher Sharon Thomas Goodman was published in the *Arcadian* newspaper with the headline "Fight the Real Problem." In 1967, as an eleven-year-old, Goodman had sung "How Great Thou Art" at the Richardson children's funeral and now taught at Memorial Elementary, where the Ray children went. It was in Arcadia, she wrote, that she first became "keenly aware of what discrimination and prejudice was."

> I was born and reared in Arcadia, . . . [and] I remember not getting to do certain things because I was Black. . . . Members of my family, just a few months ago, stopped taking their daily walks out by the Revco Drug store because of nasty racial slurs that were yelled at them—and this is 1987. Yes, we have some serious problems in Arcadia. . . . Arcadia is no island. . . . Wherever the Ray family goes there are going to be people who do not want them there.[53]

Those people included George Smith, Arcadia's mayor, who in the wake of the fire had the audacity to say on live national television that he didn't feel "it would be to their good or ours" if the Rays returned to Arcadia. He was just being honest, and that was "the general feeling in the town."[54] Meanwhile, on *Donahue,* Clifford Ray insisted that contrary to news reports, many Arcadians had helped the family. "There was a lot of them that was real good," he explained, but most were "leery because the opposition group is so strong. It's your politicians in Arcadia, starting with the mayor. It's your school board, your county commissioners, the whole opposition. They don't want the children in school."[55]

They were so adamant about keeping the kids out of school that in late September 1987, the evening of the Rays' first day at Gocio Elementary in Sarasota, the group Citizens Against AIDS in Schools followed them there, driving fifty miles from Arcadia to hold a rally at the county fairgrounds. They weren't being vindictive, they said. They were only trying to lead people there to "show them what they can do."[56]

The response to the group, however, was lukewarm. Unlike the group's rodeo rally in Arcadia that drew at least a thousand people, the Sarasota rally attracted two hundred, and outside some seventy-five members of a counterprotest group called Citizens Against Misinformation carried signs that read, "Go home, Arcadia!" and "Don't Turn Our Nice Little City into a Mean Little Town!"[57] Sheriff's deputies had to move the Arcadia group's gathering to a different building at the fairgrounds after someone called in a bomb threat. Attendees who remained witnessed a shouting match.[58]

In September 1988, Arcadia and its school board settled with the Rays for $1.1 million, paid out in installments, with some $400,000 going to attorneys' fees and court costs. The townsfolk hoped to move on. But twenty-five miles away, at a nursing home in Wauchula, a small, frail, African American grandmother mumbled, "I killed those children. . . . I killed them but I don't know why."[59] The woman's name was Betsy Reese.

THIRTEEN

THE NE'ER-DO-WELL

By September 1988, the month the Rays settled with the DeSoto County School Board, the ailing Betsy Reese, now age sixty-seven, had been in nursing homes in Highlands, Hardee, and DeSoto Counties for the previous six years. She had Alzheimer's, spent most of her days in a fetal position, and was, a physician said, unable to understand anyone at all.[1] But beginning in 1986, two caregivers at the Hardee Manor Nursing Home, Doris Harris and Belinda Romeo, claimed Reese was lucid at times and would discuss the Richardson case, saying "I poisoned them" or "I killed them" at least a hundred times. "I always tried to get her to tell me why, but I never could," said Romeo. "She'd just start praying and asking the Lord to forgive her."[2]

Eventually, word of Reese's admissions made its way to Arcadia, to the Quarters, and from there to Richardson attorney John Robinson. Still in Daytona Beach, Robinson had been defending Richardson for more than twenty years. He'd helped with his 1971 appeal, which Richardson lost, then in 1985 convinced Florida's Parole and Probation Commission to reduce Richardson's sentence by a whopping 108 years, which meant, after a single twenty-five-year term, his first possible parole date was May 31, 1993.[3] "I'm not some wild liberal trying to turn criminals loose on the public," Robinson told the commission. "I know he's absolutely innocent."[4] In 1988 Robinson told Mark Lane about Harris and Romeo.

Lane was lucky to be alive. In 1978 he'd narrowly escaped "drinking the Kool-Aid" at the infamous Peoples Temple Agricultural Project in Jonestown, Guyana. Lane had been Jim Jones's attorney, and Jones had paid Lane, handsomely, to clean up the cult's image. According to a 1979 *Mother Jones* report, that included filing Freedom of Information Act requests with the CIA and the FBI to see what they had on Jones, killing a *National Enquirer* story with threats of a defamation suit, and convincing parents of brainwashed Temple members not to sue.[5] It was seedy work, but Jones paid Lane a reported $6,000 a month in hopes he'd assist the exiled preacher in pulling an "Eldridge Cleaver," a reference to the famed Black Panther who, following the attempted murder of a police officer, fled to Algeria before becoming a born-again Christian and returning home.[6]

But Cleaver wasn't crazy; Jones was, and the cult leader embraced Lane and his CIA conspiracy theories just as California Congressman Leo Ryan came to visit. Ryan's district was the area in and around San Francisco, where the Peoples Temple had been headquartered and where parents of cult members had been pressuring Ryan to go to Guyana to get them out. After a seemingly benign meeting in Jonestown in which a small number of members elected to leave the cult but most opted to stay, Jones's Red Brigade security squad shot and killed the congressman at a nearby airstrip. That's when the apocalyptic Jones ordered his nine hundred or so followers, including children, to commit "revolutionary suicide" by drinking fruit punch laced with cyanide. If they refused, armed members of his brigade would inject them, and they planned on injecting Lane, as he and another attorney, Charles Garry, were the only non-temple members on site.

They'd been placed under arrest in a shack, and over the camp's loudspeakers they heard Jones exhorting his followers to die. As investigative reporters Tim Reiterman and John Jacobs wrote in 1982, a guard turned to Lane and said, "'We're going to commit revolutionary suicide.' ... That 'we' hung unambiguously in the air."[7] In his own 2012 memoir, Lane would recount how in a panic, he had told the guard that he should spare them so they could "tell the truth to the world about what happened that day."[8] The guard agreed, and Lane and Garry escaped into the bush. They'd survived Jonestown, and soon Lane was on tour giving college lectures at $2,700 apiece. "Probably in a year he won't be able to get that much," said the office manager at Lane's New York talent agency, "but right now I think it's even a little low."[9] The thrust of his lectures was this: the US State Department knew Jones was crazy and that he was oscillating mentally between killing all of his followers in Guyana and moving them to Russia, which Lane claimed would have been an embarrassment for the United States.

Therefore, in yet another conspiracy, said Lane, officials at the State Department kept news of Jones's craziness from Ryan in order to goad the insane preacher into killing the congressman as well as members of his cult. Lane offered no evidence but reportedly told audiences, "We will get the truth about Jonestown, and when we do, I hope we do not discover that someone in the U.S. State Department said, 'We can't have 1,000 poor women and Blacks defecting to the Soviet Union; we can't have a propaganda nightmare.' I hope we do not find that someone in the State Department said, 'Better let them die in the jungles of Guyana.'"[10]

By then, the national news media had had enough of Lane. Albeit legal, his work for Jones had been reprehensible, and critics alleged that the conspiratorial Lane had fed Jones's paranoia. Was Lane culpable? That was a stretch, but *New York Times* columnist Anthony Lewis called Lane a "ghoul." In 1978 Lewis wrote, "I have always assumed that he was just a pitchman with an exceptional talent for preying on the gullible. But there is the possibility that he believes his own visions. In any event, it is time for the decent people of the United States to tune out Mark Lane."[11]

To an extent, they did. By the early 1980s, interest in Jones had died, while the Kennedy conspiracy lecture circuit that Lane created had grown full of competitors. There were dozens of "Who shot Kennedy?" books, including the 1980 David Lifton work *Best Evidence: Disguise and Deception in the Assassination of John F. Kennedy*, in which Lifton posited bizarrely that Kennedy had been shot by multiple assassins from the front and that some unidentified party had removed and then returned the body while in transit and manipulated the bullet holes to show that Oswald, acting alone, had shot Kennedy from the back.

The theory was over the top and Lane-esque, a "shocking mish-mash," read a review in *New York* magazine, "that makes all previous speculation about the president's murder—the Oswald doubles, the CIA conspiracies, and mafia plots—look like the work of dull and sober men."[12] Nevertheless, Lifton's *Best Evidence* was a national bestseller, at 100,000 books in hardback and 200,000 books in seven editions in paperback. That success meant Lifton had displaced Lane as the newest thing on the Kennedy circuit.[13]

So Lane pivoted. He kept his legal practice but began lecturing for a fee to Muslim student groups on American college campuses in support of the

PLO, the Palestinian Liberation Organization, which had been advocating, sometimes violently, for an independent Arab state in lands controlled by Israel.[14] He was living in DC and practicing law in 1988 when Robinson gave him the news: an ailing Betsy Reese had told nurses at her retirement home in Wauchula that she'd killed the kids.

Although certainly salacious, what Reese said, allegedly, couldn't be used in court. She had dementia, and doctors and nurses at three facilities had deemed her "incompetent," "unresponsive," "unable to speak clearly," and "severely confused."[15] She needed twenty-four-hour care. In March 1988 Lane traveled to Wauchula, in Hardee County, to take notarized statements from Harris and Romeo. Romeo's statement revealed the most:

> I met Betsy Reese . . . on or about October 1986 . . . [and she] was competent. She answered questions I asked of her and clearly demonstrated that she understood my questions by her answers and through her actions. . . . I had been informed that many people in Arcadia believed that Ms. Reese had killed the seven Richardson children and that the children's father, James Richardson, was innocent. One day, while I was alone with Ms. Reese, I asked her if she had murdered the Richardson children. Ms. Reese looked at me, her eyes filled with tears and she said, "Yeah, I did it. I killed those children." . . . It was so startling to hear Ms. Reese admit that she killed the seven children that I asked her about the matter on numerous occasions. . . . I am certain that . . . more than one hundred times she admitted to me that she had killed the children.[16]

According to Romeo, Reese would also say "Charlie," in reference perhaps to Charlie Smith, the drunkard with whom Reese had a relationship and discovered the parathion in Richardson's shed.

Sworn statements in hand, in August 1988, Lane rented the auditorium at Smith-Brown School, the site of the 1967 Richardson funeral, now a community center, for what he called an "end-the-silence" meeting. "There's been twenty years of silence," he explained. "Many people know much more and are afraid to speak out."[17] Lane, then sixty-one, put up posters in Arcadia and took out ads in two newspapers to tout the event, then met with Joe Varnadore, who just so happened to be in a heated political campaign with Frank Cline.

By that point, the fifty-seven-year-old Cline had left Glades County to work as a debt collector for Tinsley's IGA, a small Arcadia supermarket. The two men despised each other. In campaign interviews Cline mocked Varnadore mercilessly for having spent twenty-eight years in the Florida Highway Patrol not pursuing criminals on patrol but "inspecting school buses."[18] Thus, when the muckraking almost mythical Lane came to town looking to criticize Cline, Varnadore welcomed him. That was still a surprise, for apart from the Rays, no one was more hated in Arcadia than Mark Lane. Townsfolk questioned his motives, insisting that, like the Rays, he'd only drummed up interest in the case for a piece of the movie rights. They stole Lane's book from the library, a reported five or six copies in eighteen years; some even threatened his life, and a local newspaper published political cartoons making fun of him.[19]

Sheriff Varnadore was a decent man, wrote Lane in his 2012 memoir, who advised him that "since the Klan was active in the community it would be important for us [Lane and his wife] to leave town before nightfall and return the next day. I told him we had rented a motel room. He sighed and urged us to leave because he could not protect us."[20] No doubt Varnadore had been on edge since the Ray case. The Rays were gone, but shortly after Lane's meeting with Richardson, members of the New York-based Lesbian and Gay Freedom Ride planned to mark the Ray family's exile by staging a protest they called a "die-in" on the DeSoto County Courthouse lawn.

That brought plans for a counterprotest from Tony Bastanzio, a thirty-one-year-old landscaper and resident of Apopka, Florida; he also was the Grand Wizard of the Florida Knights of the Ku Klux Klan. There wasn't an Arcadia klavern, and there hadn't been one for years, but Bastanzio and other sheet-wearing racists from outside of the city were monitoring the town's affairs. Not knowing what to expect, Varnadore ordered hourly patrols of Lane's motel room, and Lane put a mattress in front of the window.

Lane made it to Smith-Brown community center the following evening, Friday, August 12, 1988, and spoke to more than three hundred mostly black Arcadia residents. He had "the fervor of a fire-and-brimstone preacher," wrote a *Fort Myers News-Press* reporter who described the meeting as "a cross between a church service and a sporting event."[21] To cheers of "Amen!" and "That's right!" Lane proclaimed Richardson's innocence, insisting there would be no peace in Arcadia until the imprisoned man went free.[22] When he read Romeo's statement, there were gasps from the crowd and even tears. He played a short recording of Richardson in which the fifty-two-year-old prisoner said softly, "I thank God for you [all].... I'm kind of upset the way the situation is ... [but hope] the people of Arcadia will help me get out of prison."[23]

At that point, Lane asked anyone with information to come forward and said he was forming a Free James Richardson committee in Arcadia. As people filed out, Lane noticed a white man in his thirties in a cowboy hat waiting to talk to him. The man approached him and said he had something to tell Lane but wanted a sheriff's department officer to be present.[24] Lane found an officer, and standing in the gymnasium of the community center the three men had a chat. "If someone stole the official file in this case from the state's attorney's office," the man asked, "could he be charged with a crime?" "Hypothetically, stole it when?" replied Lane. "Ten years ago." To which Lane answered, no. "The person could not be indicted since the statute of limitations had expired, but if he was indicted I would represent him."[25] The sheriff's deputy agreed, and that's when Remus Griffin, a one-time inmate turned amateur detective, told Lane about "the box."

Robert "Remus" Griffin was a good old-fashioned DeSoto County ne'er-do-well. Born to a working-class family in 1959, he grew up on a ranch in the far east of the county but moved at age eight to Arcadia, where his father was a truck driver and his mother an aide at G. Pierce Wood state mental hospital. He had three older brothers and a sister, Kay, who remembered Remus as a sometimes bad though well-meaning boy with a good heart. "I'm older now and get my timelines confused," she said in a 2023 interview, "but shit was always going on in our family. The oldest boys were always getting into trouble, sneaking out and stealing things, so Remus, being the littlest brother, did too."[26]

Once, when the older boys crept out through a bedroom window and left Remus at home, he tried to catch up by stealing a Coca-Cola delivery truck that was parked with the keys in the ignition at a bottling plant next door. "Remus was like nine or ten," Kay recalled with a laugh, "but climbed into the cab of that truck and drove into town. He actually shifted the gears and pressed the pedals but stalled at a red light just as a patrol car pulled up. The cops couldn't see the driver, so that's how he got caught."

On another occasion, sometime in 1966 or 1967, Kay was in eighth grade when she heard at school that Remus and their brother Mark had jumped onto a departing train, thinking they'd jump off when it slowed down. However, the train didn't slow down until it came to a stop some twenty miles to the south in nearby Cleveland, Florida, on the way to Punta Gorda. "Here I was in tears," she chortled, "thinking those two dummies had gone all the way to Cleveland, Ohio. But what did I know? Remus could—and would—do anything. Even as a boy."[27]

Some ten years later, in the summer of 1976, brothers Remus and Mark got into real trouble when they committed a series of break-ins in Arcadia in which they burglarized an evidence locker at the DeSoto County Courthouse in search of a suitcase full of cocaine.[28] It wasn't the brightest of moves, and both brothers went to prison. Yet Remus was seventeen and a nonviolent offender. He should have gone to a juvenile facility but was sent instead to the DeSoto Correctional Institution, where for some reason, he spent more than two years as one of 147 teens younger than eighteen in Florida's adult prison system.[29]

Remus Griffin got out of prison in 1979. He was his usual anti-authoritarian self, drinking, drugging, and fighting, but his experiences in prison, explained Kay, had left him angry at the judicial system and the police. When his girlfriend, twenty-four-year-old secretary Maggie Albritton, told him that her boss, the former Assistant State Attorney Red Treadwell, sometimes came to the office drunk and rambling about the Richardson case, Griffin was all ears.

Albritton later explained, "Red, when drunk, was consumed with guilt that he had sent an innocent man to prison." She said that "when sober, [Treadwell] would allude to possible unfair prosecution, and evidence that did not make it to trial."[30] According to Albritton, Treadwell even said, "I helped to convict an innocent man." In coming years, Treadwell would deny Albritton's claims, calling them "ridiculous," but he did admit "a person under the influence [of alcohol] sometimes says things he doesn't mean."[31]

Truthful or no, Treadwell did have a set of Richardson files that included the exculpatory Gerald Purvis interviews that in 1968 State Attorney Frank Schaub hadn't given to the defense. Why Treadwell kept them is unknown,

Remus Griffin, 1989. Risking a return to prison, Griffin stole previously undisclosed Richardson case files from a former state attorney, setting in motion a movement to free Richardson that culminated in the man's release. Courtesy Tanman Films.

but late one night, sometime in 1979, Griffin borrowed Albritton's car and with it her keys, which he used to open Treadwell's office and steal the files. It was, as Griffin remembered it, a risk. "I could have gotten fifteen years for that," he remarked. "I'd just gotten out of prison and was on probation."[32] But, Griffin opined, "the file didn't belong to Red Treadwell. That file is the property of the people of the state of Florida. At worst, what I did is break into his office . . . and give it back to them."[33]

Griffin wasn't an idiot. He planned to get the file out of his possession and into the hands of Richardson attorney John Robinson, who, when not trying product-liability cases or defending accused murderers, was then the city attorney for South Daytona Beach, the small residential community where he lived. Robinson remembered Griffin's call but said that as a busy attorney, he got lots of calls, often from weirdos, and wanted no part of stolen evidence, if indeed what Griffin had was usable evidence at all. Therefore, Robinson said no. Next, Griffin tried the Black Arcadia city councilman and soon-to-be-mayor Eugene Hickson, but Hickson said no. He "told me to throw it away," claimed Griffin, and "that Frank Cline would kill me if he knew I had it."[34]

That's when Griffin turned to a kindred spirit in former DeSoto County sheriff's dispatcher Hazel Bowden, a thirty-seven-year-old single mother of three who absolutely hated Cline. In a 2023 interview, Bowden, in her eighties, said Cline "was crooked as a dog's hind leg," running stills along the Peace River and extorting sex from female dispatchers, which Bowden refused. "I come from old Florida stock," she said. "I wasn't going to allow a man like Frank Cline to mistreat me. So I quit my job with the sheriff's office and was working as a dispatcher at the [Arcadia] police department when Remus sought me out. He had this big box of files, and I knew that because of what was in it, we were treading on thin ice."[35] Yet Treadwell never said anything; no one knows when or how he learned that the files were missing or if he ever told Sheriff Cline.

By then, Cline was in his fourteenth year in office but was vulnerable, politically, after his son faced felony drug charges for a Sarasota marijuana arrest and a federal grand jury in Tampa investigated but did not indict the sheriff for corruption.[36] Cline hung on until October 1980, when, in a surprise landslide, he lost in the primaries to former Florida Highway Patrolman Robert Thomas.[37] Cline was still an entity, though, a former president of the Florida Sheriffs Association who, to some, was a law enforcement legend. He stayed in Arcadia and in 1981 became acting sheriff in nearby Glades County when the sheriff there took medical leave due to a brain tumor.[38] Thus, with Cline still in the area, Hazel Bowden kept the Richardson files under wraps. "I wanted to give them to someone," she said. "I really did. But just having the box was a crime, and without Robinson, there wasn't much we could do. So Remus did his thing and I did mine, and when I left Arcadia for Clewiston, for a job in the sheriff's office over there, the files went with me."[39] They'd sit in a home in a rough prairie development near an area the Seminoles called Devil's Garden for the next nine years before coming to light, with a vengeance, in 1988.

# FOURTEEN

ANATOMY OF A FRAME-UP

With the fateful meeting of Mark Lane and Remus Griffin, the long-dormant James Richardson case heated up. Griffin called Hazel Bowden, the former DeSoto County Sheriff's dispatcher who'd taken the stolen files to Clewiston. Although Bowden hated Frank Cline and claimed that he sexually harassed her and other women in the office, as a native Arcadian she hated Lane even more. "I mean, he bad-talked my town," she explained. "He just came in here, an outsider, and dredged up all this stuff. And not because he wanted to help Richardson. He only wanted to help himself. So I told Remus, I wasn't going to give Lane that box. I'd give it to the other guy, Robinson, but Lane? Not him."[1]

Robinson took some convincing. The Daytona Beach lawyer initially told Lane he feared losing his law license if he handled stolen evidence, even if it exonerated his client. He also seemed embarrassed by the work he'd done representing Richardson back in 1968 and reportedly told Lane, "What will my peers think about me if this case is reviewed?"[2] To Lane's astonishment, Robinson hemmed and hawed and spent the remainder of September 1988 deciding whether or not to take possession of the box. The press had no idea there even was a box but descended on Arcadia, yet again, as news of Betsy Reese's reported confession went viral. Even the folksy radio show host Paul Harvey covered it, and soon reporters from the *St. Petersburg Times*, the *Tampa Tribune*, and others were in town to reexamine the case.

They were joined by Charles Flowers and Peter B. Gallagher, two freelance journalists working on an article for *Tropic* magazine, the long-form weekend publication of the *Miami Herald*. Although exceptionally talented, the two men were industry misfits, especially Gallagher, who'd been an obsessive though widely respected *St. Petersburg Times* reporter and Pulitzer Prize finalist reportedly fired for insubordination. Likewise, Flowers had passed through several reporting jobs and the editorship of *Sunshine* magazine, a *Fort Lauderdale Sun-Sentinel* publication, but, as he put it, he didn't have "the world's greatest reputation."[3]

They were, though, a formidable team, and Gallagher had the backing of Chief James Billie of Florida's Seminole Indian tribe, who'd been paying the reporter $500 a week to write for the *Seminole Tribune,* the tribe's bimonthly, eight-page paper produced in Hollywood, Florida, with a circulation of 5,000. It was a tiny, Xeroxed rag with a big reach, and every newspaper and politician of note in Florida received a copy. The controversial Billie was an orphaned, two-tour Vietnam vet whose penchant for trouble—with the state, the feds, the National Indian Gaming Commission, and others—was rivaled only by his talent for making money. He had taken office in 1979 and been pushing the tribe to move beyond cigarette sales and alligator wrestling and into the realm of casinos. In a 2022 interview Gallagher recalled his agreement to write for Billie.

> Billie always used these military phrases. He knew I was a writer and had invited me out to his camp in the Big Cypress. He had all these plans, and told me, "I need a pen." I said, "You need what?" And he said, "I've got a map man, I've got a sniper, and now I need a pen." He wanted someone to write for him, to serve as a kind of mouthpiece, but let me pursue almost any other story I wanted.[4]

So Gallagher covered the Richardson case for the *Seminole Tribune* and chose as his partner Flowers, with whom he'd recently worked on a *Tribune* report on the Florida panther. When the Richardson case grew more and more complex and some of its subjects litigious, Gallagher brought the story to the *Miami Herald,* which ran a feature by the two in *Tropic* as well as several smaller articles, in parallel to what Flowers and Gallagher had published in the *Seminole Tribune.*

In September 1988, with Robinson in attendance, the two men visited Richardson at the maximum-security Tomoka Correctional Institution in Daytona Beach. There, they were met by the warden, Leonard Duggar, who told the journalists, "Men who come to prison for killing children do really hard time. They get beat up. They get tortured and killed. Nobody treats them decently. Guards, fellow inmates, staff. But this man has a totally clean record, not a single black mark in twenty-one years. Everyone knows he's innocent."[5]

At length, Richardson told the reporters his story. Then, they spoke to Griffin, who described how he'd stolen the box and given it to a woman in a place called Devil's Garden. Gallagher knew the area. It was a pancake-flat agricultural region of cattle ranches and tomato fields between Clewiston in the north and the Big Cypress Seminole Reservation to the south, where the great 1830s Seminole leader Abiaki, whom US soldiers called "The Devil," had once had a camp.

That's where Hazel Bowden lived, in a 1960s-era mobile-home subdivision called Montura Ranch Estates. Flood-prone and remote, Montura, at times, resembled less a housing development than a *Mad Max* free-for-all, with drug labs, pot farms, cockfights, anti-Castro training facilities, and in 1988 the home of Hector "Macho" Comacho, a flamboyant but troubled boxing champion who'd been arrested in February for threatening a high school student with a gun on school grounds.[6]

It was a dangerous place, but all Griffin would say was that the box was there. He then gave them the number of an after-hours phone at G. Pierce Wood mental facility, where Bowden, having left the Hendry County Sheriff's Office, now worked the night shift. "Remus didn't say 'Call Hazel' or 'Call a woman named Bowden,'" Gallagher said with a laugh. "Instead, he gave us a code name, like in a spy novel, and said 'Ask for the Contessa.'"[7]

When Gallagher called the facility, however, the Contessa freaked out. She told him where she lived and how to get there, but then, fearing undue media attention or a visit from Frank Cline, contacted Robinson and convinced him to take the box. Why he had changed his mind is unknown, but the handover took place at a gas station on the corner of state roads 70 and 27 in Lake Placid after Bowden waited for several minutes to see that Robinson hadn't been followed. But Gallagher didn't know that. He told his boss, Chief Billie, where Bowden lived, and Billie, armed with a pistol, drove Gallagher to her house. In a later interview Bowden explained,

> I just wanted a peaceful life, but having this box and knowing that people probably would've killed for it made me afraid to say anything to anyone. I just wanted it out of the house. But then Gallagher arrived and

there's this guy with him. My sons were both six feet and big, so I told them to go outside to see who it was. That's when I hear all this whooping and hollering. They said, "Hey, Mama! It's alright! It's James Billie!" You see, what this Gallagher didn't know was that my husband and Billie had gone to high school together and were old friends. He knew me, but not the Contessa, my code name. We all had a big laugh about it and sat around while I talked to Gallagher, but I'd already given Robinson the box. He was a lawyer and it just seemed safer that way.[8]

Lane, though, said when Robinson returned to Daytona Beach he considered destroying the box, for inside were 955 pages not previously made public, including witness statements and interviews that hadn't been given to the defense. If these became public, surmised Lane, the state might review the case, and Robinson's poor work in defending Richardson would be revealed.

Yet, in his defense, the Daytona Beach lawyer had defended James Richardson pro bono when no one else would. Robinson had no criminal trial experience and faced a win-at-all-costs prosecutor in a racially biased court, where a sheriff and two jailhouse snitches seemed to have perjured themselves under oath. Lane wrote that the conviction wasn't Robinson's fault when even the great lawyer Clarence Darrow might not have prevailed. After some consideration, Robinson gave Lane the box but told the lawyer, "he would not be part of any effort that sought a review."[9] Thus, for whatever reason—vanity? guilt? shame?—Robinson removed himself as Richardson's attorney. The two men remained friends, but for all intents and purposes, Robinson was through.

That left Lane, who in October 1988 added as co-counsel the controversial Florida attorney Ellis Rubin. A 1951 University of Miami law grad, the sixty-three-year-old Rubin was the king of the "Twinkie" defense, a slang term among lawyers meaning a long-shot legal defense bordering on the insane. In 1978 Rubin argued that a fifteen-year-old Miami Beach resident named Ronny Zamora had shot and killed an elderly female neighbor because of "involuntary subliminal television intoxication."

Mark Lane, Ellis Rubin, and James Richardson (*left to right*), 1989. Lane added the controversial Miami attorney Rubin as co-counsel on the Richardson case in 1988. The two lawyers didn't like each other, but in 1989 they secured Richardson's release. Courtesy Tanman Films.

In other words, cop shows on TV, specifically *Kojak,* made him do it.[10] Then there was the "porno defense" of Tampa serial killer Bobby Joe Long in 1986, in which Rubin claimed Long had raped and killed eight women because of "prolonged, intense, subliminal" exposure to pornography.[11] Neither Twinkie worked; Zamora got life and Long got the chair. But in 1987 Rubin hit pay dirt by being the first lawyer in Florida to argue convincingly that "battered-woman syndrome" had caused a thirty-year-old Broward County resident to premeditatively murder her sexually abusive stepfather.

Rubin was smart, innovative, wildly egotistical, and adept at stoking the press, a kind of Mark Lane clone. "Most people, frankly, sneered at Ellis and considered him an excessive publicity hound," said a former Miami prosecutor. "But he had some very successful litigation, and I can't remember him ever backing off from a battle."[12] Rubin was also licensed in Florida, so while Lane negotiated film rights and worked the TV circuit for Richardson, Rubin did the legal work. It was an uneasy pairing, as both wanted credit for freeing Richardson and both wanted to be in the press.

Everything, though, depended on what Lane found in the box. And what he found was that statements given in 1967 and 1968 by jailhouse snitches James Cunningham, Earnell Washington, and James "Spot" Weaver differed radically from what each had said under oath. At best, they'd told two different stories, and at worst, with perhaps a nod from authorities, they'd lied. But with Schaub in charge, the prosecution had withheld their statements as well as those of Reverend L. T. Fagan and the insurance salesman Gerald Purvis, which would have aided the defense.

Those missing statements "detailed the anatomy of a frameup," insisted Lane, and though "prosecutors had the absolute duty to produce the documents," they never did.[13] As a teaser, Lane then shared some of the documents with reporters, including Flowers and Gallagher, who in the fall of 1988 began traversing the state to confirm Richardson's story. "We wanted that box," said Gallagher. "Lane showed us some pages, but when I started taking pictures, he said, 'No! No!' and put everything away. I always thought Charles, who was a big guy, should have just grabbed the box and run out of there. What was Lane going to do? Have us arrested for stealing a stolen box?"[14]

The two men had already interviewed Richardson at Tomoka. They then met with Griffin and Bowden and were tracking down additional sources when, on October 19, 1988, Lane held a press conference in Tallahassee. He was there, he said, to present the Richardson files to Peter Dunbar, chief counsel to Florida Governor Bob Martinez, who he hoped would appoint a special prosecutor to review the case.

"This is a case, the most monumental and outrageous case of prosecutorial misconduct I have ever encountered or read about in my thirty-seven years as a lawyer," declared Lane to a throng of reporters at the Tallahassee Hilton.[15] He knew that prosecutors and overly zealous sheriffs and police departments made mistakes, he said. But "these are not mistakes. This is a deliberate plan to frame an innocent man."[16] Naming Red Treadwell, Frank Schaub, and Frank Cline in particular, Lane remarked bluntly, "They lied. They lied to the people of Florida. They lied to the jury, and they lied to the judge."[17]

He then shared passages, snippets of pages that a reporter called "difficult to interpret out of context."[18] But Lane's narrative was clear: Betsy Reese had killed the children to get back at Richardson for driving her husband to Jacksonville. Cline chose not to investigate Reese because he had a sexual relationship with Reese's daughter. And though Schaub and Treadwell had once considered dropping the case for lack of evidence, they'd prosecuted Richardson anyway.

Never mind that the files only hinted at Reese's motive or that Evelyn Black, Reese's daughter, had said openly and fervently that she'd never had sex with the sheriff and that her child wasn't his. Lane told a lugubrious tale, a salacious tale seemingly taken from a telenovela. And it just so happened that accompanying Lane that day was the Hollywood producer Steve Jaffe, the one-time super-agent to Jane Fonda, Barbra Streisand, and Ryan O'Neal, who'd been given seed money from HBO for a possible TV series.

Richardson apparently had given Lane the right to negotiate TV contracts on his behalf, and both the Free James Richardson rally and the Tallahassee press conference had been paid for by the network. However, when asked what they'd earn for the rights or what the production would cost, Jaffe said, "What Lane's doing right now, he's doing for James Richardson and not for himself, so it's inappropriate for me to comment on business."[19]

But Lane was all about business. Soon after the press conference, he entered into negotiations with the syndicated tabloid-TV program *Inside Edition,* which, in exchange for access, agreed to pay $50,000 to a Lane-controlled Free James Richardson Fund.[20] The fund was to pay legal fees for Lane and Rubin and to support Richardson if and when he got out of prison. But that depended on the governor, whose office reviewed the files, then passed them on to the Florida Department of Law Enforcement (FDLE) for a formal investigation.

The FDLE's point man was inspector John Doughtie, who in late 1988 and early 1989 dug up records and conducted interviews with people connected to the case, from Frank Cline, Frank Schaub, and Red Treadwell to Richard Barnard, Annie Mae Richardson, James "Spot" Weaver, and "Bad Boy" Boom. "The funny thing was," said Gallagher, "we were doing that, too. We'd go to Immokalee to talk to this person, and Doughtie would pass us on the way out. It got to be a joke with us. We'd say, 'See you in Arcadia!' or 'See you in Lakeland!' You know, wherever the next person would be."[21]

The two investigations, in parallel, revealed some interesting information. For one, Spot Weaver had lied. He admitted he had lied to Doughtie in an interview he conducted at the Polk County Sheriff's Office in Lakeland. He didn't say why he had lied, only that Boom had beaten him, both in a car on the way to Arcadia and at the DeSoto County jail. Doughtie reported, "James Weaver states that he was not told by James Richardson nor did he overhear James Richardson say he had killed his children."[22]

Backing up Weaver's statements was Jack Ross, an investigator for the state attorney's office in Daytona Beach who in 1981 was an independent private eye. Ross claimed he'd been hired by Robinson to find and interview Weaver for an appeal. Ross located Weaver in Lakeland, where the often-arrested gambler admitted that both he and Cunningham had perjured themselves for an early release from jail.[23] Ross said to Flowers and Gallagher, "Weaver told me that he and Cunningham were told what to say.... They had really not heard Richardson confess."[24]

Then there was the former Arcadia police chief Richard Barnard. He had never liked Cline, and since mocking the sheriff in Lane's book in 1970, he had become a probation officer in Polk County. On December 3, 1988, Barnard gave Ellis Rubin a handwritten, notarized statement, which Rubin gave to both the FDLE and the press. Barnard wrote, "I was chief of police in Arcadia, Florida, during all of the relevant times referred to in this affidavit. Based upon my investigation into the deaths of the seven Richardson children, I have concluded that James Richardson is innocent, and that he was framed... by Sheriff Frank Cline."[25]

Barnard offered no direct evidence, but an assistant FDLE investigator found something new. In the fall of 1967, Weaver had been in the Arcadia city jail on a larceny charge. He was Barnard's prisoner. Cline had called Barnard and said, "Let me have Spot," and had him transferred to the county jail to be placed in a cell with Richardson. Had Cline engineered Weaver's statement? Cline said no. But sure enough, Barnard provided the FDLE with original jail records verifying the days Weaver had been there.[26]

Things didn't look good for Cline. They looked even worse when Barnard claimed that shortly after the poisonings, when he tried to question Betsy Reese, someone from the governor's office called to inform him that Cline "was the chief law enforcement investigator in the county" and that he should "lay off."[27] Barnard didn't know who had called and didn't have a recording of the conversation. Next, Barnard claimed that shortly before the trial, Cline had said he wanted to go to Fort Myers to "look over the jury list" to see "if anyone that he knew" was on it.[28] Did he want to talk to jurors? Persuade jurors? Barnard didn't know.

Then, there was this strange tidbit, which had nothing to do with Richardson but everything to do with Cline. In one of several FDLE interviews, Barnard claimed that he had in his possession absentee ballots from the 1966 DeSoto County sheriff's election that had been marked for Cline's rival but that Judge Gordon Hays told a custodian to destroy.[29] Did Hays put Cline in office? And really, what did it matter? The election, by that point, was twenty-two years old, and Doughtie wasn't investigating Cline.

Still, the FDLE's inquiries painted a pretty bad picture of the sheriff. Doughtie's Richardson file contained a document titled "1981 FDLE/FBI Investigation" of "Frank Cline and Associates," which detailed an airborne marijuana smuggling operation that passed, in the 1970s, through DeSoto County.[30] The entries were short and factual and purported an odd relationship between Cline and a known Atlanta drug smuggler, Hubert S. Cotton, who later did thirty months in a federal prison. On one occasion, the FDLE/FBI investigation found, the DeSoto County Sheriff's Office confiscated a World War II–era C-46 airplane full of pot but then turned around and sold the plane to Cotton for less than half of what it was worth.

With Cline's blessing, presumably, the sheriff's office also sold a second plane to Cotton, reportedly below value, then backed off from confiscating a small-engine Piper Aztec owned by a known Cotton associate and drug smuggler named Gary Reynolds, who had jettisoned the plane's seats and several bales of marijuana in rural DeSoto before flying the plane to Georgia.[31] Next were complaints against the DeSoto County Sheriff's Office. "Interviews of current and former employees," read one entry, "have identified several females who were forced to have sex with Sheriff Cline under threat of losing their jobs."[32] The sheriff also had at least two girlfriends, one of whom, the FDLE and FBI investigation alleged, he gave sheriff's office property to.

As for Cline's relationship with Reese's daughter, Evelyn Black, both Cline and Black were adamant, in spite of rumors, that they didn't have an affair. The two even took and passed DNA tests paid for by the FDLE to prove it. However, in a sworn statement to Doughtie, a twenty-two-year-old African American woman and Nocatee resident, Mary Kirkland, insisted that sometime in the late 1970s, some ten years after Richardson's conviction, Cline made frequent trips, "night and day" and "noon sometimes," to Black's small trailer. "Would you know if this was work related business?" asked Doughtie. "No, it was not," replied Kirkland. "Because when the police come to people's house, they don't come that many time[s] and don't take nobody to jail."[33] Who knows if Kirkland was telling the truth; she was in Lowell State Prison the next time Doughtie spoke with her. Maybe this is where the rumor started that Cline protected Reese because he was sleeping with her daughter. Maybe Cline and Black did have an affair, but one that started after her daughter was born and after Richardson had gone to prison.

Then there was Gerald Purvis, the insurance salesman, whom Flowers and Gallagher found at his home in Ellenton, lying in his living room in a full-body iron lung. He had chronic obstructive pulmonary disease but claimed vigorously that Richardson hadn't purchased insurance and didn't think he had purchased any.[34] Purvis's story hadn't changed in twenty years.

But Doughtie found something new. In a taped phone interview, Purvis told Doughtie and reiterated yet again that he "in no way indicated to Richardson that he or his family were covered." But Doughtie learned that in 1967, Schaub had asked Purvis to attend a meeting in Tampa with Florida's deputy insurance commissioner. The reason was that Schaub and Treadwell both believed Purvis was lying and that in order to sell Richardson a policy, Purvis had fronted him the money. Therefore, Schaub attempted to pressure Purvis by holding a meeting, in person, with a state insurance regulator, and according to Purvis, by offering him immunity if he said under oath that Richardson was insured.[35] But Purvis refused. He remained as steadfast in his defense of Richardson as Schaub was in proclaiming his guilt.

FIFTEEN

BUT THEY'RE GONE HOME

"Retired now at the age of 67," wrote journalists Flowers and Gallagher in 1989, Frank Schaub "compulsively misstates known facts in the case, holds to a few, queer, unsubstantiated charges and arrogantly refuses to consider any possibility that might shed even the slightest of positive light on Richardson." As the two journalists contended, "Schaub is where he was four decades ago, stuck in a state of mind that says the criminal goes to jail, the sociologist is a fool, and the law is not an ass."[1]

Without question, members of the Manatee County Bar Association did not like Schaub as a judge. In 1982 he ranked tenth out of ten in a poll of which circuit court judges its lawyers preferred to work with. Asked to rank them in three categories—highly approve, approve, and do not approve—Schaub came in dead last, receiving one highly approve vote, seventeen approve votes, and a whopping fifty-two do not approve votes.[2]

"He won't go down ... as one of our stronger circuit judges," said a longtime Bradenton lawyer. "I think he was bored because, at heart, he is a trial lawyer. He did not have patience for inept lawyers or inefficiency. I don't think he was happy as a judge."[3] What is more, Schaub was obsessed with speedy trials, running a rocket docket with as many as eight cases a week. Sometimes he'd schedule twenty or twenty-five cases a week, so "prosecutors, defense attorneys, and numerous witnesses, like horses jammed at the starting gate, must wait, prepared and ready for trial, to see if their case comes up."[4]

Schaub was curt and abrupt and seemed as a judge almost preternaturally disposed to convict. In January 1982, when Schaub rotated from civil court to criminal court and replaced a judge named Parham, he pronounced sixty-five people guilty. But that same month a year earlier, Parham pronounced just eleven. Schaub "believes in adjudicating people guilty," explained one court clerk. "He believes in sending people to prison, and he believes in giving the maximum when the jury says guilty."[5]

Tired of being a judge, in 1984 Schaub ran for district attorney, again, and won unopposed. He then took office, reduced plea bargains, and chose not to participate in pretrial intervention programs for first-time nonviolent offenders such as polluters and trespassers. That would have saved taxpayers at least $2,000 a case, but Schaub wanted the trials.[6] In 1987 he returned to court as prosecutor for the case of twenty-eight-year-old West Bradenton resident Charles Frederick Nowitzke, the stepson of former Cincinnati Reds pitcher Clay Carroll who in 1985 shot to death his mother and stepbrother and wounded Carroll.

Nowitzke claimed insanity, but Schaub, at the trial, decimated his defense by engaging in what the Florida Supreme Court called "instances of [prosecutorial] misconduct too numerous to mention."[7] Schaub's trial strategy, such as it was, was to impeach Nowitzki's insanity plea by attacking the personal integrity of defense psychiatrist Emmanuel Tanay through six hours of questioning in which he referred to Tanay as a "hired gun," then misled the jury by saying Tanay made $600 an hour when Schaub knew he made $150.

His biggest gaffe, perhaps, was in telling jurors incorrectly that Nowitzke "would be released within eight months if he were found innocent by reason of insanity."[8] That wasn't true; therefore, in a 7–0 vote, the Florida Supreme Court reversed Nowitzke's conviction while blasting Schaub for ignoring the precepts of his office. The court wrote, "The prosecutor's primary responsibility is to see that justice is done, not to win at all costs. Schaub's conduct demonstrates a complete lack of regard for the role of prosecutor."[9] But that's what he was: a prosecutor, a deliverer of justice, who in his seemingly maniacal quest to win the Nowitzke case had utterly ignored the rules. Did he do the same thing in the Richardson case? From the contents of the stolen Treadwell file, it could be argued he did, so Richardson went to prison, where, if not for an unrelated decision that paused the death penalty nationwide, Richardson would have been executed. That's why Lane declared Schaub should've been charged with attempted murder.

However, *Sarasota Herald-Tribune* reporter L. Wayne Hicks mistakenly reported that Rubin had said it. Therefore, Schaub filed a $35 million defamation of character suit against Rubin and called a press conference to do it. Eventually Schaub amended the suit, claiming that Lane had also defamed him, but Schaub's December 1988 legal filing wasn't one he could win. In fact, Rubin welcomed it, going so far as to call Schaub's suit a "Christmas present" because if Schaub sued the two attorneys, they in turn could question him under oath.[10]

They might ask him why, for example, he hadn't given the Purvis and Fagan statements to the defense or why he had let Cline lie when the sheriff testified that Purvis's business card was a receipt. And what about Cunningham, Washington, and Weaver, the snitchy threesome, who'd said one thing under questioning, then something entirely different under oath? Should they have been witnesses? "I would hope Schaub had taken a different tack," said Bradenton attorney and fellow prosecutor Edwin Mulock, "because the train was out of the station and people wanted Richardson released."[11]

The Free James Richardson movement reached a crescendo in December 1988 when Flowers and Gallagher published "Poisoned Justice," a gripping article in *Tropic* magazine insisting that Richardson didn't do it. Then, in January 1989, Richardson himself starred in the first-ever episode of the tabloid news program *Inside Edition,* which its producers billed as "the new face of reality." Aired on some eighty stations nationwide, the show had as its field producer Craig Rivera, the brother of famed tabloid journalist Geraldo Rivera, and as host the legendary British investigative reporter David Frost. Although known for pushing the envelope, Frost had real credibility. He interviewed, in a career spanning decades, seven US presidents and was the first reporter to sit down with disgraced former President Richard Nixon following Watergate.

With episode one of *Inside Edition,* Frost introduced the Richardson story, then a reporter named John Scott narrated the tale and interviewed Richardson in Tomoka. The show left little doubt that Richardson had been framed and was innocent. Frost finished the segment by declaring, "*I* think James Richardson *is* innocent. . . . How on earth can society pay its debt to [such a man] . . . for twenty years of anguish and pain? We'll come back to that in another program. Right now, the first priority is to set him free."[12] With that, *Inside Edition* put the mailing address of Florida Governor Bob Martinez on the screen, while Frost implored viewers to send letters demanding

Richardson's release, "not next month or next year," he said, "but now! This week! By lunchtime tomorrow! If only on parole for a start!"[13]

The appeal worked. By early February, some 14,000 letters had arrived, including one from US Representative Mervyn Dymally, a Democrat from California who chaired the Congressional Black Caucus. In a one-and-a-half-page letter, Dymally listed problems with the state's case, insisting that a "blatant misconduct of trial proceedings" had cast doubt on Richardson's guilt. Therefore, he urged the governor to release Richardson while taking "appropriate action against those who . . . have seriously violated the law in the conduct of their duties."[14]

That's what Doughtie's FDLE investigation showed, that the use of unreliable snitch testimony had been troubling and that various exculpatory statements hadn't been given to the defense. Moreover, in late January 1989, just as Doughtie planned to finish his investigation, a new witness came forward, a twenty-eight-year-old African American woman named Virginia Dennis. She lived in the Quarters and in 1967 had been a seven-year-old friend and classmate of Betty Jean Richardson.

In a sworn interview with Doughtie on January 20, 1989, Dennis testified that she stopped by the Richardson residence on the morning of the murders to accompany Betty Jean to school. No adult was there, said Dennis, so she and Betty Jean and the other kids ate from a pot of grits before leaving. She did not get sick, she explained, nor did she taste or smell parathion. Here's the rub: at lunch, Dennis returned with Betty Jean, but this time Reese was there, and as the older woman prepared food for the kids, she told Dennis to go home. "I don't think Mr. Richardson did it," declared Dennis. "I believe [Reese] did it . . . because I had eaten the breakfast but not the lunch."[15]

Although chilling, Dennis's statement was problematic, as in December she had also spoken to Doughtie and failed to mention the incidents. But coming as it did on the heels of *Inside Edition* and adding yet more, albeit questionable, evidence in support of Richardson, Dennis's declaration forced the governor to act. "There were seven deaths," Martinez asserted, "We can't forget that. Seven little ones died. And someone was found guilty. If there was wrongdoing at that time, we would like to know about it. Justice ought to prevail wherever it may be."[16]

On February 1, 1989, Martinez appointed a special prosecutor to review and present the case to the governor and six elected members of his cabinet, who served as a clemency board and could pardon Richardson or commute his sentence. Martinez had chosen well. His special prosecutor was the über-ethical, not to mention popular and battle-tested Dade County State Attorney Janet Reno, who, as Florida's first female state attorney, had handled prosecutions in Miami since 1978. She was a survivor, having stayed in office through the Mariel boatlift, the police beating death of Black insurance salesman Arthur McDuffie, the riots of Liberty City, and the real-life *Miami Vice* years of the "cocaine cowboys." Now she was reviewing a case from Arcadia.

The town, which had barely caught its breath following the Ray case, was, at the time, fighting over the proposed renaming of Orange Avenue, the primary thoroughfare through southwest Arcadia and the Quarters, in honor of Reverend Martin Luther King Jr. But Orange also ran north into a white neighborhood, so when the city sent questionnaires to property owners asking if they favored the change, the responses were thirty-four for and thirty-seven against, divided along racial lines.

A white respondent wrote, "Too many concessions to minorities now. The middle-class whites are the ones being discriminated against."[17] By now, virtually anyone who knew Arcadia knew that wasn't true. According to mandatory reporting data sent to the Federal Equal Opportunity Employment Commission, for example, Arcadia had an African American population of roughly 30 percent, but as of 1991, their share of city jobs stood at less than 12 percent, with 87 whites, 12 African Americans, 2 Hispanics, and 2 Asians and/or Pacific Islanders on the payroll.[18]

Digging deeper, there were no paid administrators who were Black, and only one African American employee, a technician, received an income that would have been considered middle-class. City Councilman Eugene Hickson was Black, but there were no Black county commissioners or school board members—and never had been—because the county used a discriminatory election process of at-large voting in which, instead of choosing one candidate per district, voters chose all five candidates at once.

This diluted the Black vote intentionally and violated Section 2 of the federal Voting Rights Act of 1965.[19] Thus, as of 1989, Arcadia's Black residents, led by sixty-something former teacher's aide and NAACP president Helen Washington, were considering two lawsuits, one with the county and one with the school board, while pressing for an Orange Avenue name change and supporting Richardson.

It was a heady time, and Washington, who often made comments critical of Arcadia in the press, became a target of prank phone calls and even a death threat.[20] However, white Arcadians were surprisingly calm regarding the Richardson case. Most suspected that at a minimum, the imprisoned farmworker had been wronged but were tired of all the "town without pity" reports on TV. "It's really strange in a way," said a white librarian from Arcadia. "Everyone I talk to is fed up with all the hoopla over the Richardson thing and the Ray thing, and the way it's stirred up the whole town. But, at the same time . . . [residents] want to know what really happened twenty-one years ago. They want to know the truth."[21]

So did Janet Reno. The Dade state attorney reviewed the case and Doughtie's investigative file through February and March 1989 and planned to present her findings to the governor and cabinet at a clemency hearing on April 6. But on March 30, news leaked that Reno had uncovered serious problems in the handling of the prosecution and that she had encouraged the governor not to grant clemency but to ask the original circuit court to set aside its verdict and to grant Richardson postconviction relief. "Justice was not served in the defendant's trial," Reno told the governor. "He was deprived of a fair trial."[22]

Therefore, at Governor Martinez's urging, on April 5, 1989, the Florida Supreme Court ordered the circuit court in Arcadia to hold a hearing as to whether it should vacate Richardson's conviction. It then appointed retired judge Clifton Kelly of Sebring to manage the proceedings, which were held at the DeSoto County Courthouse on Tuesday, April 25. Not one for excuses, Kelly wasn't a pushover. In 1977 the tough-on-crime judge had sentenced a sixteen-year-old Highlands County youth to die in the electric chair for murdering an elderly widow, and he had traveled the state in retirement giving "scared-straight" lectures to schoolkids and promoting a textbook called *The Consequences of Crime*.[23]

On the day of the hearing, Kelly entered the courtroom to a packed house shortly after 9 a.m. and planned to weigh arguments from Reno, Schaub, Rubin, and Lane. The seventy-one-year-old judge forgot his gavel, though, so bailiffs gave him a miniature gavel, taken from who knows where, while searching the building for a real one. It was a bizarre scene, as Kelly tapped the tiny gavel vigorously as Richardson arrived and the raucous, mostly African American crowd roared its applause.

Annie Mae was there, as was the former state NAACP president and minister Joel Atkins and the famed Black comedian and Lane's friend Dick Gregory, who owned a health resort near Fort Walton Beach and had promised Richardson a job. They sat at attention as Reno told Kelly what she had found. "We think James Richardson's constitutional rights, under the due process clause of the Fourteenth Amendment, were violated," she said, because "the state failed to provide key exculpatory evidence."[24] She then reviewed what Purvis and Fagan had said and how the prosecution had kept in its possession "evidence that completely refuted the insurance motive" and failed to provide that evidence to the defense.[25]

Reno then criticized the use of contradictory snitch testimony and singled out Cline for lying about the supposed insurance receipt under oath. Cline wasn't there, having chosen not to face the press, but Schaub was, and when his turn came to speak he described Reno's report as a "hatchet job" and claimed the entire effort to free Richardson had been "a boondoggle and a fraud." He didn't say anything about having withheld exculpatory statements, and he attacked Richardson's character with the gusto of the old Schaub. Richardson was a "sanctimonious hypocrite," he exclaimed, and prosecuting the man, he asserted, had been the highlight of his career.[26]

Tension grew even more when Lane attacked Schaub by pointing at the prosecutor and yelling, "They presented perjured testimony!" and "They did it on purpose!" The two men screamed at each other, and sheriff's deputies "were halfway up the aisle," wrote one journalist, "before things calmed down."[27] Sheriff Varnadore said, "I was sure one of them was going to pop the other one."[28] During breaks in the hearing, Varnadore allowed Richardson to wander the courtroom and greet old friends. That's when Remus Griffin introduced himself and shook Richardson's hand. The two men chatted for a moment, then parted, a wrongfully convicted Black man and a white former parolee who a decade earlier had risked going to prison to save Richardson's life.

Now, Richardson was inches from being released. The evidence was clear. At approximately 6 p.m., some nine hours into the proceedings and following thirty minutes of deliberation, Kelly announced his decision. The defendant "did not receive a fair trial," he intoned. "Had this evidence been disclosed, the outcome may have been different. Jurors did not have the full picture." To this he concluded, "The enormity of the crime—seven children poisoned to death—is matched only by the enormity of the injustice to this man."[29]

Therefore, Kelly ordered a new trial, which Reno, speaking for the state, said there would never be, and Richardson was released. The crowd erupted. A smiling Richardson hugged his lawyers and praised Jesus, and people started to cry. "I didn't think I'd live to see it," said a tearful Helen Washington. "It hasn't been many days I didn't think about him, all twenty-one years."[30] Other Black Arcadians were angry, both at Schaub and at the system that had put Richardson in prison. He "went through hell for no reason" said one woman, and "we all knew he didn't kill them."[31]

About a month later, on Memorial Day 1989, Richardson returned to Arcadia for a service at St. John Missionary Baptist Church in the Quarters, next door to where the Richardsons' apartment once stood. The congregants lit candles, one for each of the seven Richardson kids; after a sermon and some hymns, they drove to the cemetery to visit the children's graves. Richardson had been stoic, but as seven local kids sang the Sunday school hymn "Jesus Loves Me," the bowed, graying man started to cry. "I'm looking at the little children hoping they were mine," he shuddered. "But they're gone home."[32] Cameras whirred and clicked as Richardson knelt at each of the graves and prayed. Betty Jean, Alice, Susie, Doreen, Vanesa, James Jr., and Diane. He hadn't seen them in twenty years. "Take them God!" he yelled. "Into your hands of glory. . . . They're not alone anymore."[33] The congregants wept. The children wept. And Richardson was free.

SIXTEEN

I DIDN'T LOSE MY BATTLE

In October 1992 an emaciated, eighty-two-pound Ricky Ray entered All Children's Hospital in St. Petersburg. Now in the third and final stage of HIV, his fifteen-year-old body had started to wilt due to an onslaught of opportunistic infections. He had pneumonia, internal bleeding, and an inflamed pancreas; his legs were partially paralyzed, and he could no longer see through his right eye. Yet Ricky would tell people, "It just isn't my time," so the day before Thanksgiving he asked to go home. He was in hospice, staring death in the face as a teenager, with the courage and acceptance of an adult.

Since leaving Arcadia, Ricky and his family had been living in Sarasota, whose school board, shortly before the Rays' September 1987 arrival, had passed what observers called "the most comprehensive bill of rights for AIDS-infected students" in the United States.[1] For one, the policy guaranteed anonymity and stated that students with HIV could attend regular classes as long as their condition posed no threat to others. However, if the student showed symptoms of AIDS, they would be removed from class while the superintendent, in consultation with doctors, decided if the student should stay in school or learn from home.

The policy showed "reasoned caution" and "common sense," a *Bradenton Herald* editorial declared, and stood in "sharp contrast to the ignorant, inhumane policy of the DeSoto County School Board."[2] And, as for the board, Judge Elizabeth Kovachevich's August 1987 ruling for the Rays included the caveat that the board sponsor a public talk by a legitimate medical professional to educate the community about AIDS. Although board members didn't want to do it, they hired the head of the Sarasota County Health

Department, who was a doctor, to give a two-hour lecture at DeSoto Middle School that only five people attended.

"I think it's unfortunate that we didn't have more of a turnout," said Superintendent Larry Browning. "I think it would have been very beneficial to people to find out the history ... [of the disease] and what's being done through research."[3] But what did Browning expect? He and the board had castigated the Rays, which, in tight-knit, conservative Arcadia, meant giving the boys and their parents a scarlet letter. Had they pushed the AIDS issue to get reelected? Or did they honestly believe what they were saying? It's difficult to know.

But Browning, members of the DeSoto County School Board, Arcadia's mayor, and its county commissioners all went out of their way to stoke hatred toward attorney Judith Kavanaugh and especially Louise and Clifford Ray. The couple didn't care about the children, their critics said. The Rays and their uppity attorney only wanted money. Yet even if they did want money, as many Arcadians believed, the town's political elite hadn't the slightest inkling that legally, morally, or medically isolating the Ray boys had been wrong.

"There are still Arcadians who wear their ignorance like a crown," wrote Stephen Buckley of the *St. Petersburg Times* in a 2001 retrospective. "They've read about AIDS and listened to the most authoritative doctors talk about it. They've heard again and again that AIDS is passed through sexual contact, shared needles, or tainted blood. And still they don't believe."[4] As proof, Buckley interviewed James Westberry Jr., who in 1987 had been chairman of the DeSoto County School Board and who continued to insist, "They're going to find out us dumb country folk were right" and that those doctors knew "lots more than they let on."[5]

However, Arcadians who agreed with the school board didn't necessarily fear doctors. What they feared were state and federal governments telling them what to do, as many had with desegregation. Presumably that is why only five residents bothered to learn about AIDS at the court-ordered information session but upward of a hundred, still fired up and ready to speak, squeezed into the DeSoto County Commission chambers for a hearing in October 1987 of the state's legislative task force on AIDS. The task force came to Arcadia to gather testimony as to whether the state should pass laws regulating AIDS in the classroom. As it stood, Florida didn't have any laws to that effect, only guidelines for school boards suggested but not ordered by state Education Commissioner Betty Castor.

Following the Sarasota model, Castor wrote that as a general rule, HIV-positive students who were "not debilitated or posing a threat of transmitting... [AIDS] should be taught in the regular classroom." If they were sick and suffering from AIDS, they should be taught separately, either in school or at home. Anonymity was a must, and decisions regarding students were best made on a case-by-case basis by a county health director, a school administrator, the student's parents, and their doctor.[6]

The head of the task force was Florida House Representative Louise Frankel, a Democrat from West Palm Beach, who favored passing either the Sarasota model or Castor's State Department of Education guidelines into law. Frankel selected Arcadia for the hearing because fellow Representative Vernon Peeples, whose district included DeSoto County, asked her to. Peeples said Arcadians had suffered a traumatic experience and had something to share.[7]

But if Frankel wanted a diversity of views at the meeting, she didn't get it. For nearly three hours Superintendent Browning, County Commissioner John E. Johnson, and Citizens Against AIDS in Schools members Danny Tew, Robert Werner, and Melody Patton, among others, criticized the state for not barring children with HIV. "The legislative bodies have been sitting on their duff," said Werner, "worrying about me strapping a gun to my shoulder... [and] worrying about the lottery." The state should have started a task force back in 1982, not in 1987, he said. "This is like locking the chicken coop door after the fox has been in and stole all the chickens."[8]

Tew complained that by merely suggesting guidelines, Castor had usurped the authority of local school boards, but he didn't have a problem with state legislators passing laws banning infected students or requiring testing for AIDS. Lawmakers in Tallahassee didn't have the stomach for that. In June 1988, the Florida legislature came to a compromise and passed a bill, which Governor Bob Martinez signed into law, that made it illegal to discriminate against people with AIDS but allowed for the arrest and quarantining of infected residents, prostitutes mainly, who knowingly spread the disease.

The law also required the state's Department of Health and Rehabilitative Services to develop AIDS-related educational materials for cosmetologists, barbers, beauticians, child-care workers, health-care workers, massage therapists, inmates and correctional officers, and police, while mandating AIDS education at middle school and high school levels. "We're going to get tough with AIDS," said Frankel, "but not with AIDS patients."[9] Florida's 1988 AIDS law allowed victims to sue employers, landlords, insurance companies, businesses, and state and municipal entities for discrimination, with penalties of $5,000 or actual damages for those who acted intentionally or recklessly.[10]

By this point, the Rays were already suing the DeSoto County School Board, and in 1990 they also sued the factor VIII manufacturers Cutter Laboratories (a division of Bayer) and Armour Pharmaceutical in federal court. "That pharmaceutical case was crazy," said Judith Kavanaugh. "Cutter and Armour settled, but first a judge dismissed the case, then reinstated the case, and then we had a mistrial, but the big shock came in discovery."[11] Kavanaugh contended that Cutter and Armour should have prevented HIV-positive donors from giving blood and that once the companies had learned of AIDS, they should have put warning labels on their products.

In response, a lawyer for Cutter claimed that the company had made factor VIII "as safe as we could with what we knew at the time."[12] But during discovery, the pretrial procedure in which Kavanaugh and her team requested documents and other materials from the defense, a distracted Cutter attorney accidentally included a memo written in 1982 by a member of the Cutter family who also served as its counsel recommending that Cutter warn hemophilia sufferers of the connection between factor VIII and AIDS.[13]

Company officials instead played dumb and wouldn't add warnings to factor VIII labels until 1984, by which time hundreds if not thousands of hemophiliac patients including the Rays had been infected. Cutter tried to suppress the memo by claiming attorney-client privilege. When that failed, its lawyers said in court that the memo was just an opinion. The company heard lots of opinions, and besides, they argued, adding specific warning labels was "a lengthy, government-mandated process" and not something the company could quickly or easily do.[14]

Although Kavanaugh couldn't prove which of the two companies had infected the Rays, she didn't have to. A 1990 ruling by the Florida Supreme Court found that when a plaintiff didn't know which defendant had caused an injury that clearly resulted from a product they made, the defendants could be held liable under what jurists called "market share alternate liability" theory, in which courts assigned damages by the size of the market share each company owned.

The jury accepted the theory, but after thirteen hours of deliberations jurors deadlocked as to whether Cutter and Armour, knowing what they knew at the time, could've prevented their products from infecting the boys with AIDS. That is, the jury found that Cutter and Armour had caused the boys to be sick but not that they'd been negligent. So in April 1991, a judge in Tampa declared a mistrial.

The two sides were set to do it again before the same judge in a second trial in November 1991, when they came to a settlement: the Rays received a reported $1 million for their suffering, but neither Cutter nor Armour admitted to negligence. "My biggest hope is that this family can get on with their lives," said Cutter attorney Duncan Barr. "There's no way to measure the tragedy involved. It's very, very sad when the medicine that would have enabled these kids to live ... may ultimately shorten [their lives]."[15]

Yet even in Sarasota, where students, teachers, and the community had welcomed the Rays with open arms, they'd never live normal lives. They were celebrities. A *Palm Beach Post* reporter described a visit with the family in June 1991.

> It's Friday afternoon, and Louise Ray is tired.... The phone rings about once every minute, and she picks and chooses like she's shopping for ripe fruit. "*Women's World* and Sally Jessy Raphael are about to drive me insane," she said, skipping a call from a Florida reporter but grabbing the receiver when someone from *Geraldo!* calls. No two ways about it: Louise and Clifford Ray, both 33, have moxie.... They took their story and spoke their minds with Oprah Winfrey, Phil Donahue, Sally Jessy Raphael, Larry King, and Ted Koppel. And America tuned in to listen to the tale of the three dying brothers.[16]

The family said it wanted privacy, but appearances on talk shows, trips to Washington, New York, and Los Angeles, and meetings with (and swag from) movie stars and sports stars and singers had given the Rays what Clifford called the "celebrity syndrome."[17] On a trip to California, the Rays visited Disneyland, Universal Studios, and Knott's Berry Farm and met with Hollywood stars Michael J. Fox and Tina Yothers. They rode a stagecoach at Burt Reynolds' ranch, met Reynolds' wife, Lonnie Anderson, and played Monopoly with famed *Playboy* publisher Hugh Hefner. They shook hands with Ted Kennedy, Whoopi Goldberg, and Oprah Winfrey, among others; they met players and coaches from the Tampa Bay Buccaneers and even went to the Super Bowl.[18]

Then, there was the money. With two $1 million settlements, in 1988 and 1991, plus who knows how much in donations, the family got a lot. But much of it went to lawyers' fees or came in installments, over decades, while payments to the children went into trusts. The DeSoto County School Board paid the Rays $1.1 million, but roughly 40 percent of it, $437,500, went to court costs and attorneys' fees. Then, Ricky, Robert, and Randy each received $819.43 a month for a period of ten years, with much of it going to a trust, while Clifford and Louise got lump sums of $50,000 each plus payments of $298.73 a month over thirty years.[19] The terms of the Cutter and Armour settlement, though most likely similar, weren't disclosed.

"People think we're rich," bemoaned Clifford, who bought a house and a truck and paid lots of overdue bills, but most of it was in a trust fund for the kids. "If I don't work," he said, "we don't eat."[20] What rankled Arcadians at first was the Rays' TV movie deal, a reported $100,000 from a producer at ABC, but due to a writers' strike in 1988 and the fact that a Ryan White drama already had a script, the deal fell through.[21] Yet, money or no and their status as celebrities notwithstanding, Clifford and Louise faced a terrible reality: their boys were dying.

"There are days when I'm very angry," said Louise. "I'll be driving down the street and see healthy kids playing. I know they're going to grow up and have their own kids. I think 'Why my kids instead of them?'"[22] Both Clifford and Louise took antidepressants, and during the first four years they lived in Sarasota, the police were called to their residence at least twenty times, for threatening phone calls, stolen property, switched campaign signs, domestic spats, and a suicide attempt.

Clifford carried a gun, and the Rays spent nights getting in and out of bed whenever they heard anything. "Sometimes . . . you hear noise," he said, "like when there's rain and . . . thunder. We'll come straight out of bed, our feet on the floor, looking out the window. The dog starts barking and we're out of bed again."[23]

Often phone calls came unsolicited from distraught parents whose children had AIDS and whose small towns had acted much the same as Arcadia. They wanted advice, even help, and in one instance the Rays offered to drive to Illinois to pick up a woman and an HIV-positive child who'd received death threats. "I said, 'We don't know you, but Cliff and I will come and get you if you want,'" remembered Louise. "I was desperate. It was Arcadia all over again."[24]

The worst stories involved the kids. Ricky and Robert, the oldest two boys, were wasting away. They also had mood swings and depression from prescribed drugs and from AIDS-related changes to the brain. Louise told a newspaper reporter in 1990, "After a really bad episode of being sick in the bathroom, [Ricky] ... lay down on the couch and said, 'Mom, I'm just so tired of being sick. I wish it could be all over with.' I said, 'Well, Ricky, you'll feel different in the morning.' He settled down ... [but] I went outside and lost it."[25]

However, it was in Sarasota that, socially at least, Ricky thrived. At Booker Middle School, he wore a stylish magnetic earring to avoid bleeding, ran for school treasurer, handed out business cards that read, "Don't Be Picky, Vote for Ricky," and won student of the month. He also swam at the Boys Club

Wenonah Lindberg and Ricky Ray, 1991. Fourteen-year-old Ricky caused a second media firestorm that year when he announced his engagement to his sixteen-year-old girlfriend, Wenonah. As Ricky's health deteriorated, the couple called off the engagement, and Ricky died near Orlando in 1992. Courtesy *Tallahassee Democrat*/Imagn Images.

and in 1991 found a girlfriend, sixteen-year-old classmate Wenonah Lindberg. She was older and taller, a pretty girl who dwarfed the razor-thin, four-foot-eleven, wan and sickly Ricky, who was fourteen.

They dated for a time, and in June 1991, the couple caused a TV and tabloid firestorm by announcing their engagement. "I don't know if I've got two years left or a hundred and forty years," explained Ricky. "All I know is we want to be together for as long as I have."[26] Their parents agreed, and Ricky and Wenonah spoke openly about sex—they weren't going to have it—and said they'd speak to health professionals about being intimate. In addition, they planned to start a family through artificial insemination, and when Ricky died he wanted to include Wenonah in his will.

Then came the media tour, and the Rays, Wenonah in tow, did one program after another: *Larry King Live* via satellite, the *Oprah Winfrey Show* in Chicago, *Geraldo!* in New York. Were they educating people about AIDS? Or were they basking in the media attention and enjoying free trips? Probably both. The Rays themselves had contacted the press to give them the news that Ricky and Wenonah were getting married. "Basically, rumors were getting out in the schools and were being carried home," said Clifford. "And there was a lot of talk. So me and [Louise] ... called one of my friends from the *Sarasota Herald* ... before things got out of hand. So we're the ones who brought it out."[27]

Clifford explained that they were a "public family" and had "been public since 1986. There is no escaping it."[28] But, after four years of normalcy, of living in a welcoming town with residents who accepted them, maybe causing a second brouhaha, this one self-inflicted, wasn't the right thing to do. "Should a fourteen-year-old boy who has AIDS marry his sixteen-year-old girlfriend?" asked an editorial in the *Tampa Tribune*. "Maybe there's no definitive answer, but boy-oh-boy, there's no shortage of opinions on that question."[29]

Concerned citizens wrote letters, hundreds of them, called TV talk shows and radio news shows, and also called the Rays. Teenagers wanted help. Their boyfriends or girlfriends had AIDS and they planned to marry, but their parents didn't approve. Some worried about kissing or cuddling or the dangers of unprotected sex.

Then there were the cranks. The Rays received death threats, including one from a caller who said, "If this marriage goes through, both families are going to die." Another said, "If you think Arcadia was bad, you haven't seen anything."[30] That's when Clifford got three dogs and put up a privacy fence, then took the family into hiding. A Sarasota County sheriff's lieutenant said of the threats, "Whether implied or real or whatever, we're taking it seriously. He fears for the safety of his family."[31]

Through it all, Ricky and Robert declined physically. In August 1991 Ricky spent time at a National Institutes of Health hospital in Bethesda, Maryland, with an eye infection and at All Children's Hospital in St. Petersburg with a fever. He had leg problems, too, an "unexplained and transient paralysis," his doctor called it, and was, even then, on morphine.[32] The travel, the lawsuits, the interviews, and the stress had gotten to him, and the Rays, who lived on modest settlement payouts plus Clifford's income as a prison guard, were broke.

They were so broke, in fact, that in 1991, they offered local TV stations a taped video of Ricky for $1,000, but the stations said no. "I haven't seen it and I don't want it," said Tampa's WTSP news director Mel Martin. "I was taken aback. We don't pay for news."[33] Neither did most stations, but the Rays were desperate enough—and some said greedy enough—to try. *Tampa Tribune* columnist Mary Toothman opined, "When once-normal people or families become well known ... notoriety can take its toll." The Rays have "helped spotlight AIDS discrimination problems and enlightened the public that anyone can suffer from the virus." However, their recent offer to sell a videotaped interview of Ricky "was just outrageous." The Rays deserved compassion and sympathy, she wrote, but they "overestimate their own importance" in selling a child's illness.[34]

In sending Ricky and Wenonah on a media tour, they'd also turned their story from one of discrimination and acceptance to something carnivalesque. In 1991 Ricky and Wenonah joined a *Geraldo!* lineup that included "Women of the Klan: Women Who Hate" and "Sex in the Office: How to Survive from 9 to 5." The truth is that talk shows were tawdry, a "daily parade," wrote one journalist, "of frivolous celebrities, colorful loonies, airheads, weirdos, and sex freaks. Much of it may be entertaining, but none of it is worthwhile."[35]

Indeed, to the public, Ricky and Wenonah weren't teenagers fighting to find love in the midst of an AIDS epidemic as much as they were entertainment, and by late 1991, Americans had had plenty of entertainment regarding teenagers with AIDS. There had been at least three made-for-TV movies on the subject, *An Enemy Among Us* in 1987, *Go Toward the Light* in 1988, and then in 1989 *The Ryan White Story*, which had edged out a movie on the Rays.

Whatever the case, by the winter of 1991–1992, the Rays' days as talk-show celebrities were over. Ricky was sick, and he and Wenonah canceled their wedding plans that November. "I don't know if we will get married," said a weakened Ricky in a last interview of him and Wenonah. "There's been too much publicity . . . too much stress." Wenonah added, "Too much everything. It's been difficult to go out and do stuff. Everyone says, 'There's Ricky!' 'There's Wenonah!'"[36]

In the spring of 1992 the Rays moved to a suburb east of Orlando to be closer to Clifford's work at a different prison, and it's there that Ricky's condition worsened. He checked into an Orlando hospital in June for an undisclosed condition, then in October moved to All Children's Hospital in St. Petersburg. He was gravely ill, the family said, and by November they were keeping a vigil. "He talks to me, but he's very tired," said their longtime family doctor Jerry Barbosa. "He's a very stoic person and only asks for medication when the pain gets intolerable."[37] In and out of consciousness and suffering from jaundice, Ricky took a phone call from President-elect Bill Clinton, whom Ricky admired for his AIDS stance, then the day before Thanksgiving went home. He died near Orlando on Sunday, December 13, 1992, at the age of fifteen.

Ricky "asked that people not mourn his death so much as celebrate his life," explained a tearful Louise. To which Clifford added that Ricky absolutely hated when people said Ryan White had lost his battle with AIDS. "He got so mad," said Clifford. "[He'd say,] 'Ryan didn't lose his battle. Ryan don't have AIDS. Ryan don't have no pain anymore. I don't want no one to say I lost my battle. I didn't lose my battle. I won. I'm going to a better place.'"[38] The press nationwide eulogized Ricky as a hero, a fighter, and with his death revisited the events in Arcadia. As a result, the "town without pity" returned to the news.

SEVENTEEN

AN ISOLATED ISLAND OF A PLACE

"Somewhere in DeSoto County," wrote Mary Toothman of the *Tampa Tribune* two days after Ricky Ray died, "there are people who should be hanging their heads in shame. They're the people who harassed the family of young Ricky Ray and who eventually drove the Rays from their town. Unfortunately, there are many who have the same ignorant, not-our-problem attitudes about [AIDS]. They live in DeSoto County, still, and . . . all over the nation."[1] *USA Today* even sent a reporter to Arcadia and ran an article with the headline "'Town without Pity' Reflects on Treatment of Brothers with AIDS."[2]

Its tone was noncommittal. There were those who thought the Rays had been wronged and those who thought the school board had been right. But, the pastor of Arcadia's Grace Lutheran Church said, the town had "grown a great deal," and he was confident that there "wouldn't be such a controversy" now.[3] A recurring theme was the fire. The Rays, newspaper accounts noted, had been purposely burned out, their home destroyed by an "arsonist," a "coward," and a "villain."[4]

But in August 1991, on the four-year anniversary of the fire, Florida's statute of limitations on arson investigations ran out, and no one could explain how Andy Ray had been home, sleeping, when the fire started inside the house. Rumors would persist, and on one side, said Florida State Attorney's Office investigator John Fugate, were Arcadians who called the fire a hate crime and on the other, Arcadians who said it was not a hate crime and was done on purpose for publicity.[5]

Either way, the story that the Rays had been firebombed, like in a scene from the 1988 civil rights film *Mississippi Burning,* would proliferate. Arcadia would have to live with it. Like it or not, true or untrue, it was the town that had burned out children with AIDS. Just before Ricky's death, a full five years after the incident, a Japanese film crew traveled from Tokyo to ask Arcadians, in the words of their translator, "why someone got upset and arsoned the home?" They were shooting a documentary titled AIDS: *There's Nothing to Be Afraid Of* and told a reporter that Arcadia was a "bad example to learn from" and they "wanted to make a show to help people understand."[6]

The Rays had moved on. "Naturally, I never anticipated what would happen," insisted Louise. "I was born in Arcadia and I lived there for twenty-eight years. I went to school there. I grew up there.... [But] when you hate somebody it makes you bitter. I don't want to be bitter. Arcadia doesn't matter anymore. Arcadia is part of our past."[7] With Ricky gone, the Rays clung tightly to their kids and dove head first into lobbying Florida's state government and the federal government to establish assistance programs for hemophilia sufferers with AIDS.

In 1993 they attended the Clinton inauguration as guests, and in 1994 an emboldened Louise ran for a Florida House of Representatives seat as a Democrat representing rural portions of Volusia, Seminole, and Orange Counties. Her focus was "education, education, education," she said, not just AIDS, and as a working-class nurse whose husband was a correctional officer, she knew her constituents. "I mean, let's face it, it's no secret where we come from—a dumpy shack in Arcadia."[8]

She'd also say, "I've had to stand in food stamp lines. I've had to figure out how to pay the electricity bills, just like everybody else. But we've also been at the other end of the baton. We've been forced into the public eye, we've eaten dinner with the president and the vice-president. I think all of this gives me a good perspective."[9] Louise lost, handily, in a surprisingly bitter campaign with incumbent conservative Marvin Couch, who had the backing of ranchers and farmers, and the Pat Robertson–led Christian Coalition. She was socially liberal and fiscally conservative, but Couch tied Louise and her AIDS work to Florida's gay and lesbian community to win in a landslide, 62 percent to 38 percent.

"This race was a learning experience and I gave it my best," Louise explained. "I got into this because I wanted to make a difference and still can, whether I'm in office or not."[10] As proof, she worked tirelessly as a private citizen with US Representative Porter Goss of Sanibel, a Republican, to promote the Ricky Ray Hemophilia Relief Fund Act. The bill would establish a $1 billion trust fund to give HIV-positive hemophilia patients and their family members a one-time, tax-free payment of $125,000. The reasoning was that the federal government bore at least partial responsibility for failing to protect its blood supply and thus owed those with hemophilia compensation.

"This legislation isn't about charity," said Goss. "And it isn't about making everything all right for the victims." It was about the federal government "owning up to a share of the responsibility for what happened."[11] The other responsible party was the factor VIII industry, which would settle with HIV-positive hemophilia patients and their families in a series of class-action and individual lawsuits through the 1990s. The manufacturers got off cheap, paying some 6,000 claimants a mere $100,000 apiece. So did the US government, which in October 1998, after three years of wrangling and pressure from Florida Senators Bob Graham and Connie Mack, finally passed the Ricky Ray act into law.[12] However, the act's language failed to assign blame to either factor VIII manufacturers or the government and stated that the payments were compassionate rather than compensatory in nature. They were also $100,000, not $125,000.[13]

By this point, AIDS-stricken hemophilia sufferers were dying at a rate of roughly two a day. The Rays had already lost Ricky, and by 1998 Robert was dying too. He hung on until October 2000, when he died of complications from the disease at All Children's Hospital in St. Petersburg. He was just twenty-two. "I can't tell you what it's like to be a father, and know you're supposed to protect your kids, get in between them and anything that might hurt them, and you can't," said Clifford. "When Robert was dying, I just wanted to pick him up in my arms, like he was still a baby. But I couldn't."[14]

Clifford considered suicide but through therapy and medication came to a state of acceptance both of his boys' lot in life and of how he and his family had been treated in Arcadia. The town was "just another place to us now," he explained after Robert died. He wasn't mad or bitter or vindictive, he said, because "nothing that happened to us compares to the pain we've suffered since then."[15]

Be that as it may, a lot had changed in the town in the thirteen or so years since the family left. Although it grew only marginally, from 6,488 in 1990 to 6,604 in 2000, Arcadia's compact, old downtown had been revitalized by a large number of antique shops, some of whose owners were gay. Apparently, few cared. "I'm here as a business person," said store owner Robert Judd in 2001. "I have never had anyone swearing and yelling at me. It's how you carry yourself and present yourself with people.... I don't know whether it's tolerance or acceptance or what."[16]

Day trippers from the coast found Arcadia cool, even quirky, and downtown chambers of commerce in other old Florida towns wanted what it had: heavy foot traffic through a conglomeration of eight gift shops and twenty-two antique stores. The *Bradenton Herald* called Arcadia a "gleaming example" for Bradenton's own downtown and looked on in envy when in 1993 author Norman Crampton, in his book *The 100 Best Small Towns in America*, named Arcadia the best small town in Florida.[17]

Never mind that Crampton had never been there or that he'd only visited fifteen of the one hundred towns he'd written about; Arcadia's leaders made use of the moniker, and the name stuck. For years, as you drove into Arcadia, you saw a sign that read, "The Best Small Town in Florida." However, in June 1993, *Miami Herald* writer Lori Rozsa called Crampton for a comment. What about James Richardson? she asked. And what about the Rays? To which Crampton replied, Those were "very sorry situation[s]. But I measure the response of the community since then. In my conversations, I was impressed that the situation has changed there."[18]

One definite way Arcadia had changed over time was demographically. It now had Hispanics, lots of them, who for the most part had come as migrant agricultural workers and stayed. A countywide Hispanic population of 610 in 1980, roughly 3 percent of the county's residents, jumped to 8,019 by 2000, about 25 percent of DeSoto County residents.[19] And that didn't count seasonal workers, whom farmworker advocates numbered at 25,000 a year.[20]

Yet DeSoto's migrant influx and increased Hispanic population had not been unexpected, as freezes in the 1980s forced growers to move the state's central Florida citrus belt some one hundred miles to the south, to places like DeSoto County where the weather was warmer.[21] There, they planted millions of new trees, which matured and bore fruit beginning in the 1990s. As a result, DeSoto County had almost as many migrant workers during the October to May harvesting season as it had residents. Its economy depended upon them.[22] DeSoto did have its rodeo, which, by the early 2000s, pumped a reported $2.4 million dollars a year into the local economy. It still had its evangelical churches and revivals as well as occasional gospel concerts in the parking lot of the Walmart, and as always elected officials said prayers before meetings of the school board, whose post-Ray superintendent was Adrian Cline, a cousin of former sheriff Frank Cline.[23]

In 2002, following a spate of deaths and several gruesome accidents, including one in which an unsupervised patient cut off his hands with a table saw, the infamous G. Pierce Wood facility finally closed its doors.[24] That meant the loss of more than 1,100 jobs that a reporter noted had "offered state benefits, stability, and something citrus groves and ranches could not: the possibility of a middle class life."[25] To ameliorate the effects of the closure, the state shuttered G. Pierce Wood in phases, then shifted a reported 750 workers to a new juvenile detention facility and to the Florida Civil Commitment Center (FCCC) for sexual offenders.[26]

Like G. Pierce Wood, both institutions were in rural DeSoto County outside of Arcadia. And reputation-wise, they were bad, especially FCCC, which, beginning in 2000, housed some of the most depraved criminals in the state. G. Pierce Wood "gave a young person a better chance to make money and not have to do such dirty work for it," said Amber Price, a therapeutic aide whose parents had also worked at the hospital. "But the choices they give you now, it's not something you're proud of."[27]

To be sure, FCCC was controversial in the extreme—"I don't want them predators in DeSoto County," said one woman—but residents needed the jobs, and no one in government bothered to ask anyone if they wanted 408 sexual offenders, including murderers and child molesters, living in their community.[28] No doubt, G. Pierce Wood had been atrocious; to some it was a poorly run, *One Flew Over the Cuckoo's Nest* warehouse for ill Floridians, but the FCCC was even worse. Its premise, made legal by a five-to-four US Supreme Court decision, was that states could continue to incarcerate sexual offenders as threats to society even after they'd served their sentences.

"They tell you you have to repay your debt to society," said an inmate from West Palm Beach who'd spent eight years in prison for molesting his stepdaughter, "then they tell you you have lifelong interest to pay on that debt."[29] Theoretically, inmates earned their release through an Alcoholics Anonymous–like step program that included honest admissions, but inmates and their attorneys feared that telling the truth would only get them into trouble. So more than 60 percent said nothing, and at a cost of $50,000 a year per person, they lived in Arcadia indefinitely, never to be reformed, in a kind of sex-offender purgatory.[30]

Things got worse when Liberty Behavioral Health, the private company paid by the state to run FCCC, increased the number of inmates but not the staff. By 2004, resident sex offenders outnumbered employees more than two to one. A *Miami Herald* reporter wrote in 2006 that "drugs, alcohol, sex, child pornography, and a band of disgruntled offenders disrupted a calm therapeutic setting, . . . [and] the facility had no way of maintaining order."[31]

With headlines that read "Arcadia Center 'a Powder Keg'" (*Bradenton Herald*) and "Treatment Center or Cesspool?" (*Orlando Sentinel*), Arcadians wondered what they'd done to deserve such a facility at all.[32] And that was before Florida's most notorious rapist escaped; Bruce Alan Young, a former Citrus County hospital nurse, had preyed on unconscious women and girls in the recovery room. He was caught in February 2008 walking down an Arcadia street.[33]

In the years following the Richardson and Ray cases, Arcadia's most notorious story, and one that found its way into the national press, was the murder of Greg and Kimberly Malnory, a young Punta Gorda couple, by Greg's coworker James Dennis "Jimbo" Ford. The murder occurred on a rural sod farm in eastern Charlotte County, but Ford was from a well-known Arcadia family with deep Florida roots. It was a dastardly crime: Ford and the Malnorys were friends, ostensibly, and had gone hunting and fishing together at a remote camp on the edge of the sod farm's property in April 1997. That's when something bad happened, something inexplicable.

The timeline is murky, but it's possible that while Greg was hunting, Ford raped Kimberly, then shoved a gun into the roof of her mouth and pulled the trigger. Then, when Greg came back, Ford hacked at his head with a hatchet or some other tool, cut his throat, then shot him in the face. He drove away, covered in blood, leaving the Malnorys' twenty-three-month-old daughter screaming in hysterics and strapped into a car seat. Deputies found her more than twenty hours later, dehydrated and covered in mosquito bites, but alive.³⁴

Although this was a Charlotte County crime, jurisdictionally, Ford was from Arcadia. He was Remus Griffin's cousin and had long been suspected in the disappearance of two other cousins, twenty-one-year-old Kellie Jo Krum and her eight-month-old daughter, Kelsi, from their home in Arcadia in 1994.³⁵ Ford had been the last person to see the young mother and her baby alive, so, as he was charged in the Malnory case, rumors swirled. Was he a serial killer? And if so, who else had he killed? "I grew up in Arcadia and knew Kelli Crum [sic]," read an anonymous comment to a Malnory-murder article on the *Florida Issues* blog. "She was a great person. Everyone in town knew that Jimbo killed her and her daughter in '94. My only regret is that I didn't end him a couple of years earlier. Rip Kelli sorry."³⁶ In April 1997, then-DeSoto Sheriff Vernon Keen had Ford polygraphed regarding the disappearance, but when Keen's technician found Ford "deceptive," Ford "invoked his right to silence" and never spoke of the matter again.³⁷

Punta Gorda attorney Paul Sullivan represented Ford in the Malnory murders and recalled that sometime prior to the trial, news broke that in 1976, when Ford was a teenager, he and his father allegedly got into a fistfight with a fifty-two-year-old housemate named Johnny C. Brown. Friends said Brown was a harmless drunk, but had come to fisticuffs with one or both of the Fords and ended up dead. "It must have been around 1980," said Brown's friend Jack Lanier, who was a bartender at the Arcadia honky-tonk The Corral, when Ford began mouthing off. "For years I'd been asking people" what had happened to Brown, and one day Ford said Brown was "probably that old son-of-a-bitch they found ... dead some years back. We took the body out and buried it."³⁸

The Fords, father and son, dug graves at Arcadia's cemetery, but for some odd reason didn't identify Brown. Neither did a negligent DeSoto County Sheriff's Office, headed at the time by Frank Cline. There also wasn't an autopsy. So Brown, a John Doe, rested in lot 13, block 2, space 5, unit 3 of Arcadia's Oak Ridge Cemetery until 1986, when Brown's sister hired a detective to find him. The detective did what any detective would do: he retrieved Brown's death photos from the mortuary, showed them to friends and family members, and identified him. It took just a day.³⁹ However, no one questioned

Jimbo Ford, and since the DeSoto County Sheriff's Office failed to investigate the burial, Brown stayed buried.

His story reappeared, though, in 1997, when journalists, law enforcement officers, residents, and victims' family members began trying to tie Ford to other crimes. "So here I am the defense attorney in the Jimbo Ford trial," said Sullivan, "and they're attempting to link Jimbo to this Brown guy, when a different story broke that [Ford's] grandfather's brother, a guy named Squash Ford, had been mixed up in some killings as well, way back in the 1930s."[40] Local historian Lindsey Williams noted Lawrence E. "Squash" Ford, Jimbo's great-uncle, worked as a cowboy for the powerful Parker ranching family of Arcadia and was a key and perhaps even murderous participant in Florida's last range war, a small but nasty affair that pitted the Parkers against a rival cow-hunting clan known as the Nortons.

In 1930 Norton family head Milton Norton was driving in a truck in rural Glades County when he was ambushed. Shot several times and woozy, Norton managed to exit the truck and hide in the bush before escaping. His assailant, he told deputies, was the Parker family boss and Arcadia cattle baron Zeb Parker. But Parker provided an alibi, so the charges were dismissed.[41] It is unclear what happened in the meantime, but in 1933, the Parker-Norton cattle feud escalated when four men lay in wait near Gator Slough, also in Glades County, and shot down Milton Norton's brother and two others. No one knew who did it at the time, but witnesses testified that Squash Ford, at the behest of Zeb Parker, had been involved. Ford was indicted in 1935, but he and his codefendants were acquitted, in spite of witness-intimidation claims, when a woman recanted.[42]

"Of course, I didn't want the jury to hear the Squash Ford story," explained Sullivan, "or really any other stories, either. They were prejudicial. But it got me thinking about Arcadia. I mean, this was a rough place. And I'm from Mississippi. I know the South. And I always told people that trying cases there was like trying cases at home. But Arcadia was rougher."[43]

Just days before Ford's trial in January 1999, the Charlotte *Sun-Herald* printed a "Jimbo Ford Timeline," with snippets from the Squash Ford case and the Johnny C. Brown case at the top. The timeline included an unsolved 1984 murder of a young Arcadia mother named Janet Sass, the missing-persons case of Ford's cousins Kellie Jo Krum and her daughter Kelsi, and important dates from the Malnory case, some fourteen entries in all. The insinuation was that all of these cases were connected.

Yet the timeline wasn't just an indictment of Ford, who got the death penalty. It was also an indictment of Arcadia. A range war in the 1930s?! Joe DiMaggio visited the beach and did his spring training in Florida in the 1930s. Johnny Weissmuller shot Tarzan movies in Florida in the 1930s. But gunfights, over cows? And what about Johnny C. Brown? How had authorities failed to identify a well-known town drunk? Unsolved murders, missing persons, and inept law enforcement—this was a town steeped in violence with a penchant for making the news.

A different question is how, in the face of unceasing development in Florida, Arcadia has continued to exist. In 2025 it's the same small agricultural town with the same economic base—cattle and oranges—that it was in 1925. In fact, a recent report by the US Department of Agriculture found that today's DeSoto County had nearly 294,000 acres of ranches and farms, more than Charlotte (99,711), Lee (91,202), and Sarasota (71,878) Counties combined.[44]

It wasn't traditionally this way, as Southwest Florida's coastal counties had once been agricultural too. As late as the 1950s, Charlotte County was one big ranch, or really a collection of ranches, with some, such as the Frizzell and Babcock holdings, nearly 100,000 acres each in size. Things changed during the post–World War II period with the advent of interstates and air-conditioning, the dredging and filling of coastal areas, new assembly-line-like techniques in home construction, and an insecticide called DDT. Suddenly, Southwest Florida wasn't swampy or malarial anymore; it was livable.

So people moved to the coast, where farms and ranches gave way to housing developments, indeed entire cities. In Charlotte and Sarasota Counties, the Frizzell Ranch became Port Charlotte and North Port; in Lee County, the Lucky Lee Ranch became Lehigh Acres. But as people moved in, mostly to the west of Interstate 75, farming and ranching moved out, to the east, to DeSoto, Hendry, and Glades Counties, where land was cheap. "I've been around here for a few years," said a fourth-generation Fort Myers farmer in 2022. "I've seen a few changes, from this being an agricultural area here to not so much."[45]

As a result, Southwest Florida's coastal areas diversified into billion-dollar economies based on tourism and construction, plus banking, medicine, insurance, real estate, utilities, government, transportation, education, and retail trades. By contrast, DeSoto County didn't diversify. It didn't have tourists or large numbers of housing starts, only ranches and farms. These were augmented by what industries coastal counties didn't want: G. Pierce Wood, the mental institution; the DeSoto Correctional Institution; and the infamous sexual-predator internment camp, FCCC.

So Arcadia lived on, "an insulated, isolated island of a place," wrote an observer, where it was acceptable for authorities to railroad an innocent farm worker, and for elected school officials, not to mention residents and parents, to vilify children with AIDS.[46] But was it a town without pity? No. Not everyone in Arcadia wanted to crucify James Richardson or cast out or segregate the Rays. They just didn't have power, and for every hate-spewing Danny Tew, there was a Helen Washington; for every Frank Cline, a Remus Griffin. "There are some real good people in Arcadia," said Kaye Mercer, the owner of a clothing store, in 1992. "But it seems like we only ever get bad publicity, because that's what makes the news."[47]

In 2002 Arcadia again made headlines when Vicky Davidson, a DeSoto fish-farm manager, purchased a reported 25,000 shotgun shells and instructed employees "to gun down anything that posed a threat to the fish."[48] Over a period of several months, the workers killed more than 4,000 birds, including herons, egrets, eastern meadowlarks, highly endangered wood storks, and black neck stilts. Davidson had broken at least a half-dozen state and federal laws, but a judge in DeSoto County gave her a laughably small $5,000 fine, which, including court costs, came to $1.30 a bird.[49]

In 2004 Hurricane Charley struck. The category 4 monster with 150 mile-per-hour winds veered from the Gulf and up US 17 to Arcadia, where it blew down the town's water tower, ripped the roof off of its hurricane-shelter civic center, and destroyed or damaged countywide some 8,000 homes. By one estimate, the hurricane left 17,000 people homeless in a county of 34,000.[50] "I think the hardest thing," said a town employee, "was manning the phones, and hearing people calling and crying for help, that they were trapped in their homes, that the storm was coming and their house was coming apart on them and there was . . . nothing we can do."[51]

Charley was so strong that it blew down oaks, scattered telephone poles and powerlines, and spewed raw sewage at the high school. It killed a man who'd hidden with his wife in a metal crate that in a wind gust had flipped over and crushed him.[52] "It's surreal," said one resident. "There's no words to describe what I've seen. The wind just came and took it away."[53]

Hit especially hard were DeSoto's cattle and citrus industries. Ranches lost few cows—"They're smarter than most people. They got low in the barn and stayed put," said a cowboy—but miles of destroyed fences, downed barns and sheds, a closed Arcadia livestock market, and cows that wouldn't eat due to mosquitos, which were swarming, meant huge losses, a reported $4 million for the Arcadia market in August 2004 alone.[54]

Citrus fared even worse, with 50 to 75 percent of area groves critically damaged or destroyed.[55] Fruit was everywhere, rotting, and an estimated 90 percent of migrant farmworker housing needed to be torn down. Growers were in recovery mode, said the director of a citrus association in Arcadia in 2005. "They've gotten past the emergency situation of living day-to-day and have now moved on to realizing they may be bankrupt. I've heard several growers say . . . they just can't afford it anymore. It's a heartbreaking thing. You're talking about not just a livelihood. It's a way of life."[56]

To that, add brutal outbreaks of twin bacterial citrus diseases called canker and greening that more or less killed trees. There wasn't a cure for either, but canker, spread by wind through Hurricane Charley, made for a terrible 2005. That's because the state mandated that every tree within 1,900 feet of an infected tree be destroyed; therefore, growers uprooted and burned more than 1.4 million trees in all. And that was just in DeSoto County. Statewide, they burned 11 million citrus trees.[57] "The sad saga of the citrus sizzle continues," wrote reporter Robert Bowden. "On the horizon, rising smoke can be seen in DeSoto County."[58]

Although the state reimbursed growers $26 per tree for a maximum of $4,004 per acre, the money wasn't enough. Workers didn't work, and migrants, who had few places to live in DeSoto County anyway, didn't get paid. With nowhere to go but up, or so they thought, things got worse for Arcadians during the subprime mortgage crisis of 2008, when Southwest Florida's real estate market and economy imploded. DeSoto County's real estate market was minuscule by comparison, but residents who commuted to other counties, particularly for jobs in construction, had little work. Agriculture also declined. "Why grow plants you can't sell?" asked a near-bankrupt nursery owner. Soon DeSoto was the poorest county in the state.

According to a 2012 MSN Money report, the county had a poverty rate of 32 percent, more than twice the US average of 15.1 percent. What is more, nearly one in four people living in DeSoto County received food stamps, and the median household income for the county was just $33,966, far below the state median income of $47,661.[59] A *Sarasota Herald-Tribune* reporter wrote, "The recession hit Florida's Gulf Coast hard, but it hit DeSoto County even harder. With a rural economy based on agriculture and construction, DeSoto has nowhere near the money or the social-service safety net of its coastal neighbors. The need for food, the most basic of basic requirements, has gone through the roof."[60] Things improved somewhat in 2013, when the poverty rate dropped and employment ticked upward, and battered Arcadia saw someone it hadn't seen in more than twenty years: James Richardson.

EPILOGUE

THINGS THAT WEREN'T SO GOOD

Seventy-seven years old and in ill health, James Richardson had been living in Wichita, Kansas, and his life had taken a circuitous route since his release from prison. Somehow his job with activist and comedian Dick Gregory had ended, and by the early 1990s Richardson was at his sister's home in Jacksonville, Florida, penniless. He'd learned to read in prison and become a minister but had trouble finding jobs and lived on small movie-rights advances from Hollywood producer Steve Jaffe.

He and Annie Mae had divorced and Richardson had remarried, but Annie Mae claimed in court that Richardson owed her half of any movie deal, should one materialize, as well as half of any wrongful-conviction settlement with the state. In 1996 a US district court in Tampa threw out a $35 million lawsuit filed by Richardson against State Attorney Frank Schaub, while Richardson's long-awaited film contract, negotiated by Jaffe with CBS, paid just $50,000, with the caveat being no movie, no deal. "He was happy, but he's been through this before," explained Jaffe. "He said, 'Do you really think it's going to happen this time?'"[1]

The answer was no because in Hollywood, optioned story ideas sometimes sit for years before dying, and in Richardson's case, it was he who nearly died. The day after he signed his contract, he had a heart attack and soon ended up in Wichita, where a wealthy cardiologist named Joseph P. Galichia offered to treat him for free. Galichia then gave Richardson a job as a caretaker on his four-hundred-acre ranch, where Richardson lived with his wife, Teresa, and minded Galichia's daughter, who had Down syndrome.[2]

Broke but comfortable, the aging man settled into a simple life. His Florida attorney Ellis Rubin died in 2006, but in 2008, when the Florida state legislature passed the Victims of Wrongful Incarceration Compensation Act, which authorized payment of $50,000 a year for false imprisonment for a maximum of $2 million, Rubin's partner Robert Barrar got into the act. In August 2008 Barrar filed a petition for Richardson in DeSoto County court seeking more than $1 million in compensation, but the court, citing language in the act requiring victims to show "verifiable and substantial evidence" that "actual innocence exists," said no.[3]

An assistant state attorney from DeSoto County argued, "While there may be bias . . . [and] while there may be prosecutorial misconduct, none of those individually or together establish verifiable and substantial evidence of innocence."[4] But how could Richardson prove he was innocent? It'd been forty years and the prosecuting attorney, Frank Schaub, had died. Betsy Reese had died. Attorney John Robinson had died. And soon, so would Frank Cline. There was nothing left to say, nothing new to discover, no new DNA evidence to incriminate Reese, who herself had handed authorities a bag of parathion. Witnesses had recanted. Evidence had disappeared. Therefore, Richardson couldn't prove what he didn't do. As his lawyer Robert Barrar opined, he couldn't prove a negative.

When in 2009 a state administrative judge and a circuit court judge both upheld the decision that Richardson wouldn't get paid, Barrar switched tactics and began pressuring the Florida legislature to change the language of the law. It seemed impossible, as Florida's conservative politicians enjoyed a stranglehold on the state House and Senate and were notoriously tough on crime. Some wished to limit claims like Richardson's and supported a system that had signed off on just 19 out of 105 compensation requests in three years.

Yet slowly but surely, Barrar made inroads. With support from Democratic Senator Geraldine Thompson of Orlando and Representative Dave Kerner of Lake Worth, by 2013 several key Republicans had offered to help, including Senate Budget Committee Chairman Joe Negron of Stuart and Senate Judiciary Committee Chairman Tom Lee of Brandon. Lee actually met Richardson in Tallahassee during a visit with Barrar in the spring of 2013. "What impressed me most," said Lee, "was that James seemed to possess no malice . . . [over] what happened to him. His level of humility, his grace—it just compelled me . . . [to help] him."[5]

In October 2013, through the generosity of a local ministerial association,

Richardson returned to Arcadia for what the association called a "healing ceremony" where he met with lawmakers Thompson and Kerner and heard Sharon Thomas Goodman sing. The last time he'd heard Goodman sing was in 1967. She was the little girl who had performed "How Great Thou Art" at his children's funeral, and since then Goodman had gone to college, earned a doctorate, and become a community leader. In 1997 Goodman became mayor, Arcadia's third African American mayor and the first woman, Black or white, to hold the office.

In her fifty-plus years as a resident, Goodman had seen a lot of change. From a segregated elementary school, she'd gone to an integrated junior high, where race relations were tense. Goodman tried to be friends with everyone, she explained in 1993. "My Black friends would say, 'You're a honky lover,' and whites would say, 'N****r, stay in your place!'"[6] But Goodman didn't stay in her place. She attended the almost entirely white Florida Southern College in Lakeland, where she studied music, but rather than sing professionally, she returned to Arcadia as a teacher. "Friends and colleagues said I was crazy," she recalled. "One teacher said, 'You disgust me. You've got a chance to go anywhere and you're blowing it. . . . [You] could've been somebody important.'"[7]

Yet, in Arcadia, Goodman was important, both as a role model for other African Americans, especially women, and for the community at large. She despised racism, and in 1995 when a fellow city councilman, white former sheriff's deputy Robert W. Heine, told a *Miami Herald* reporter that Arcadia's Hispanic residents had found out from Black people that if they quit work they could get benefits, Goodman forgave him but warned that if he spouted racist remarks like that again, she'd nail him to the wall.[8] Thirty years earlier, Goodman's criticism of a white man would have been inconceivable, let alone her position on a municipal board, but times had changed, and Arcadia wasn't a town without pity anymore.

The Rays had returned there; students with AIDS attended school there unmolested, and in 2013 Richardson himself came home. At a ceremony at the Mount Zion African Methodist Episcopal Church, Goodman sang "How Great Thou Art" once more, and Richardson received the keys to the city. In the audience was Charles Flowers, the *Seminole Tribune* writer who, along with Peter B. Gallagher, had so adeptly covered the case, as well as Flowers's son Ty, who was shooting a documentary film.[9]

(Like Richardson, Flowers and Gallagher had sold their own movie rights for a kind of Woodward and Bernstein story to David L. Wolper Productions, the company that made the series *Roots*. The movie didn't happen, nor did Flowers and Gallagher receive the Pulitzer Prize, but in 1990 they took second place in the prestigious Robert F. Kennedy Awards for Excellence in Journalism.[10])

"Thank you, God, for Brother Richardson," intoned Goodman, and for "his life and his legacy."[11] "He had turned the nation's eyes onto a little Southern town in Florida and put some light on some things that weren't so good."[12]

Goodman was happy to have Richardson for a visit; she'd been among his biggest supporters and had been tied to the case, since singing at the children's funeral that sad day in 1967, for forty-six years. She was ready to move on. Arcadia was ready to move on. And as Goodman told a reporter in April 2013, "This town has suffered enough shame over the years over what happened to those children and their father. . . . Arcadia is a much different place now than it was in the 1960s. It's a wonderful place and we want the world to know we are good people here."[13]

Soon calls for compensation snowballed, with pro-Richardson editorials in the *Miami Herald,* the *Lakeland Ledger,* the *St. Petersburg Times,* and the *Sarasota Herald-Tribune.* Then, in early 2014, the Florida Legislative Black Caucus, chaired by Democrat Alan Williams of Tallahassee, wrote a letter bearing the signatures of each of its members to House Speaker Will Weatherford, a Republican from Pasco County, asking him to encourage a recalcitrant House Criminal Justice Subcommittee to approve HB 227, a bill written by Kerner that would allow Richardson to qualify for payment.

Drawn up specifically for Richardson, the bill covered wrongfully incarcerated people sentenced to life in prison or death before 1980 and in whose cases a special prosecutor had reviewed the conviction and issued a *nolle prosequi,* an indefinite adjournment of the case without an acquittal. That meant officially exonerated or not, Richardson could collect compensation, which is what happened in April 2014 when the House Criminal Justice Subcommittee, under the chairmanship of Republican Matt Gaetz of Shalimar, voted 11–0 to let the bill pass.

With votes of 116–0 in the House and 38–0 in the Senate, on June 21, 2014, Governor Rick Scott signed the bill into law. "It's been a hectic journey

James Richardson outside the state capitol, Tallahassee, 2014. With the input of attorney Robert Barrar and others, in 2014 the Florida legislature passed a bill granting Richardson some $1.2 million in compensation. He died in 2023, four months after the last Ray brother. Courtesy Peter B. Gallagher.

and a big sigh of relief for all of us," said Representative Kerner. "I don't think Mr. Richardson was looking for money. It's one thing to release you from prison; it's another thing to say we're sorry for what we did."[14] Beginning in 2015, Richardson would receive ten annual checks totaling $112,000 each, but $25,000 per check went to attorney and lobbyist fees.[15] He'd be out of prison twenty-six years before receiving his first reparations, while having been in prison for twenty-one. It was a long time to wait.

"Prison cost me a lot of things," Richardson said. "It cost me my health, my marriage, and my freedom. I was almost like a blind man when I got out."[16] Richardson resided quietly in Wichita before passing away at age eighty-seven in September 2023. He would outlive by four months the last Ray boy, Randy, who, at forty-three, had defied expectations by living into adulthood.

Richardson and the Rays, two gut-wrenching tales that once defined Arcadia as a town without pity. They're largely forgotten today, as is the community's stigma. There are no monuments or plaques and no commemorations, only seven small graves belonging to the Richardson kids in Arcadia's Oak Ridge Cemetery. The Ray brothers are buried in Sarasota, exiled in death as they were so cruelly exiled in life. Victims of race and class, respectively, Richardson and the Rays had no power.

And while local authorities were bigoted and deceitful enough to knowingly condemn an innocent man, they also stoked fear in residents to drive terminally ill children out of town. Why? They wanted control, first over Blacks in the Quarters as desegregation in Florida heated up. Then, with the threat of AIDS in America and people's anxiety over gays, they turned their distaste for federal mandates on the Rays.

Could two similar events have happened in other towns? Of course. But in the late 1980s, as the Rays fled to Sarasota and Richardson emerged from prison, they happened in this Florida town, a confluence of two headline-grabbing stories at the same time. Perhaps Arcadia deserved its infamy. A vestige of the Deep South with all that it implies, it was insular and poor and racist, yet so close to the coast. Arcadia was a holdout, a place that resisted change, but while clinging hard to its traditional values, it had very little pity for Richardson and very little pity for the Rays. "You know, Arcadia's got a bad reputation," said former mayor Eugene Hickson in 1992. "But not everyone in Arcadia deserves the blame for killing the Richardson children, framing Richardson, and burning out the Rays. I'll say this: it happened."[17]

ACKNOWLEDGMENTS

This was a difficult book to write: boys with AIDS and a grieving father who spent years in prison for a crime he didn't commit. I couldn't think of worse stories to examine, nor could I imagine that they would happen just a year apart in one Florida town. (The Rays returned to school and lost their home in August 1987, while the Free James Richardson campaign began in earnest in August 1988). But they did, and growing up just twenty-five miles away in Punta Gorda, I remember the two events vividly as well as the fear we felt toward AIDS but, conversely, the anger we felt toward the town.

In college in North Carolina, my friends would say, "Hey, Florida boy! How was your spring break?" And I'd respond, almost viscerally, with "Have you ever been to Punta Gorda? No . . . forget Punta Gorda. You ever been to Arcadia? I DO NOT live on the beach." It was, in effect, my go-to response to people's preconceived notions of what Florida should be. Arcadia was tough, swaggeringly authentic, unapologetically Southern, and real. So this is my deep dive into the town and my best attempt at understanding the Richardson and Ray cases and of figuring out how, as Southwest Florida grew and changed exponentially, year after year, tiny, seemingly changeless Arcadia continued to exist.

As for my acknowledgments, I spoke with numerous DeSoto County residents who were uneasy about appearing in the book. They'd tell me incredible stories, then say, "Please don't print that." Or "Don't use my name." So, to honor their wishes, I won't, nor will I list various town supporters who were helpful with their time, even gracious, but who, I can only guess, will not be pleased with the conclusions I've reached in the book. Thus, in no particular order, I wish to thank the following people and institutions for their help, however great or small, in assisting me with this book: staff members of the State Library and Archives of Florida in Tallahassee and of the DeSoto County Courthouse in Arcadia; public records officers of the

Florida Department of Law Enforcement and the Federal Bureau of Investigation; Paul Sullivan, Max Forgey, Wayne Daltry, Judy Earl, Robert Barrar, Sian Hunter, Gary Mormino, Craig Pittman, Ty Flowers, Pete Gallagher, Bettinita Harris, Wayne Hicks, Hazel Bowden, Glenn Sapp, Bill Clement, Lynn Harrell, Tracy Peck, Laura Griffin, Richard Bowers, Edna Tree, Kay Harrison, Marcille Wallis, Claudia Jones, John Jones, Lori Belleza, Cheryl Cook, Judi Duff Addison, Tom Ankerson, Brandon Jett, Tony Palermo, Jason Green, Alton Peacock, Joe Craig, Erin Greb, Susan Hoffman, Kurt Piehler, Susan Piehler, Chris Nank, Gary Helinski, James Faison, Canter Brown, Todd Moye, Mike Denham, Greg Cantrell, Stephanie Cole, Derek Zimmer, Jeff Glas, and Kelly Vuic Oliva; as well as my beautiful wife, Kara Dixon Vuic, and our fantastic children, Asher and Imogene. Thank you.

NOTES

INTRODUCTION

1. "Race Bans Oust Band from Arcadia," *Miami Herald*, 1 March 1958.
2. Quoted in Steven Petrow, "Ray Boys Show More Bravery Than Adults in Arcadia," *Fort Myers News-Press*, 6 September 1987.
3. Steven Petrow, *Dancing against the Darkness: A Journey through America in the Age of AIDS* (Lexington, MA: Lexington, 1990), 27.
4. Quoted in "Judge to Decide If 3 Boys with AIDS Virus Will Be Allowed to Return to Florida School," *Greenville News* (SC), 3 August 1987.
5. John Donnelly, "Family Says Publicity Takes Its Toll on AIDS-Infected Sons," *Austin American-Statesman*, 25 December 1991.
6. Petrow, "Ray Boys Show More Bravery."
7. Jeffrey Schmalz, "Aids Issue Lingers in Florida Town," *New York Times*, 7 October 1988.
8. Kim Murphy, "A Pitiless Place," editorial, *Evening Express* (ME), 1 September 1987.
9. Myra MacPherson, "The Children and the Flames of Fear," *Washington Post*, 15 September 1987.
10. Dorothy Garza, quoted in Mary Toothman, "Ray Issue in Poetry and Prose," *Tampa Tribune*, 21 September 1987. Poem used with permission of Garza's daughter Lori Belleza.
11. Mark Lane, *Arcadia* (New York: Holt, Rinehart, and Winston, 1970), 15.
12. John Allard, "Media Becoming 'Court of Appeal' for Accused Killer," *Bradenton Herald*, 22 January 1989.
13. Quoted in Bill Sloat, "Fort Myers, Arcadia Blasted for Discrimination," *Fort Myers News-Press*, 30 May 1976.
14. Quoted in Patty Shillington, "Lawsuit Challenges Election System, DeSoto Traditions," *Miami Herald*, 15 January 1991.
15. Lucy Morgan, "Poisoning Case Flawed, Attorney Finds," *St. Petersburg Times*, 30 March 1989.
16. John W. Allman, "Arcadia 'Won't Be the Same, but It'll Be OK,'" *Tampa Tribune*, 22 August 2004.

ONE / Upstream in the River of Time

1. Craig Pittman, "Arcadia Harks Back to Days of Bone Mizell," *St. Petersburg Times*, 3 July 1992.

2. D. B. McKay, "Preacher Named Arcadia for Little Girl Who Baked Birthday Cake for Him," *Tampa Tribune*, 24 May 1959.

3. "Discovery of Phosphate in 1881 Brought Land Boom to Peace River Area," *Tampa Tribune*, 17 May 1953.

4. Quoted in McKay, "Discovery of Phosphate in 1881."

5. McKay, "Discovery of Phosphate in 1881."

6. "All About Fair Arcadia," *Weekly Tribune* (Tampa), 21 July 1897.

7. Quoted in Stuart McIver, "Remington's Last Roundup," *Sunshine Magazine*, 5 January 1986, 20.

8. For an impressive discussion of the Cracker phenomenon in Florida, see Dana Ste. Claire, *Cracker: The Cracker Culture in Florida History* (Gainesville: University Press of Florida, 1998).

9. Derek Herscovici, "A History of the Florida Cracker Cowboys," *Tampa Magazine*, December-January 2017, https://tampamagazines.com/florida-cracker-cowboys-history/.

10. Frederic Remington, "Cracker Cowboys of Florida," *Harper's Magazine*, August 1895, 339; Julian M. Pleasants, "Frederic Remington in Florida," *Florida Historical Quarterly* 56, no. 1 (July 1977): 5.

11. Quoted in Mike Morgan, "Who Still Recalls the Cattle Wars?" *Miami Herald*, 18 January 1959.

12. Morgan, "Who Still Recalls the Cattle Wars?"; Nixon Smiley, "Big Blaze of '05 Burned Out Orneriness of Arcadia," *Miami Herald*, 27 August 1967.

13. Quoted in Nixon Smiley, "Bloodshed on the Big 90," *Miami Herald*, October 3, 1965.

14. "A Murderer Murdered," *Courier-Informant* (Bartow, FL), 24 November 1897.

15. James A. Able, "The Last Cowhunter," *St. Petersburg Times*, 4 April 1997; Jim Bob Tinsley, *Florida Cow Hunter: The Life and Times of Bone Mizell* (Gainesville: University Press of Florida, 1991), 57.

16. Remington, "Cracker Cowboys of Florida," 342.

17. Stetson Kennedy, *Palmetto Country* (New York: Duell, Sloan, and Pierce, 1942), 216.

18. Spessard Stone, "Ziba King," *Cracker Barrel* (blog), 17 April 2009, https://sites.rootsweb.com/~crackerbarrel/ziba.html.

19. "Cattle King of Florida," *Morning News* (Savannah, GA), 16 January 1898.

20. D. B. McKay, "Story of Mrs. Blount Recalls Rugged Days," *Tampa Tribune*, 26 September 1948.

21. "The Passing Throng," *Atlanta Constitution*, 9 March 1901.

22. Quoted in Remington, "Cracker Cowboys of Florida," 341. See also Jim Bob Tinsley, *Florida Cow Hunter*, 69–72.

23. "Corbett Wins," *Boston Daily Globe*, 26 January 1894.

24. "Zeba King's Bankroll," *Morning News* (Savannah, GA), 19 March 1898; Dean Dixon, "Cattle Baron Ziba King Filled Court Dockets," *Herald-Tribune* (Sarasota, FL), 19 August 2002.

25. Vernon Peeples Sr., *Punta Gorda: In the Beginning, 1865–1900* (Port Charlotte, FL: Book-Broker Publishers of Florida, 2012), 54; Henry Leifermann, "High Noon in Arcadia," *Fort Lauderdale Sun-Sentinel*, 12 February 1989.

26. "Judge Ziba King, Cattle King of Florida, Dead at Arcadia," *Tampa Morning Tribune*, 8 March 1901; "Judge King Played Indian," *Tampa Weekly Tribune*, 28 March 1901.

27. "The Law," *St. Petersburg Times*, 28 September 1901.

28. "Many More Arcadia Notes," *Tampa Tribune*, 20 September 1901

29. C. C. Worthington, "Arcadia Is a Live Town with a Livelier Future," *Tampa Daily Times*, 19 March 1918; "Indian Cattle Are a Success," *Tampa Daily Times*, 31 March 1914.

30. Ian Trontz, "Arcadia Booms 90 Years after Emerging from the Ashes," *Tampa Tribune*, 30 November 1995.

31. "DeSoto's Development," *Punta Gorda Herald*, 17 December 1908.

32. "Statistics of DeSoto County Show Its Remarkable Diversity of Products," *Tampa Tribune*, 10 January 1909; G. L. Walton, "Arcadia's Growth Steady and Its Future Is Assured," *Tampa Tribune*, 12 December 1915.

33. Mike Baxter, "Arcadia," *Tropic*, 4 May 1969, 35.

34. Jerrell H. Shofner, "Custom, Law, and History: The Enduring Influence of Florida's 'Black Code,'" *Florida Historical Quarterly* 55, no. 3 (January 1977): 289–290.

35. For a fascinating study of how a nearby Florida city implemented Jim Crow laws, see Jonathan Harrison, "The Rise of Jim Crow in Fort Myers," *Florida Historical Quarterly* 94, no. 1 (2015): 40–67.

36. "Give the Negroes a Fair Deal," editorial, *Arcadia News*, reprinted in the *Tampa Tribune*, 3 August 1911.

37. "Negroes at Arcadia Contribute Fund for Extra School Month," *Tampa Tribune*, 30 April 1925.

38. "Teacher Pay Scale Is Upheld by Court," *Bradenton Herald*, 25 July 1939.

39. "Need Negro School," editorial, *Arcadian*, reprinted in *Tampa Times*, 9 August 1941.

40. In Arcadia's defense, in 1945 the DeSoto County Sheriff's Office did hire the first Black deputy in the state of Florida. However, he was permitted to work solely in the Quarters and was only paid per arrest. Mary Toothman, "Police Work under His Skin," *Tampa Tribune*, 28 July 1987.

41. Richard Nellius, "Arcadia: Profile of a Small Florida Town," *The Floridian* (*St. Petersburg Times* supplement), 18 February 1968, 9.

42. Remington, "Cracker Cowboys of Florida," 342.

43. Lindsey Williams and U. S. Cleveland, *Our Fascinating Past: Charlotte Harbor, the Early Years* (Punta Gorda, FL: Charlotte Harbor Area Historical Society, 1993), 354.

44. Quoted in Williams and Cleveland, *Our Fascinating Past*, 352–353.

45. "Chance for Someone to Pick up $300," *DeSoto County News*, 17 June 1915.

46. The Arcadia klavern was Klavern number 82. "Mapping the Second Ku Klux Klan, 1915–1940," Virginia Commonwealth University Library, https://labs.library.vcu.edu/klan/learn.

47. "Herndon Is Asked to Quit Position in Arcadia School," *Tampa Tribune*, 15 August 1925.

48. "Preventive Punishment," *Ocala Evening Star*, 30 October 1906.

49. "Negro Is Lynched at Arcadia for Attempting an Assault," *Tampa Tribune*, 16 June 1909.

50. "In Orderly Manner," editorial, *Arcadia Champion,* reprinted in *Tampa Tribune,* 22 June 1909.

51. "Another Lynching at Arcadia," *Ocala Evening Star,* 16 June 1909.

52. Quoted in "Negro Raids Post Office to Start His Troubles," *Tampa Tribune,* 9 September 1917.

TWO / Old Habits Die Hard

1. "Ex-Mayor of Arcadia, Paul P. Speer Dies," *Tampa Tribune,* 8 January 1972; George M. Goolsby, "Goolsby Tells How Fight for Division Was Waged," *Tampa Tribune,* 24 April 1921.

2. Ted Bryan, "Arcadia Rodeo Goes Back a Long Way," *Fort Myers News Press,* 4 June 1968; "Arcadia Legion Post Again to Present Rodeo," *Tampa Tribune,* 2 October 1930; "Finals Begin Today at Arcadia Rodeo," *St. Petersburg Times,* 4 July 1967; "Possettes Planning November Show," *St. Petersburg Times,* 22 September 1966.

3. "Beauty and Beasts Will Reign in July," *Fort Lauderdale News,* 16 June 1963.

4. "Failing to Feed the Hungry," *Fort Myers News-Press,* 3 July 1968.

5. "80,000-Acre Ranch Near Arcadia Sold," *Tampa Times,* 25 March 1963.

6. Quoted in Henry Leifermann, "High Noon in Arcadia," *Fort Lauderdale Sun-Sentinel,* 12 February 1989.

7. Quoted in Pittman, "Arcadia Harks Back to Days of Bone Mizell." Arcadia Mayor Eugene Hickson also recounted whites lassoing Blacks, in Jeffrey Cardenas, "Arcadia Makes History with Black Mayor," *Fort Myers News-Press,* 6 October 1979.

8. Nellius, "Arcadia," 9.

9. Quoted in "Employer's View of Surplus Food," *Tampa Tribune,* 6 January 1963. "Food Program Role Rejected by DeSoto County," *Tampa Tribune,* 4 July 1968.

10. Peter Kramer, "The Citrus Pickers: A Long, Long Day," *St. Petersburg Times,* 22 February 1965.

11. Quoted in Selena Roberts, "Patriots' Rembert Served Well by Tough Childhood," *Tampa Tribune,* 30 October 1990.

12. Ralph Sumner, "2 Cuban Refugees Busy with DeSoto Missionary Work," *Tampa Tribune,* 19 April 1962.

13. Milton Plumb, "Florida Flatlands' Pine Stumps Bringing New Wealth to State," *Tampa Tribune,* 9 November 1958.

14. George Lane Jr., "Orange Groves Changing Face of DeSoto Plain," *St. Petersburg Times,* 6 September 1970.

15. "Arcadia Airbases Made Available for State Mental Hospital Annex," *St. Petersburg Times,* 27 September 1946.

16. Quoted in Bob Morris, "G. Pierce Wood: A Quiet Place for Troubled Minds," *Fort Myers News-Press,* 1 August 1976.

17. Fred Smith, "Facilities at Arcadia Hospital Rapped," *Tampa Tribune,* 5 August 1966; "Potential Scandal Brewing at Arcadia Sunland Unit," (quote), *Tampa Times,* 10 July 1968.

18. M. J. Potter, "Dorr Mental 'Hospital' Reeks of Misery," *Orlando Sentinel,* 29 July 1968.

19. John Frasca, "Legislature Holds Fate of Mental Health Center," *Tampa Tribune,* 19 April 1969.

20. Quoted in "Anti-Nepotism Bill Unopposed," *Tampa Times,* 13 June 1969.

21. "Rioters Raiford Bound," *Fort Myers News-Press,* 8 September 1972; Al Lee, "Rape, Racial Conflict Invade Prison," *Tampa Tribune,* 20 September 1974.

22. Quoted in John Lear, "DeSoto Leaders Seek Industry to Help Economy," *Tampa Tribune,* 20 September 1978.

23. "Three Cross Burnings Reported," *Tampa Tribune,* 8 May 1970; "DeSoto Parade Cheered," *Tampa Tribune,* 24 January 1963; "Arcadia Band Gets Confederate Flag," *Tampa Tribune,* 21 November 1957.

24. George Lane Jr., "The New Black City Councilman: 'The Eyes of Arcadia Are upon Me,'" *St. Petersburg Times,* 12 September 1971.

25. Jeffrey Cardenas, "Arcadia Makes History with Black Mayor," *Fort Myers News-Press,* 6 October 1979.

26. Lane, "New Black City Councilman."

27. Quoted in James Kerr, "20th Century Is Trickling into Once Sleepy Arcadia," *Fort Lauderdale News,* 17 October 1971.

28. Ralph Sumner, "Old Armory Now Recreation Center," *Tampa Tribune,* 1 December 1972.

29. Quoted in Jim McGee, "In Arcadia, Racism Isn't Just Black and White," *Fort Myers News-Press,* 1 May 1977.

30. Claudia Jones, phone interview with the author, 19 November 2020.

31. Brett McMurphy, "Bowers Breaks Color Barrier Long Before Modern-Day Pioneers," *Tampa Tribune,* 9 December 1990.

32. Ernie Neff, "Second Arcadia Police Officer Resigns," *Tampa Tribune,* 12 April 1979.

33. Quoted in Kevin Bouffard, "Churches Bring Races Together," *Tampa Tribune,* 14 February 1994.

34. Quoted in Abdon M. Pallasch, "Three Generations: The Joneses," *Tampa Tribune,* 19 May 1991.

35. Jim McGee, "In Arcadia, Racism Isn't Just Black and White."

36. Quoted in McGee, "In Arcadia, Racism Isn't Just Black and White."

THREE / Ever Put a Penny in Your Mouth?

1. Mary Farris, "Nuclear Weapons: For $69.60, You Can Kill Nearly a Million People," *Fort Myers News-Press,* 25 April 1968.

2. Quoted in "Humans vs. Bugs: What Cost Insecticides," *Miami Herald,* 17 December 1967.

3. "Boy Eats Fried Chicken, Dies," *Miami Herald,* 30 September 1964.

4. Verne O. Williams, "Parathion, Not Bump, Was Killing Boy," *Miami News,* 28 July 1966.

5. Quoted in Mary Farris, "Workers Are Lax in Using Deadly Spray Materials," *Fort Myers News-Press,* 22 May 1968.

6. Williams, "Parathion, Not Bump, Was Killing Boy."

7. Farris, "Nuclear Weapons."

8. "Parathion Still Found in River," *Tampa Tribune*, 4 February 1965.

9. Pete Schmidt, "River Board Has Stormy Session on Pollution," *Tampa Tribune*, 5 December 1964.

10. Farris, "Nuclear Weapons."

11. Ralph Sumner, "Well Field Tests Set Near Arcadia Despite Protests," *Tampa Tribune*, 5 May 1965.

12. Testimony of Myrtice Jackson, 28–31 May 1968, *State of Florida vs. James Joseph Richardson*, 12th Judicial Circuit, case number 3302-D, pp. 1083–1084. Richardson's original trial transcript and other evidentiary files were accessed through a public records request with the Office of the Attorney General, State of Florida, November 2021. The files were received in a single 1,787-page PDF. Because some documents had page numbers and others didn't, citations from the Office of the Attorney General file refer to the PDF page number. These case documents are cited hereafter as *State of Florida vs. James Joseph Richardson* (OAG).

13. Testimony of Ruby Faison, *State of Florida vs. James Joseph Richardson* (OAG), pp. 1127–1128.

14. Quoted in Constance Johnson, "Dad Still Denies Poisoning 7 Kids," *Orlando Sentinel*, 9 October 1988.

15. Ralph Sumner, "Burns Names Widow as DeSoto Sheriff," *Tampa Tribune*, 24 June 1965; Jack McClintock, "She's a Sheriff," *Tampa Tribune*, 8 August 1965.

16. Larry Coy, "FBI Probing Pistol-Whipping," *Miami Herald*, 29 April 1954; "South Bay Decision Reversed," *Miami Herald*, 3 November 1954.

17. Quoted in Nellius, "Arcadia," 8.

18. Quoted in Lane, *Arcadia*, 233.

19. Ralph Sumner, "DeSoto Sheriff Praises Work of Two Auxiliaries," *Tampa Tribune*, 15 August 1967.

20. James Faison, phone interview with the author, 26 April 2021.

21. Karl Vick, "Former Sheriff under Fire," *St. Petersburg Times*, 7 May 1989.

22. Quoted in Ernie Neff, "Cline: I Won't Run for Sheriff Again," *Tampa Tribune*, 9 October 1980.

23. Faison, interview, 26 April 2021.

24. Ralph Sumner, "Turpentine Extractor Explodes, Burns," *Tampa Tribune*, 25 January 1967.

25. "Peace River Fish Die," *Orlando Sentinel*, 15 March 1967.

26. Name of source withheld upon request, phone interview with the author, 27 April 2021.

27. "Sheriff Breaks Foot in Simulated Escape," *Tampa Tribune*, 28 January 1969.

28. Ted Bryan, "Man Killed in Shootout with Sheriff," *St. Petersburg Times*, 23 September 1967.

29. Quoted in "Killer Shot Down in Arcadia in Gun Battle with Sheriff," *Fort Myers News-Press*, 24 September 1967.

30. Ralph Sumner, "Man Slays Former Wife, Dies in Police Gunfire," *Tampa Tribune*, 23 September 1967; "Autopsy Shows Victim of Shootout Shot Self," *St. Petersburg Times*, 3 October 1967.

31. Quoted in Lane, *Arcadia*, 97.

32. The transcript of the prosecution's 1 December 1967 interview of Minister L. T. Fagan appears as exhibit C in "Response to Motion for Post-Conviction Relief," filed 12 April 1989, by Florida State Attorneys Janet Reno, Don L. Horn, and Richard L. Shiffrin, *State of Florida vs. James Joseph Richardson*, vol. 4. This and other case documents accessed at DeSoto County Courthouse, Arcadia, Florida, are cited hereafter as *State of Florida vs. James Joseph Richardson* (DC).

33. Testimony of Judge Gordon Hays at a coroner's inquest in Arcadia, 25 March 1968. Hays died of a heart attack shortly before Richardson's trial, so his testimony from the coroner's inquest was included in Richardson's trial transcript as exhibit 26, *State of Florida vs. James Joseph Richardson* (OAG), p. 1493.

34. Charles Whited, "How Many More Lives Are Wasted," *Miami Herald*, 27 April 1989.

35. Testimony of Annie Mae Richardson, *State of Florida vs. James Joseph Richardson* (OAG), p. 1535.

36. Peter B. Gallagher, "Poisoned Justice," *Freedom Magazine*, January/February 2017, 32.

37. Karl Vick, "Former Sheriff under Fire," *St. Petersburg Times*, 7 May 1989; Rick Buck, "Probe Points to Cover-Up in Poisonings," *Tampa Tribune*, 22 May 1989.

38. Karl Vick, "Author Accuses 3 of Cover-Up in Murders," *St. Petersburg Times*, 20 October 1988.

39. Charles Flowers and Peter B. Gallagher, "Poisoned Justice," *Tropic*, 11 December 1988, 26.

40. Karl Vick, "Blood Test Results Deepen Murder Mystery," *St. Petersburg Times*, 4 May 1989.

41. Richard Nellius, "Seventh Child Dies of Poison," *St. Petersburg Times*, 27 October 1967.

42. Charlie Smith, interview by Frank Cline and John Treadwell, 27 October 1967, transcript, *State of Florida vs. James Joseph Richardson* (OAG), pp. 548–557.

FOUR / A Stubborn and Purposeful Man

1. Quoted in Francis Gilpin, "Feisty Schaub at Home in Legal Battle Zones," *Tampa Tribune*, 13 June 1988.

2. John D. MacDonald, *No Deadly Drug* (New York: Doubleday, 1968), 8.

3. Quoted in Bob Dart, "Carl Coppolino: Hub of Macabre Circle," *Atlanta Constitution*, 15 October 1979.

4. Bob Talbert, "F. Lee Bailey, Esq.," *The State* (Columbia, SC), 27 February 1967.

5. MacDonald, *No Deadly Drug*, 9.

6. F. Lee Bailey with Jean Rabe, *When the Husband Is the Suspect* (New York: Tom Doherty Associates, 2008), 37.

7. Richard Nellius, "Coppolino Case: Points of Thriller," *St. Petersburg Times*, 2 April 1967.

8. Nancy Beth Jackson, "Coppolino Trial: Women Star in a True-to-Life-Soap Opera," *Miami Herald*, 27 April 1967.

9. Richard Nellius, "Coppolino's Attorney Tries to Put Prosecution on Trial," *St. Petersburg Times*, 6 April 1967.

10. Bailey with Rabe, *When the Husband Is the Suspect*, 37.

11. "Schaub No Match for Bailey?," *Tallahassee Democrat*, 4 May 1967.

12. "'Drug Killed Mrs. Coppolino'; Lawyers Get Jail Warning," *Miami News*, 14 April 1967.

13. Pete Schmidt, "Judge Threatens Two Lawyers with Jail," *Tampa Tribune*, 15 April 1967.

14. Peggy Poor, "Drug Death Challenged," *Orlando Sentinel*, 21 April 1967.

15. June Frank, "Schaub Relaxes after Big Trial" (quote), *Bradenton Herald*, 30 April 1967; Wanda Dionne, "Attorney Bailey to Be TV Host," *Tampa Tribune*, 5 April 1967.

16. "Schaub Lists 95 Per Cent Convictions," *Bradenton Herald*, 15 July 1969.

17. Quoted in John Allard, "Schaub's Career Is Marred," *Bradenton Herald*, 21 May 1989.

18. Gerald Purvis, interview by James Foy, 26 October 1967, exhibit A in "Response to Motion for Post-Conviction Relief," *State of Florida vs. James Joseph Richardson* (DC), vol. 4.

19. Gerald Purvis, interview by John Treadwell, 27 October 1967, exhibit B in "Response to Motion for Post-Conviction Relief," *State of Florida vs. James Joseph Richardson* (DC), vol. 4.

20. "Kids Insured before Deaths," *Orlando Sentinel*, 28 October 1967; Jon Nordheimer, "Lawmen: 7 Deaths Planned," *Miami Herald*, 28 October 1967.

21. Purvis interview by Treadwell, 27 October 1967.

22. Purvis interview by Treadwell, 27 October 1967.

23. United Life Insurance Company, "Agent's Report to Manager on New Business, Revivals, and Transfers," week of Monday, 23 October 1967, exhibit 8, *State of Florida vs. James Joseph Richardson* (OAG), p. 31.

24. Nordheimer, "Lawmen: 7 Deaths Planned."

25. Quoted in Flowers and Gallagher, "Poisoned Justice," *Tropic*, 14.

26. Dave Behrens, "Seven Little White Coffins Stood in a Row," *Miami Herald*, 30 October 1967.

27. "Sobs Resound at Children's Funeral," *Tampa Bay Times*, 30 October 1967.

28. "Arcadia Mourns at Mass Funeral," *Fort Myers News-Press*, 30 October 1967.

FIVE / No Workinghard Man

1. "This Is How the AP Covers the World," *Idaho State Journal*, 19 January 1968.

2. "6 Children Die of Crop Poison," AP, in *Tucson Daily Citizen*, 26 October 1967.

3. Bill Hackney, "Slightly Hackneyed," editorial, *The Arcadian*, 2 November 1967.

4. Jon Nordheimer, "Timetable of Tragedy: How Children Died," *Miami Herald*, 28 October 1967.

5. Nordheimer, "Timetable of Tragedy."

6. "Seven Poisoning Victims Buried," *Tallahassee Democrat*, 30 October 1967.

7. Editor's preface to Nellius, "Arcadia," 8.

8. Nellius, "Arcadia," 8.

9. Nellius, "Arcadia," 11.

10. Frank Caperton, "GOP's Dream of Capturing Senate Fades," *Tampa Tribune*, 20 October 1968.

11. DeSoto County Historian Howard Melton, interview by Steve Frangos, 19 January 1987, Florida Memory, State Archives of Florida, https://www.floridamemory.com/items/show/236628; Claudia Jones, interview, 19 November 2020.

12. Nellius, "Arcadia," 8.

13. Quoted in Flowers and Gallagher, "Poisoned Justice," *Tropic*, 15–16.

14. "Five Other Child Deaths Probed," *Tampa Times*, 1 November 1967.

15. Grace Smith, "Veteran Judge Is Dead at 65," *The Arcadian*, 2 May 1968.

16. "DeSoto Negro Held in Slaying," *Tampa Tribune*, 24 December 1955.

17. Quoted in Bill Hackney, "Coroner's Jury Gets Detailed Story at Poisoning Inquests," *The Arcadian*, 9 November 1967.

18. Quoted in Hackney, "Coroner's Jury Gets Detailed Story."

19. Fred Farris, "Father of Poisoned Children Is Charged with Murder," *Fort Myers News-Press*, 3 November 1967.

20. Jon Nordheimer, "Dad of 7 Charged in Deaths," *Miami Herald*, 3 November 1967.

21. "Duval Records Checked in Probe of Poisonings," *Tampa Tribune*, 4 November 1967.

22. Causes of death are listed in a Duval County Sheriff's Office report, *State of Florida vs. James Joseph Richardson* (OAG), pp. 79–80.

23. Quoted in Jon Nordheimer, "No Workinghard Man Ever Killed His Children," *Miami Herald*, 4 November 1967.

24. Quoted in Nordheimer, "No Workinghard Man Ever Killed His Children."

25. Bruce Beard, "The Stubborn Little President," *St. Petersburg Times*, 21 May 1967; Lane, *Arcadia*, 36–37.

26. "NAACP Asks for Parathion Probe," *St. Petersburg Times*, 7 November 1967.

27. Drew McKillops, "Press Voices Opposition to Trial News Code," *Honolulu Advertiser*, 5 August 1967.

28. Paul C. Reardon, "The Fair Trial—Free Press Standards," *American Bar Association Journal* 54 no. 4 (April 1968): 348.

29. Quoted in Jon Nordheimer, "Sheriff Says He's Set to Act as Jury Mulls 7 Poisonings," *Miami Herald*, 2 November 1967.

30. "Sheriff Sees Insurance Plot: Coroner's Jury to Look into 7 Poison Deaths at Arcadia," *Fort Myers News-Press*, 2 November 1967.

31. "Poison Motive Established," *Pensacola News*, 1 November 1967; "Kids Killed for Insurance," *Miami News*, 1 November 1967; "Sheriff Sees Poison Death Plans Motivated by Insurance Benefits" *Panama City News*, 2 November 1967.

32. "Sheriff Says He's Ready to Act on Murder Charge in Poisonings," *The Arcadian*, 2 November 1967.

33. Jim Warters, "John Robinson: 'A Terrible Injustice Was Being Done,'" *Florida Magazine*, 26 July 1970, 8F; Lane, *Arcadia*, 34–41; "Lawyer Seeks Accused Killer's Freedom," *Pensacola News*, 8 November 1967.

34. Quoted in Lane, *Arcadia*, 36–37.

35. Quoted in Lane, *Arcadia*, 42.

36. Lane, *Arcadia*, 51.
37. Quoted in Lane, *Arcadia*, 45.
38. Quoted in Lane, *Arcadia*, 245.
39. Quoted in Rick Barry, "Bad Boy Boom," *Florida Accent*, 10 August 1975, 6.
40. Homer Bigart, "Squalor Found at Florida Camp," *News and Observer* (Raleigh, NC), 17 February 1969.
41. "'Poor' Migrant Probe Report Kicks up Dust," *Orlando Sentinel*, 27 December 1967.
42. Quoted in Dwight Otwell, "Bad Boy Boom Is Tough but Fair," *Naples Daily News*, 23 June 1974.
43. Quoted in Otwell, "Bad Boy Boom."
44. Quoted in Otwell, "Bad Boy Boom."
45. Boom admitted to beating Richardson in an interview with Charles Flowers and Peter B. Gallagher in 1988. Peter B. Gallagher, phone interview with the author, 17 May 2022.
46. Quoted in Lane, *Arcadia*, 274–275.
47. Quoted in Gallagher, "Poisoned Justice," *Freedom Magazine*, 36.

SIX / Quid Pro Quo

1. The transcript of the prosecution's 18 November 1967 interview of James Dean Cunningham appears as exhibit D in "Response to Motion for Post-Conviction Relief," *State of Florida vs. James Joseph Richardson* (DC), vol. 4.
2. Transcript of L. T. Fagan interview, 1 December 1967, exhibit C, "Response to Motion for Post-Conviction Relief," *State of Florida vs. James Joseph Richardson* (DC), vol. 4.
3. "Grand Jury Begins Probe of 7 Deaths," *St. Petersburg Times*, 5 December 1967.
4. "Richardson Trial Here," *Miami Herald*, 26 March 1968.
5. "Richardson Murder Case Witness Killed," *Palm Beach Post*, 15 April 1968.
6. "Judge in DeSoto Dies," *Fort Myers News-Press*, 30 April 1968.
7. Ashley A. Smith, "Lee Lagged in Integration," *Fort Myers News-Press*, 17 May 2014; Jewell Dean, "Council Agrees to Desegregate City Facilities: Would Delay Teen Club and 3 Pools until 1968," *Fort Myers News-Press*, 31 March 1965; David A. Milliron, "Fort Myers Police Reunion Mixes History, Reminiscing," *Fort Myers News-Press*, 23 October 1994.
8. Suzanne Jeffries and Lee Melsek, "A Legacy of Struggle," *Fort Myers News-Press*, 26 February 1989.
9. Quoted in Betty Parker, "Councilwoman Departs with Legacy," *Fort Myers News-Press*, 16 April 2007.
10. Steve Dougherty, "Dunbar: Segregation Legally Ended in Fort Myers in 1963," *Fort Myers News-Press*, 20 July 1975.
11. Quoted in Jeffries and Melsek, "Legacy of Struggle."
12. Jeffries and Melsek, "Legacy of Struggle."
13. Eileen Bernard, interview by David E. Dodrill, 1 January 1986, Lee County Collection, Samuel Proctor Oral History Program, University of Florida, https://ufdc.ufl.edu/UF00006586/00001.

14. Steve Ruediger, "NAACP Leader Blasts County Agency Bias," *Fort Myers News-Press,* 22 August 1968.

15. "New Jury List Sealed in Box," *Fort Myers News-Press,* 8 January 1960.

16. Quoted in Lane, *Arcadia,* 62.

17. "Poison Charges Made at Hearing," *Tallahassee Democrat,* 26 March 1968; "Witness in Poison Case Slain," *Tampa Tribune,* 14 April 1968.

18. Robert Bowden, "Deaths of 7 Children Traced in Poison Trial," *St. Petersburg Times,* 29 May 1968.

19. Lane, *Arcadia,* 80.

20. Comments made by Assistant State Attorney LeRoy Hill to the court, 28–31 May 1968, *State of Florida vs. James Joseph Richardson* (OAG), pp. 1204–1205.

21. Testimony of Sheriff Frank Cline, *State of Florida vs. James Joseph Richardson* (OAG), p. 1241.

22. Testimony of Bernice Hartley, *State of Florida vs. James Joseph Richardson* (OAG), p. 1579.

23. Testimony of Sarah E. Jones, *State of Florida vs. James Joseph Richardson* (OAG), p. 1597.

24. Testimony of Annie Mae Richardson, *State of Florida vs. James Joseph Richardson* (OAG), pp. 1540–1541.

25. Quoted in Steve Ruediger, "Richardson Draws Sentence of Death," *Fort Myers News-Press,* 1 June 1968.

26. The 1968 courtroom scene is recounted in L. Wayne Hicks, "After 20 Years in Prison, Father Says He's Innocent," *Sarasota Herald-Tribune,* 25 October 1987.

SEVEN / The Lawyer-Turned-Pamphleteer

1. Quoted in Mary Reinholz, "Mark Lane, 89, Leading J.F.K. Conspiracy Theorist," *The Villager* (NY), 26 May 2016.

2. Mark Lane, *Citizen Lane: Defending Our Rights in the Courts, the Capitol, and the Streets* (Chicago: Chicago Review Press, 2012), 39.

3. Jack W. Germond, "Colleagues Shun Carlino-Baiting Lane as Upstart," *Evening Press* (Binghamton, NY), 7 January 1962.

4. Jack W. Germond, "It's Carlino 143–1, Lane Alone," *Evening Press* (Binghamton, NY), 22 February 1962.

5. Jack Germond, "Lane, Not Carlino, the One out on Limb," *Elmira Star-Gazette* (NY), 4 January 1962; Germond, "Colleagues Shun Carlino-Baiting Lane as Upstart."

6. "21 More 'Riders' Jailed, Including N.Y. Assemblyman," *Rochester Democrat and Chronicle,* 9 June 1961.

7. Jack Severson, "Mark Lane Always Near a Tragic Event," *Detroit Free Press,* 24 November 1978.

8. "All Around Town Hall," *Hamburg Sun and Erie County Independent,* 31 May 1962.

9. "Lane Quits Politics to Write Book," *Buffalo News,* 25 May 1962.

10. Lane, *Citizen Lane,* 150.

11. Mark Lane, "Lane's Defense Brief for Oswald," *National Guardian*, 19 December 1963.

12. Vincent Bugliosi, *Reclaiming History: The Assassination of President John F. Kennedy* (New York, W. W. Norton, 2007), 989.

13. Hugh Aynesworth, *November 22, 1963: Witness to History* (Dallas: Brown Books, 2013), 190.

14. "Sellout Crowd Hears Mother Defend Oswald," *New Brunswick Daily Home News*, 19 February 1964.

15. Bob Katz, "Mark Lane: The Left's Leading Hearse-Chaser," *Mother Jones*, August 1979, 27.

16. Gary Wills, "Latest Mark Lane Book Victimizes the Victims," *Dayton Daily News*, 13 January 1971.

17. Lane, *Citizen Lane*, 187–188.

18. Ron Csillag, "JFK Conspiracy Theorist Mark Lane Made Mountain out of a Knoll," *Toronto Star*, 22 May 2016.

19. Lane, *Citizen Lane*, 188–189.

20. Mike Baxter, "Raiford: No Place for the Insane," *Miami Herald*, 9 November 1970.

21. Jack Roberts, "Killer Dogs, Deviates, Life on Death Row," *Miami News*, 12 February 1969; Peggy McLaughlin, "Executions Take Seven Minutes," *Orlando Evening Star*, 2 July 1968; George Waas, "County Leads on Death Row," *Palm Beach Post*, 24 April 1966.

22. McLaughlin, "Executions Take Seven Minutes."

23. Lane, *Arcadia*, 267–268.

24. Lane, *Arcadia*, 271.

25. Lane, *Arcadia*, 271–272.

26. "Girl May Talk at Shaw Trial," *Philadelphia Inquirer*, 4 February 1969.

27. Mark Lane, "Seven Poisoned Children," *Playboy*, March 1969, 48.

28. Lane, "Seven Poisoned Children," 50.

29. Rick Fleitas, "*Arcadia* by Mark Lane," *Orlando Sentinel*, 26 July 1970; David E. Clement, "Neither Fact nor Fiction," *Tampa Tribune*, 29 November 1970; Marion K. Pinsdorf, "In a Southern Town, a Rush to Convict," *The Record* (Hackensack, NJ), 28 June 1970.

30. Pinsdorf, "In a Southern Town, a Rush to Convict."

31. Clement, "Neither Fact nor Fiction."

32. Katz, "Mark Lane," 22.

33. Lane, *Arcadia*, 258.

34. Lane, *Arcadia*, 259.

35. Quoted in Lane, *Arcadia*, 260.

36. Quoted in Lane, *Arcadia*, 260.

37. Lane, *Arcadia*, 249–250.

38. "Immunity Bid Defended by Shevin," *Miami Herald*, 21 September 1970; Charles Hendrick, "Immunity Pledge Rapped," *Tampa Tribune*, 30 March 1969.

39. Quoted in Lane, *Arcadia*, 251–252.

40. Quoted in Lane, *Arcadia*, 253.

41. Quoted in Lane, *Arcadia*, 3.

42. Quoted in Lane, *Arcadia*, 254.

43. Quoted in Lane, *Arcadia*, 254.

EIGHT / A Florida Enigma

1. Quoted in Lane, *Arcadia*, 233.
2. Lane, Arcadia, 234–235.
3. Lane, Arcadia, 239–240.
4. Bill Hackney, "Slightly Hackneyed," *The Arcadian*, 6 February 1969.
5. The Wildmon column discussing *Playboy* appeared nationally February 1968; the *Arcadian* ran the column in February 1969. Donald E. Wildmon, "Whatsoever Things," *The Arcadian*, 6 February 1969.
6. "Letters Ask for Clemency," *Daytona Beach News-Journal*, 16 September 1971.
7. "Nat Schlossberg Answers *News Journal*," opinion, *The Arcadian*, 23 April 1970.
8. "Boca Ciega: 37 Suspended," *St. Petersburg Times*, 24 April 1969.
9. "Cross-Burnings," *The Arcadian*, 7 May 1970.
10. Quoted in Lane, *Arcadia*, 23.
11. Lane, *Arcadia*, 24–25.
12. Ralph Sumner, "Peace Valley Views," *Tampa Tribune*, 29 June 1970.
13. Deposition of Roosevelt Johnson, in *Brenda M. Johnson, et al., vs. DeSoto County Board of Commissioners, et al.*, US District Court for the Middle District of Florida, case no. 90-366-CIV-FTM-15(D), 5 June 1992, pp. 8–10.
14. Deposition of Roosevelt Johnson, p. 41.
15. Marcille Wallis, phone interview with the author, 17 November 2022.
16. Wallis, interview, 17 November 2022.
17. Quoted in Sally Davenport, "DeSoto School Board Plans Action in Future High School Disruptions," *Sarasota Herald-Tribune*, 8 April 1970.
18. Quoted in Joyce Shuemake, "Negroes Boycott DeSoto Schools," *Sarasota Herald-Tribune*, 6 March 1971.
19. Shuemake, "Negroes Boycott DeSoto Schools."
20. "Black Students Return to School," *Sarasota Herald-Tribune*, 9 March 1971.
21. Lane, *Arcadia*, 14–15.
22. Karen Lachenauer, "Cheap Watermelons, a Home-Cooked Meal, a Whiff of Fresh Backwoods Air—Arcadia Offers These and More," *Tampa Times*, 21 May 1977.
23. Quoted in Sandra Zec, "Port Charlotte Is Bustling with Growth," *Tampa Tribune*, 9 February 1982.
24. Ernie Neff, "Study, Drivers Agree: U.S. 17 is Treacherous," *Tampa Tribune*, 5 February 1980.
25. Paul L. McGorrian, "U.S. 17 on the Road to Four-Lane Expansion," *Tampa Tribune*, 8 June 1984.
26. Rick Buck, "U.S. 17: The Waiting Game," *Tampa Tribune*, 5 April 1989.
27. Eric McFail, "'Bridesmaid' Road Still Hoping," *Orlando Sentinel*, 22 May 1970.
28. "DeSoto Principal Is Killed in Wreck," *St. Petersburg Times*, 21 December 1960; "3 Injured in DeSoto Crash," *Tampa Tribune*, 7 April 1962; "Polk Man Kill in Crash Near Arcadia," *Tampa Tribune*, 25 April 1964; "2 Die in DeSoto Accident," *Tampa Tribune*, 30 December 1965; "Where One Died," *Tampa Tribune*, 25 June 1966; "Man, 79, Dies from Car Crash Injuries," *St. Petersburg Times*, 15 December 1967; "Contract Seen This Month

on 4-Lane Job," *Tampa Tribune*, 8 July 1969; "Arcadian Killed," *Sarasota Herald-Tribune*, 19 December 1970; "Crash Kills Family of 5-Year-Old Boy," *Tampa Tribune*, 30 September 1975.

29. Doug Nurse, "Road Is Truckers' Path of Least Resistance," *Tampa Tribune*, 6 April 1989.

30. Buck, "U.S. 17: The Waiting Game."

31. "Hard Facts of Geography," editorial, *Fort Myers News-Press*, 22 October 1954.

32. Quoted in Chip Wilson, "DeSoto Endorses Plan Giving Addresses to Rural Homes," *Tampa Tribune*, 15 February 1984.

33. Rosemary Farley, "Florida Enigma," *New York Times*, 11 December 1960.

34. Frances D. Williams, "Arcadia Is a Quiet Town Unspoiled by Progress," *Fort Myers News-Press*, 20 February 1982.

35. George Lane Jr., "PGI's New Ranch: A 'Semi-Wilderness,'" *St. Petersburg Times*, 18 September 1972.

36. "Deer Run Approval Sought from County Commission," *Fort Myers News-Press*, 19 June 1973.

37. "DeSoto Postpones Platting of PGI's 'Deer Run' Project," *St. Petersburg Times*, 30 June 1973.

38. Mike Fuery, "Huge Deer Run Community Indicated," *Fort Myers News-Press*, 4 November 1973.

39. Quoted in Dave Schultz, "DeSoto County, Developer Are Facing Crucial Week," *Tampa Tribune*, 15 April 1974.

40. Jack Hillhouse, "DeSoto Proposes Deer Run District," *Fort Myers News-Press*, 21 February 1974.

41. Jim Pratt and Bob Schofield, "PGI Will Not Develop Deer Run," *Fort Myers News-Press*, 3 December 1975.

42. George Lane Jr., "Industry Is Closed; One-Plant Town Hurt," *St. Petersburg Times*, 3 October 1971; "Arcadia to Lose Passenger Train Service on May 1," *Tampa Tribune*, 20 April 1971.

43. Quoted in Bill King, "Oct. 25, 1967: An Infamous Day in Arcadia," *Tampa Tribune*, 25 October 1977.

44. Quoted in Ernie Neff, "High Turnover of Teachers Continues in DeSoto County," *Tampa Tribune*, 5 June 1980.

45. Chip Wilson, "DeSoto Officials Dispute Figures on College-Bound Students," *Tampa Tribune*, 12 June 1984; Mark Potok, "Stats Show Broward is College Bound," *Miami Herald*, 19 July 1985; Mark Silva, "Vocational Education Is Only Partly Doing the Job," *Miami Herald*, 12 June 1983.

46. Gregory Spears, "Agronomics 'Lucked Out' in Freeze," *St. Petersburg Times*, 30 December 1983; Jane Musgrave, "Villages of Desoto 'Dead,' Says GDC, after County Stand," *Fort Myers News-Press*, 20 May 1982.

47. Sandra Zec, "Firm Delays Building National Headquarters," *Tampa Tribune*, 24 July 1982.

48. "Hospital Death Rate Probe Asked," *Orlando Sentinel*, 20 January 1981.

49. Ernie Neff, "Mental Patients Accused in Theft, Shooting Spree," *Tampa Tribune*, 10 May 1979.

50. Ernie Neff, "Patient Leaves Hospital, Walks into Truck's Path," *Tampa Tribune*, 13 September 1979; Chip Wilson, "Deputy Injured in Attack at Mental Institution," *Tampa Tribune*, 27 August 1983.

51. "Arcadia Realizes What Hospital Means to Town," *Fort Myers News-Press*, 30 October 1995.

52. Barbara Boyer, "Inmate: Guards Too Few To Protect against Gangs," *Tampa Tribune*, 2 June 1991.

53. Sandra Zec, "Payroll Eases Drawbacks of Life Near Prison," *Tampa Tribune*, 20 October 1982.

54. Quoted in Zec, "Payroll Eases Drawbacks."

55. Barbara Johnson, "Mann, Others, Tour Area's Institutions," *Fort Myers News-Press*, 12 December 1978.

56. "Prison Gates Open—and the Guards Are Leaving," *Tampa Tribune*, 14 May 1979.

57. Bill Kaczor, "Prison Guards Turnover Cited as Pay Hike Is Urged," *Fort Myers News-Press*, 1 March 1979.

NINE / Factor VIII

1. There are other genetic maladies that produce hemophilia in women, too, but at far smaller rates than men. Susan Resnik, *Blood Saga: Hemophilia, AIDS, and the Survival of a Community* (Berkeley: University of California Press, 1999), 5.

2. Roger Schlueter, "Football Helmets, Bleeding, Needles: A Hemophiliac's Life," *Belleville News-Democrat* (IL), 11 October 1982.

3. "Hemophiliacs Considered at High Risk of Contracting AIDS," *The Expositor* (Brantford, Canada), 28 September 1985; Sue Prater, "Cygnet 10-Year-Old Leads Normal Life While Bearing the Burden of Hemophilia," *Daily Sentinel-Tribune* (Bowling Green, OH), 14 April 1982.

4. Quoted in Dianne C. Gordon, "Hemophilia Boys Are Her Second Family," *Intelligencer Journal* (Lancaster, PA), 13 July 1976.

5. Quoted in Joseph D. Whitaker, "Financial Relief Being Sought for the Nation's Hemophilia Victims," *Indianapolis Star*, 10 November 1974.

6. Quoted in Irene H. Wright, "Home Transfusions Free Formerly Shackled Hemophiliacs," *Cincinnati Enquirer*, 14 June 1978.

7. Cindy Creasy, "Hemophiliac: He Masters Tennis and His Illness," *Richmond Times-Dispatch*, 1 April 1979.

8. George Getze, "Hemophiliac Given New Hip Joint by Surgery," *Los Angeles Times*, 12 April 1968; "Hemophiliac Has Heart Surgery," *Baltimore Sun*, 4 February 1971; Arthur Page, "Area Hemophiliac Has First Bypass Operation," *Buffalo News*, 12 May 1977.

9. Mindy O'Mary, "Sellers May Be Transmitting Hepatitis or Malaria along with the Blood's Proteins," *Chula Vista Star-News* (CA), 18 January 1979.

10. Stephen Pemberton, *The Bleeding Disease: Hemophilia and the Unintended Consequences of Medical Progress* (Baltimore, MD: Johns Hopkins University Press, 2011), 229.

11. Quoted in Elaine DePrince, *Cry Bloody Murder: A Tale of Tainted Blood* (New York: Random House, 1997), 53.

12. Emmanuel M. Rappaport, "Hepatitis Following Blood or Plasma Transfusions," *Journal of the American Medical Association* 128, no. 13 (28 January 1945): 939. See also Eric Weinberg and Donna Shaw, *Blood on Their Hands* (New Brunswick, NJ: Rutgers University Press, 2017), 36–37.

13. "Surgeon Says Paid Donor Blood Causes Hepatitis," *Modesto Bee*, 17 February 1970.

14. Quoted in Weinberg and Shaw, *Blood on Their Hands*, 104.

15. Erik Berntorp, William Archey, Günter Auerswald, Augusto B Federici, Massimo Franchini, Sigurd Knaub, Wolfhart Kreuz, et al., "A Systematic Overview of the First Pasteurised VWF/FVIII Medicinal Product, Haemate P/Humate-P: History and Clinical Performance," *European Journal of Haematology* 80, supplement 70 (2008): 10.

16. Quoted in Gilbert M. Gaul, "America: The OPEC of the Global Plasma Industry," *Philadelphia Inquirer*, 28 September 1989.

17. Lauren B. Leveton, Harold C. Sox Jr., and Michael A. Stoto, eds., *HIV and the Blood Supply: An Analysis of Crisis Decisionmaking* (Washington, DC: National Academy Press, 1995), 93.

18. Quoted in MacPherson, "The Children and the Flames of Fear."

19. Quoted in Mary Voboril, "The Castaways: Fears about AIDS Drive Three Boys from Home," *Life*, October 1987, 100.

20. Michael McLeod, "AIDS Hits Home," *Florida Magazine*, 21 June 1987, 13.

21. Quoted in Sue Miller, "Nurse-Nun Faults Nurses Who Avoid AIDS Patients," *Asbury Park Press* (NJ), 29 December 1985.

22. Quoted in Gino del Guercio, "Fear Spreads Faster Than Virus," *Daily News-Journal* (Murfreesboro, TN), 29 September 1985.

23. "Pneumocystis Pneumonia—Los Angeles," *Morbidity and Mortality Weekly Report* 30, no. 21 (5 June 1981): 251.

24. Quoted in Jeff Kunerth, "Myths Aside, It's Everybody's Problem," *Orlando Sentinel*, 29 January 1985.

25. Stephanie Innes, "Sherlockian Effort to Find Origin of AIDS Took 8 years," *Arizona Daily Star*, 2 October 2008.

26. Preston A. Marx, Phillip G. Alcabes, and Ernest Drucker, "Serial Human Passage of Simian Immunodeficiency Virus by Unsterile Injections and the Emergence of Human Immunodeficiency Virus in Africa," *Philosophical Transactions of the Royal Society of London* 356, no. 1410 (2001): 911–920.

27. Rebecca Creston, "The Sea Has Neither Sense nor Pity: The Earliest Known Cases of AIDS in the Pre-AIDS Era," *Discover Magazine*, 22 October 2012, https://www.discovermagazine.com/planet-earth/the-sea-has-neither-sense-nor-pity-the-earliest-known-cases-of-aids-in-the-pre-aids-era.

28. Steve Hendrix, "A Mystery Illness Killed a Boy in 1969. Years Later, Doctors Believed They'd Learned What It Was: AIDS," *Washington Post*, 15 May 2019.

29. M. Worobey, Thomas D. Watts, Richard A. McKay, Marc A. Suchard, Timothy Granade, Dirk E. Teuwen, Beryl A. Koblin, et al., "1970s and 'Patient 0': HIV-1 Genomes Illuminate Early HIV/AIDS History in North America," *Nature*, November 3, 98–101; Donald G. McNeil Jr., "H.I.V. Arrived in the U.S. Long Before 'Patient Zero,'"

New York Times, 26 October 2016; Richard Severo, "Impoverished Haitians Sell Plasma for Use in the U.S.," *New York Times,* 28 January 1972.

30. "Epidemiologic Notes and Reports: Pneumocystis carinii Pneumonia among Persons with Hemophilia A," *Morbidity and Mortality Weekly Report* 31, no. 27 (16 July 1982): 366.

31. Weinberg and Shaw, *Blood on Their Hands,* 80.

32. Donna Shaw, "Hemophilia Foundation Chief Knew of AIDS Risk in 1984," *Philadelphia Inquirer,* 3 November 1994.

33. Quoted in Michael McCleod, "Bad Blood," *Orlando Sentinel,* 19 December 1993.

34. Paul Jacobs, "Immune System Disease Spreads, Children Infected," *Los Angeles Times,* 10 December 1982.

35. Quoted in McCleod, "Bad Blood."

36. John Omicinski, "AIDS Threat Scares Hemophiliacs from Treatment," *Florida Today,* 2 May 1983.

37. Quoted in Sheryl Stolberg, "Cruel Link: Hemophilia and AIDS," *Los Angeles Times,* 31 August 1994.

TEN / The Coward's Way Out

1. Chip Berlet and Joel Bellman, "Lyndon LaRouche's Dirty Little Secret," *Reader,* 8 January 1987.

2. Bob Lewis, "Poll Shows AIDS Myths Persist in Ohio," *The Tribune* (Coshocton, OH), 12 December 1987.

3. George Gallup Jr., "Many Cling to False Ideas about AIDS," editorial, *Palm Beach Post,* 27 November 1987.

4. Quoted in "Poll Disturbs AIDS Workers," *San Francisco Examiner,* 20 December 1985.

5. Todd Spangler, "Community's Fear of AIDS Forced Man to Flee for His Life," *Buffalo News,* 27 July 1987.

6. Quoted in "Firefighter Dismissed for Refusing AIDS Patient," *Bradenton Herald,* 11 June 1987.

7. Andy Knott, "AIDS Fear Infecting City's Police Officers," *Chicago Tribune,* 5 April 1987.

8. Eric Zorn, "AIDS Fear Has Police Fighting Crime with Rubber Gloves," *Chicago Tribune,* 29 July 1987.

9. Quoted in Lisa M. Hamm, "Doctor, Wary of AIDS, Refuses to Treat Man," *Philadelphia Inquirer,* 10 July 1987.

10. Quoted in "An RU Historian's Perspective on AIDS," *Central New Jersey Home News,* 12 May 1986.

11. "Americans Fear Cancer More than Any Other Disease," *Durham Morning Herald* (NC), 11 November 1985; "Questions and Answers in New Poll on Diseases," *Tyler Courier-Times* (TX), 11 May 1987.

12. Quoted in Rosemary Goudreau, "AIDS Signs Keep 3 out of School," *Orlando Sentinel,* 9 September 1984.

13. "Court Mandates No Segregation of the Retarded," *New York Times*, 1 March 1979.

14. Marianne Constantinu, "Triplets with AIDS Start Kindergarten in Isolation," *Miami Herald*, 13 October 1984.

15. Yves Colon and Marianne Constantinu, "Let Diseased Triplets Learn, Experts Say," *Miami News*, 11 September 1984.

16. Quoted in Larry Rohter, "11,000 Boycott Start of Classes in AIDS Protest," *New York Times*, 10 September 1985; Jeffrey Page, "Parents Voice Fear of AIDS in School," *The Record* (Hackensack, NJ), 11 September 1985.

17. "Parents Plan to Continue AIDS Boycott at School," *The Record* (Hackensack, NJ), 27 October 1985.

18. Quoted in "Parents Launch Boycott over AIDS Issue," *Asbury Park Press* (NJ), 25 October 1985.

19. Quoted in "Growing Up Isolated," *Paducah Sun* (KY), 1 August 1985.

20. Quoted in Hank Klibanoff, "13-year-old AIDS Victim Scared but Keeps Smiling," *Wichita Eagle*, 26 August 1985.

21. "Ryan White: 'It's How You Live Your Life That Counts,'" *Clarion-Ledger* (Jackson, MS), 9 April 1990.

22. "Louganis Wins 38th Title, Gives Medal to AIDS Victim," *Orlando Sentinel*, 21 April 1986. For an examination of how Ryan White became the face of AIDS awareness in America, see Paul M. Renfro, *The Life and Death of Ryan White: AIDS and Inequality in America* (Chapel Hill: University of North Carolina Press, 2024).

23. Quoted in Sharon Cohen, "Kokomo, 'City of Firsts,' Is Torn over the AIDS Issue," *Birmingham Post-Herald* (AL), 29 April 1986.

24. Quoted in Neal Rubin, "A Town Torn Apart by AIDS," *Detroit Free Press*, 9 March 1986.

25. Rogers Worthington, "Kokomo Bristles over Publicity on AIDS Boy's Plight," *Chicago Tribune*, 4 March 1986.

26. Kim Ode, "AIDS, Uproar, Can't Break Ryan's Spirit," *Star and Tribune* (Minneapolis, MN), 11 May 1986.

27. Quoted in "53 Stay Home, Four Withdraw upon White's Return to School," *The Republic* (Columbus, IN), 12 April 1986.

28. Steve Tiberi, "Belle Glade Students Hurt by AIDS Stigma," *Fort Lauderdale News*, 11 October 1985.

29. Quoted in Pat Borzi, "AIDS Panic Infects Playing Fields," *Miami Herald*, 20 September 1985.

ELEVEN / We Treated Them Young 'Uns Wrong

1. Lawrence Fletcher, "Arcadia Pastor Condemns Criticism of Him, Church," *Tampa Tribune*, 21 September 1987.

2. Henry Leifermann, "High Noon in Arcadia," *Fort Lauderdale Sun-Sentinel*, 12 February 1989.

3. Ernestine Williams, "'Maybe I Shouldn't Have Told Anyone' about Sons' Illness," *Palm Beach Post*, 25 August 1987.

4. Quoted in Michael McLeod, "The Outcasts," *Fort Lauderdale Sun-Sentinel*, 23 August 1987.

5. Quoted in Bettinita Harris, "Fear, Ignorance Force Family to Flee," *Tampa Tribune*, 12 April 1987.

6. Quoted in Harris, "Fear, Ignorance Force Family to Flee."

7. Quoted in Fletcher, "Arcadia Pastor Condemns Criticism."

8. Harris, "Fear, Ignorance Force Family to Flee."

9. Quoted in "'We Didn't Run Those People Out'—Florida Town Hates Being the AIDS Ogre," *San Francisco Chronicle*, 12 September 1987.

10. Quoted in Beth Francis, "ARCADIA, Fla.—Ricky Ray Is in Tears," *USA Today*, 10 July 1987.

11. Testimony of Clifford Ray, September 11, 1987, US Congress, Senate, Committee on Labor and Human Resources, AIDS Federal Policy Act of 1987 Hearings before the United States Senate, 101st Congress, 1st session, 1987, 12.

12. Quoted in MacPherson, "The Children and the Flames of Fear."

13. Harris, "Fear, Ignorance Force Family to Flee."

14. Bettinita Harris, phone interview with the author, 5 June 2023.

15. Mike Thomas, "Attorney Loves a Good Fight, and Got One Defending Rays," *Orlando Sentinel*, 29 September 1987.

16. Quoted in Peter West, "Sarasota Attorney a Champion for AIDS Victims," *Fort Myers News-Press*, 2 November 1988.

17. Judith Kavanaugh, phone interview with the author, 2 June 2023.

18. Kavanaugh, interview, 2 June 2023.

19. Quoted in "Ruling Seen Aid to AIDS Victims," *Philadelphia Daily News*, 3 March 1987.

20. Al Kamen, "AIDS Ruled A Protected 'Handicap'; Court Says Coverage of Bias Law Extends to Contagious Ills," *Washington Post*, 4 March 1987.

21. Ellis Berger, "Schools Hope Education Will Calm Fears," *Miami News*, 4 June 1987.

22. Quoted in Cathy Shaw, "3 with AIDS Virus Go to Regular Classes," *Miami Herald*, 15 May 1987.

23. L. A. Maxwell, "Separate Classes Urged for AIDS Patients," *Tampa Tribune*, 5 May 1987.

24. "AIDS Antibody Isolates Three Boys," *Orlando Sentinel*, 24 May 1987.

25. Quoted in Diedtra Henderson, "Arcadia Brothers Offered Isolated Classroom," *Bradenton Herald*, 23 May 1987.

26. Quoted in Henderson, "Arcadia Brothers Offered Isolated Classroom"; "Rays Go to Court to Get Children to School," *Fort Myers News-Press*, 10 July 1987.

27. Rick Buck, "School Executive Takes Tough Stand," *Tampa Tribune*, 21 September 1987.

28. Quoted in Bettinita Harris, "Fla. AIDS Family Fights for Survival," *Tampa Tribune*, 8 June 1987.

29. Quoted in Mary Voboril, "Children of the Plague," *Miami Herald*, 18 June 1987.

30. Quoted in Jeff Barker, "Koop Promotes Services for Kids Who Have AIDS," *San Francisco Examiner*, 7 April 1987.

31. "Guidelines for AIDS Students," *Tampa Tribune*, 10 June 1987.
32. Quoted in Judy Hill, "Will I Die?" *St. Petersburg Times*, 28 August 1983.
33. Michael McCleod, "AIDS Hits Home," *Florida Today*, 21 June 1987.
34. Quoted in Bettinita Harris, "Doctor Won't Stop Caring Just Because a Patient Dies," *Tampa Tribune*, 12 July 1987.
35. Quoted in Voboril, "Children of the Plague."
36. Quoted in Voboril, "Children of the Plague."
37. Kavanaugh, interview, 2 June 2023.
38. "Reagan Didn't Grasp AIDS Problem," *Spokane Chronicle*, 1 September 1989.
39. Marlene Cimons, "AIDS Funds: Tardy but Catching Up," *Los Angeles Times*, 26 November 1985.
40. Karen Tumulty, *The Triumph of Nancy Reagan* (New York: Simon and Schuster, 2022), 414.
41. Quoted in Harris, "Fla. AIDS Family Fights for Survival."
42. "County Officials Call on Reagan to Retract Comment about Town," *Stuart News* (FL), 6 September 1987.
43. The June 25, 1987, ABC Nightly News report "A Town without Pity?" is available upon request through the Vanderbilt University Television News Archive, record #109914.

TWELVE / Hatesville, USA

1. James M. Denham, *Fifty Years of Justice: A History of the U.S. District Court for the Middle District of Florida* (Gainesville: University Press of Florida, 2015), 178.
2. Milo Geyelin, "Judge Pushes for Swift Justice," *St. Petersburg Times*, 30 August 1987.
3. Mark A. Stein, "Judges Hint at Backing Teacher in AIDS Case," *Los Angeles Times*, 11 November 1987.
4. Quoted in "Teacher with AIDS Wants to Return to Classroom," *Daily Press* (Victorville, CA), 12 November 1987.
5. James F. Grutsch Jr. and A.D.J. Robertson, "The Coming of AIDS," *American Spectator*, March 1986, 14.
6. Neville Hodgkinson, "Aids Expert Wants National Screening," *Sunday Times* (London), 26 October 1986.
7. Quoted in Diedtra Henderson, "Boys' Fate in AIDS Case Is on Hold," *Bradenton Herald*, 11 June 1987.
8. Bentley Orrick, "Rays Told to Retest for AIDS," *Tampa Tribune*, 11 July 1987.
9. Quoted in Cory Jo Lancaster, "Education Is Aim of AIDS Taskforce in Brevard," *Orlando Sentinel*, 9 July 1997.
10. Quoted in Bayard Steele, "Demonstrators Take Heat on AIDS Issue," *Tampa Tribune*, 11 July 1987.
11. Quoted in Bentley Orrick, "Ray Boys Win Fight to Go to School," *Tampa Tribune*, 6 August 1987.
12. Quoted in Orrick, "Ray Boys Win Fight."
13. "Striking Down Ignorance in DeSoto County Schools," editorial, *Tampa Tribune*, 6 August 1987.

14. Quoted in Beth Francis, "DeSoto School Board Delays Action on AIDS Ruling Appeal," *Fort Myers News-Press*, 11 August 1987.

15. Quoted in Francis, "DeSoto School Board Delays Action."

16. Quoted in Francis, "DeSoto School Board Delays Action."

17. Brian Craven and Christina Kent, "Cleared DeSoto Deputy out of Job," *Sarasota Herald-Tribune*, 1 March 1982.

18. Beth Francis, "Off to School—In Fear," *Fort Myers News-Press*, 24 August 1987.

19. Quoted in Dave Nicholson, "Parents Organize to Fight Ruling on Ray Children," *Tampa Tribune*, 22 August 1987.

20. Lawrence E. Lockman, "A Homosexual Quarantine to Stop the Spread of AIDS," opinion, *Bangor Daily News* (ME), 10 January 1986.

21. Mario Moretto, "Democrats Want Lawmaker to Resign: State Rep Ripped for 'Hateful, Vicious' Comments Gays, Abortion," *Sun-Journal* (ME), 26 February 2014.

22. Moody Adams, *AIDS: You Just Think You're Safe* (Baker, LA: Dalton Moody, 1986), 71.

23. Adams, *AIDS*, 114.

24. F. V. Cresswell, J. Ellis, J. Hartley, C. A. Sabin, C. Orkin, and D. R. Churchill, "A Systematic Review of Risk of HIV Transmission through Biting or Spitting: Implications for Policy," HIV *Medicine* 19, no. 8 (September 2018): 532.

25. Quoted in Linda Gibson, "Uncertainty Breeds Hysteria," *Tampa Tribune*, 20 September 1987.

26. Quoted in Ellen Goodman, "Anxious Arcadia Overreacted to the Remote Risk of AIDS," *Palm Beach Post*, 4 September 1987.

27. Chris Quinn, "Sorry That the Rays Left Angry; Some in Arcadia Are Glad to See AIDS Fear," *Orlando Sentinel*, 31 August 1987.

28. Kavanaugh, interview, 2 June 2023.

29. MacPherson, "The Children and the Flames of Fear."

30. MacPherson, "The Children and the Flames of Fear."

31. Quoted in Steven Petrow, *Dancing in the Darkness: A Journey through America in the Age of* AIDS (Washington, DC: Lexington, 1990), 31.

32. Petrow, *Dancing in the Darkness*, 22.

33. Petrow, *Dancing in the Darkness*, 23, 33.

34. Holt Hackney, "Sonrise Christian Academy May Set New Enrollment High," *The Arcadian*, 13 August 1987.

35. Quoted in Beth Francis, "Boycott Greets Ray Boys," *Fort Myers News-Press*, 25 August 1987.

36. Francis, "Boycott Greets Ray Boys."

37. Quoted in "3rd Bomb Threat Empties School, but Attendance Up," *Fort Lauderdale News*, 27 August 1987.

38. Quoted in Bettinita Harris, "Light at End of Tunnel was Fire," *Tampa Tribune*, 20 September 1987.

39. Beth Francis, "Arson Ruled Cause of Ray Fire," *Fort Myers News-Press*, 23 September 1987.

40. Rick Buck, "DeSoto County Sheriff Expects to Make Arrest in Case," *Tampa Tribune*, 23 September 1987.

41. Kavanaugh, interview, 2 June 2023.

42. Quoted in Tom Schroder and Stephanie Zimmerman, "Sheriff: Media Holding Up Arcadia Fire Report," *Florida Today*, 3 September 1987.

43. Quoted in Karl Vick, "Neighbor Says He's Suspected in Arcadia Fire," *St. Petersburg Times*, 10 September 1987.

44. "Rays: Arcadia 'Waited Too Long' to Help," *Palm Beach Post*, 1 September 1987.

45. Quoted in Bridget Bidwell, "No Protest Marks Ryan's School Day," *Noblesville Daily Ledger* (IN), 31 August 1987.

46. Quoted in John Flora, "Seminars Paved Way for Ryan White," *Indianapolis News*, 3 September 1987.

47. "Two Towns Called Arcadia," *Chicago Tribune*, 2 September 1987; "Two Arcadias, Two Responses to AIDS in Schools," *Arizona Daily Star*, 2 September 1987; James G. Driscoll, "Tale of Two Arcadias: One without Pity, the Other with a Hug for a Dying Boy," *Fort Lauderdale News*, 6 September 1987.

48. Quoted in Chris Cooper, "Arcadians Lash Out Again at AIDS Rally," *Fort Myers News-Press*, 6 September 1987.

49. Quoted in Chris Cooper, "Arcadia Tells Critics It's Not 'Hatesville,'" *Florida Today*, 6 September 1987.

50. Quoted in Larry Perl, "Some Residents of 'Town without Pity' Have Change of Heart," *Fort Myers News-Press*, 14 December 1992.

51. Joan Les, letter to the editor, *Miami Herald*, 5 September 1987.

52. Chuck Stone, "Southern Discomfort," opinion, *Times and Democrat* (SC), 9 September 1987.

53. Sharon Thomas Goodman, "Fight the Real Problem," letter to the editor, *The Arcadian*, 17 September 1987.

54. Quoted in Michael Lasalandra and Ellis Berger, "Ray Family Seeks School in 'Enlightened' District," *Miami News*, 1 September 1987.

55. Quoted in Chris Downey, "Ray Family Takes Story to Nation," *Bradenton Herald*, 12 September 1987.

56. Hayley Gorenberg, "3 AIDS-exposed Brothers Find New School Friendlier," *Sacramento Bee*, 24 September 1987.

57. Rick Barry, "Very Special Greeting for Ray Brothers," *Tampa Tribune*, 24 September 1987.

58. Barry, "Very Special Greeting for Ray Brothers."

59. Quoted in "1967 Mass Murder Takes Twist," *St. Petersburg Times*, 8 December 1988.

THIRTEEN / The Ne'er-Do-Well

1. "Diversicare Physicians Determination" for Betsy Reese, signed by Dr. Gammad, 16 October 1987, *State of Florida vs. James Joseph Richardson* (DC), vol. 5.

2. Quoted in "Babysitter Who Helped Free Man in Poisoning Case Dies," *St. Petersburg Times*, 1 November 1992.

3. Richardson had been tried and convicted for murdering just one child, eight-year-old Betty Jean, and first-degree murder in Florida carried a twenty-five-year mandatory minimum sentence. Apparently, Schaub tried only one case, so if he lost, he would have six more opportunities to convict.

4. Quoted in "Arcadia Man Gets Murder Sentence Reduced by 108 Years," *Fort Myers News-Press,* 27 June 1985.

5. Bob Katz, "Mark Lane: The Left's Leading Hearse-Chaser," *Mother Jones,* August 1979, 30–31.

6. Tim Reiterman and John Jacobs, *Raven: The Untold Story of the Rev. Jim Jones and His People* (New York: Dutton, 1982), 438.

7. Reiterman and Jacobs, *Raven,* 541.

8. Lane, *Citizen Lane,* 312.

9. Quoted in Kathy Canavan, "Historian Tells of Guyana for Pay," *Pensacola Journal,* 2 December 1978.

10. Quoted in Katz, "Mark Lane," 31.

11. Anthony Lewis, "Abroad at Home: The Mark of Zorro," *New York Times,* 30 November 1978.

12. Thomas Powers and Alan Rich, "Robbing the Grave," *New York,* 23 February 1981, 46–47.

13. Lee Green, "His J.F.K Obsession," *Los Angeles Times Magazine,* 20 November 1988, 24.

14. Ben L. Kaufman, "U.S. Aid to Israel Should Depend on PLO Discussions, Author Says," *Cincinnati Enquirer,* 16 May 1982; "Pro-Palestinians Challenge Some Jewish Groups' U.S. Tax Status," *Philadelphia Inquirer,* 7 October 1983.

15. Betsy Reese's nursing home medical records appear as exhibit 39 in a report titled "Arguments against a Grant of Clemency and Exhibits in Support Thereof," by Frank Schaub, *State of Florida vs. James Joseph Richardson* (DC), vol. 5.

16. Belinda Romeo affidavit, sworn in Hardee County, Florida, 27 March 1988, *State of Florida vs. James Joseph Richardson* (OAG), pp. 97–99.

17. Quoted in Rick Buck, "Author Claims Man Was Not Murderer," *Tampa Tribune,* 10 August 1988.

18. Rick Buck, "Varnadore Faces 2 Challengers," *Tampa Tribune,* 29 August 1988.

19. Rick Buck, "Author's Visit Resurrects Ill Feelings," *Tampa Tribune,* 12 August 1988; Lance Oliver, "Cheers and Hugs of Celebration," *Orlando Sentinel,* 26 April 1989. The *DeSoto County Times* political cartoons appeared on 17 November 1988 and 26 April 1989.

20. Lane, *Citizen Lane,* 196.

21. William Sabo, "Author Points to Babysitter as Murderer in 1968 Case," *Fort Myers News-Press,* 13 August 1988.

22. Sabo, "Author Points to Babysitter as Murderer."

23. Richardson's taped statement is re-created from two sources: L. Wayne Hicks, "21 Years Later, Thousands Gather to Listen to Father's Story," *Sarasota Herald-Tribune,* 13 August 1988, and Sabo, "Author Points to Babysitter as Murderer."

24. Lane, *Citizen Lane,* 197.

25. Lane, *Citizen Lane,* 197.

26. Kay Harrison, phone interview with the author, 24 January 2023.

27. Harrison, interview, 24 January 2023.

28. Rick Buck, "Unsung Hero Key to Richardson's Freedom," *Tampa Tribune*, 7 May 1989; "Two Charged in DeSoto Robbery," *Tampa Tribune*, 21 August 1976.

29. Cathy Lynn Grossman, "Legislators Want Get-Tough Laws against Violent Teens," *Miami Herald*, 2 May 1977.

30. Charles Flowers and Peter B. Gallagher, "Investigators Probe Secretary, '57 Death," *Miami Herald*, 28 December 1988.

31. Constance Johnson, "Secretary: Prosecutor Said Richardson was Innocent," *Orlando Sentinel*, 13 January 1989.

32. Quoted in Patti McGee, "Resident Recalls Stealing Richardson Files," *DeSoto County Times*, 5 April 1989.

33. Quoted in Buck, "Unsung Hero."

34. Quoted in Charles Flowers and Peter B. Gallagher, "'Contessa,' Plus Stolen Papers, Helped Unravel Case," *Miami Herald*, 26 April 1989.

35. Hazel Bowden, phone interview with the author, 25 January 2023.

36. Ernie Neff, "Will Son's Drug Arrest Hurt Cline?" *Tampa Tribune*, 3 June 1980; Charles Hendrick, "DeSoto Sheriff Appears before U.S. Grand Jury," *Tampa Tribune*, 19 May 1977.

37. Frances D. Williams, "Veteran DeSoto Sheriff Is Defeated in Primary," *Fort Myers News-Press*, 8 October 1980.

38. Karen Bair, "Former DeSoto Sheriff Named Glades Chief Deputy," *Fort Myers News-Press*, 10 March 1981.

39. Bowden, interview, 25 January 2023.

FOURTEEN / Anatomy of a Frame-Up

1. Bowden, interview, 25 January 2023.

2. Quoted in Lane, *Citizen Lane*, 198.

3. Quoted in Joel Achenbach, "Soon to Be a Major Motion Picture," *Tropic*, 20 August 1989, 11.

4. Peter B. Gallagher, interview with the author, 17 May 2022, St. Petersburg, FL.

5. Quoted in Gallagher, "Poisoned Justice," *Freedom Magazine*, 33.

6. "Four Arrested in Cocaine Seizure," *Fort Myers News-Press*, 8 January 1986; Mike Hoyem, "4 More Sought in Pot-Growing Ring," *Fort Myers News-Press*, 14 January 2005; "71 Arrested at Hendry Cockfight," *Fort Myers News-Press*, 20 January 1985; "Cuban Exile Commandos Prepare for Fidel Castro's Overthrow," *Tampa Tribune*, 1 May 1980; Dave George, "Mucho Trouble for Macho," *Palm Beach Post*, 9 February 1988.

7. Gallagher, interview 17 May 2022.

8. Bowden, interview, 25 January 2023.

9. Lane, *Citizen Lane*, 200.

10. "Violence on TV Blamed for Death," *Tampa Tribune*, 19 August 1977.

11. Milo Geyelin, "Porn Drove Long to Murder, His Attorney Says," *St. Petersburg Times*, 11 July 1986.

12. Quoted in Elinor J. Brecher and Even S. Benn, "Lawyer Known for the Odd Defense Dies," *Miami Herald*, 12 December 2006.
13. Lane, *Citizen Lane*, 198.
14. Gallagher, interview, 17 May 2022.
15. Quoted in Daniel McLaughlin, "'Suppressed' Evidence Show Murder Frame-Up, Writer Says," *Tampa Tribune*, 20 October 1988.
16. Quoted in George Hatch, "Author Says Documents Dispute Results of Murder Probe, Trial," *Sarasota Herald-Tribune*, 20 October 1988;
17. Quoted in Karl Vick, "Author Accuses 3 in Cover-up in Murders," *St. Petersburg Times*, 20 October 1988.
18. Karl Vick, "Author Accuses 3 in Cover-up in Murders."
19. Quoted in Karl Vick, "A Dramatic New Twist," *St. Petersburg Times*, 18 October 1988.
20. Achenbach, "Soon to Be a Major Motion Picture," 12.
21. Gallagher, interview, 17 May 2022.
22. John Doughtie, "Florida Department of Law Enforcement Investigative Report," 16 November 1988, p. 21, FDLE case number 100-26-0144, accessed by the author through an FDLE public records request, May 2022.
23. John Doughtie, "Florida Department of Law Enforcement Investigative Report," 20 January 1989, FDLE case number 100-26-0144, p. 151.
24. Flowers and Gallagher, "Poisoned Justice," *Tropic*, 17.
25. Sworn affidavit of Richard Barnard, Orange County, Florida, 3 December 1988, exhibit 21, filed 31 March 1989 by Ellis Rubin, "Response to Motion for Post-Conviction Relief," *State of Florida vs. James Joseph Richardson* (DC), vol. 6.
26. Richard Barnard, interview by Steve Davenport, "Florida Department of Law Enforcement Investigative Report," 7 December 1988, FDLE case number 100-26-0144, p. 141.
27. Barnard, interview, 7 December 1988, p. 140.
28. Barnard, interview, 7 December 1988, p. 140.
29. Barnard, interview by Steve Davenport, "Florida Department of Law Enforcement Investigative Report," 20 January 1989, FDLE case number 100-26-0144, p. 263.
30. "Frank Cline and Associates," 1981, FDLE/FBI Investigation, FDLE case number 100-26-0144, pp. 121–127.
31. "Frank Cline and Associates," pp. 122–123.
32. "Frank Cline and Associates," p. 123.
33. Mary Lalah Kirkland, interview by John Doughtie, 11 January 1989, "Florida Department of Law Enforcement Investigative Report," FDLE case number 100-26-0144, p. 305.
34. Gallagher, "Poisoned Justice," *Freedom Magazine*, 36.
35. Gerald Purvis, interview by John Doughtie, 21 November 1988, "Florida Department of Law Enforcement Investigative Report," FDLE case number 100-26-0144, p. 149.

FIFTEEN / But They're Gone Home

1. Peter B. Gallagher and Charles Flowers, "Inside the Hard Head of Frank Schaub," *Sarasota*, May 1989, 55, 58.

2. Christine Wolff, "Hensley Tops Poll of Lawyers," *Bradenton Herald,* 31 July 1982.

3. Quoted in Susan Burns, "Frank Schaub: Silent Strength in the Office of State Attorney," *Bradenton Herald,* 6 October 1985.

4. Christine Wolff, "Things Move Fast with Frank Schaub in the Courtroom," *Bradenton Herald,* 21 February 1982.

5. Quoted in Wolff, "Things Move Fast."

6. Burns, "Frank Schaub."

7. John Gibeaut, "Victim Will Go through Pain of Step-Son's Trial Again," *Tampa Tribune,* 10 December 1990.

8. Beth Muniz, "Schaub to Face Misconduct Trial," *Bradenton Herald,* 30 April 1992.

9. Quoted in Kathleen Beeman, "High Court Suspends Ex-Prosecutor," *Tampa Tribune,* 14 May 1993.

10. William Sabo, "Defense Sued for Slander in Arcadia Murder Case," *Fort Myers News-Press,* 23 December 1988.

11. Quoted in John Allard, "Schaub's Career Is Marred," *Bradenton Herald,* 21 May 1989.

12. Quoted in Karl Vick, "A Made-for-Media Freedom Crusade," *St. Petersburg Times,* 16 January 1989.

13. Quoted in Howard Rosenberg, "CBS's 'Inside Edition' Puts a Chill on TV's Hard News Coverage," *Los Angeles Times,* 11 January 1989.

14. Quoted in L. Wayne Hicks, "Congressman Asks Martinez to Free James Richardson," *Sarasota Herald-Tribune,* 15 November 1988.

15. "New Story Supports Jailed Dad," *Orlando Sentinel,* 22 January 1989.

16. Quoted in Peter B. Gallagher and Charles Flowers, "Martinez Steps Up Probe of Child-Poisoning Case," *Miami Herald,* 2 February 1989.

17. Quoted in Rick Buck, "Tradition at Root of Issue," *Tampa Tribune,* 20 March 1989.

18. "State and Local Government Information Report (EEO-4)," submitted by the city of Arcadia, FL, to the U.S. Equal Opportunity Employment Commission for the year 1991, plaintiff's exhibit ER6-3-92 in *Brenda M. Johnson, et al., vs. DeSoto County Board of Commissioners, et. al.,* US District Court for the Middle District of Florida, case no. 90-366-CIV-FTM-15(D), 5 June 1992, in box 2, folder 3, Gary Mormino Papers, MS-2010-06, University of South Florida Libraries, Special Collections.

19. Heather M. Iarusso, "DeSoto Board Appeals Ruling on Election," *Tampa Tribune,* 16 November 1994.

20. Shillington, "Lawsuit Challenges Election System."

21. Quoted in Barry Millman and Brian O'Donnell, "Release Stirs Emotions in Arcadia," *Tampa Tribune,* 27 April 1989.

22. Quoted in "Richardson Was Deprived of a Fair Trial, Reno Says," *Miami Herald,* 12 April 1989.

23. Dave Nicholson, "Judge Kelly Announces Plans to Retire," *Tampa Tribune,* 16 April 1983.

24. Quoted in Mark Silva, "Man Jailed in '68 Murder Gets Boost from the Governor," *Miami Herald,* 1 April 1989.

25. Rick Buck, "Prosecutor Insists 1968 Trial Was Fair," *Tampa Tribune,* 12 April 1989.

26. Karl Vick, "Man in Poisoning Case Set Free," *St. Petersburg Times,* 26 April 1989.

27. Karl Vick, "Man in Poisoning Case Set Free," *St. Petersburg Times*, 26 April 1989.
28. Quoted in Vick, "Man in Poisoning Case Set Free."
29. Quoted in John Allard, "Judge Frees Richardson," *Bradenton Herald*, 26 April 1989, and Peter B. Gallagher and Charles Flowers, "Slaying Conviction Overturned," *Tallahassee Democrat*, 26 April 1989.
30. Quoted in Lance Oliver, "Cheers and Hugs of Celebration," *Orlando Sentinel*, 26 April 1989.
31. Quoted in Brian O'Donnell, "Arcadia's Black Are Glad," *Tampa Tribune*, 26 April 1989.
32. Quoted in Karl Vick, "Richardson Visits Graves," *St. Petersburgh Times*, 30 May 1989.
33. Quoted in Bart Greenwald, "Richardson Visits Graves of Seven Children," *Bradenton Herald*, 30 May 1989.

SIXTEEN / I Didn't Lose My Battle

1. Rick Barry and Frank Jackman, "Sarasota Approves AIDS Plan," *Tampa Tribune*, 2 September 1987.
2. "Sensible AIDS Policy," editorial, *Bradenton Herald*, 4 September 1987.
3. Quoted in "Few Arcadia Residents Attend Court-Mandated AIDS Talks," *Naples Daily News*, 17 December 1987.
4. Stephen Buckley, "Slow Change of Heart," *St. Petersburg Times*, 2 September 2001.
5. Quoted in Buckley, "Slow Change of Heart."
6. Quoted in Kit Lively, "Castor: Let AIDS Kids Attend Regular Classes," *Orlando Sentinel*, October 16, 1987.
7. "Group Wants School AIDS Testing," *Miami Herald*, 1 November 1987.
8. Quoted in Diedtra Henderson, "AIDS Policymakers Hear Arcadia's Story," *Bradenton Herald*, 31 October 1987.
9. "Sweeping Legislative Package on AIDS Becomes Law," *Miami Herald*, 8 July 1988.
10. Robin Epstein, "Florida Tries to Deal with AIDS," *St. Petersburg Times*, 12 July 1988.
11. Kavanaugh, interview, 2 June 2023.
12. Quoted in "Suit Blames Firms for AIDS Cases," *Miami Herald*, 17 April 1991.
13. Tom Brennan, "Slip-Up Reveals Memo Warning of AIDS Danger," *Tampa Tribune*, 18 May 1990.
14. Deborah Sharp, "Ray Family Testifies: It's Been Very Hard," *Fort Myers News-Press*, 18 April 1991.
15. Quoted in "Rays Agree to Settle with Drug Companies," *St. Petersburg Times*, 8 November 1991.
16. Emily J. Minor, "AIDS, Media Circus Turn Rays Family's Life Inside Out," *Palm Beach Post*, 10 June 1991.
17. John Donnelly, "Learning to Live with It: Rays Protect Childhood, against All Odds," *Miami Herald*, 22 August 1990.
18. Michael McLeod, "Another Loss Draws Family Closer," *Orlando Sentinel*, 1 November 2000; Billy Cox, "Life without Ricky," *Florida Today*, 13 January 1993.
19. Pat Leisner, "School District Settles AIDS Case," *Stuart News* (FL), 30 September 1988.

20. Quoted in Cox, "Life without Ricky."
21. "TV Movie on Rays Called Off," *Fort Lauderdale News*, 26 June 1988.
22. Quoted in Deborah Sharp, "Living with AIDS," *Fort Myers News-Press*, 13 April 1991.
23. Quoted in "After Year as Symbol of AIDS Bias, Ray Brothers Settling in New Home," *Atlanta Journal-Constitution*, 3 October 1988.
24. Quoted in "After Year as Symbol of AIDS Bias."
25. Quoted in Mark Zaloudek, "When Three of Your Children Have AIDS," *San Francisco Chronicle*, 4 October 1990.
26. Quoted in Francis Gilpin, "14-Year-Old with AIDS to Marry," *Tampa Tribune*, 3 June 1991.
27. Clifford Ray, *Larry King Live*, 3 June 1991.
28. Quoted in Minor, "AIDS, Media Circus."
29. Mary Toothman, "AIDS, Teens, and Marriage Raise Issues," editorial, *Tampa Tribune*, 5 June 1991.
30. Quoted in "AIDS Boy's Family Gets New Death Threat," *Miami Herald*, 8 June 1991.
31. Quoted in "AIDS Boy's Family Gets New Death Threat."
32. "Hospitalized Ricky Ray Tries to Stay Upbeat," *Fort Myers News-Press*, 16 August 1991.
33. Quoted in Donna Vavala, "Ricky Ray Video for Sale by Family," *Tampa Tribune*, 16 August 1991.
34. Mary Toothman, "Selling Ray Interview Is in Poor Taste," editorial, *Tampa Tribune*, 19 August 1991.
35. Tom Shales, "TV Talk Shows Aim for Sensationalization," editorial, *Florida Today*, 27 November 1988.
36. Quoted in John Donnelly, "Rays Withdraw from Limelight," *Miami Herald*, 23 December 1991.
37. Quoted in "Family Maintains Bedside Vigil for 'Gravely Ill' Teen with AIDS," *St. Petersburg Times*, 4 November 1992.
38. Quoted in Craig Basse and Lisa Frederick, "Ricky Ray Dies of AIDS," *St. Petersburg Times*, 14 December 1992.

SEVENTEEN / An Isolated Island of a Place

1. Mary Toothman, "Rays Battle with AIDS, Attitudes," editorial, *Tampa Tribune*, 15 December 1992.
2. Larry Perl, "'Town without Pity' Reflects on Treatment of Brothers with AIDS," *USA Today*, 13 December 1992.
3. Perl, "'Town without Pity' Reflects on Treatment."
4. "Ricky Ray, 15, Dies; Known for AIDS Case," *New York Times*, 14 December 1992; "The Life and Death of Ricky Ray," *Tampa Tribune*, 15 December 1992; Deborah Mathis, editorial, "Ricky Ray and His Family Offer Us All Lessons in the Tenacity of Living," *Clarion-Ledger* (Jackson, MS), 15 December 1992.
5. Barbara Boyer, "Deadline Nears for Charges in Torching of Rays Home," *Tampa Tribune*, 22 August 1991.

6. Quoted in Cheryl Waldrip, "Arcadia: A Town without Pity?" *Tampa Tribune*, 31 August 1992.

7. Quoted in Billy Cox, "Life without Ricky," *Florida Today*, 13 January 1993.

8. Quoted in Beth Francis, "Headlines and Heartache Aside, the Ray Family Is Moving Forward," *USA Today*, 27 January 1994.

9. Quoted in Beth Francis, "Education Main Issue in Election, Ray Believes," *Fort Myers News-Press*, 13 December 1993.

10. "Election Day Notebook," *Fort Myers News-Press*, 8 November 1994.

11. Quoted in Peter Eisler, "Goss Offers Help for Hemophiliacs Who Got AIDS," *Fort Myers News-Press*, 24 February 1995.

12. "$600 Million for Hemophiliacs," *Toronto Star*, 8 May 1997.

13. Larry Wheeler, "Senate Passes Ricky Ray Bill," *Fort Myers News-Press*, 22 October 1988.

14. Quoted in Michael McLeod, "Another Loss Draws Family Even Closer," *Orlando Sentinel*, 1 November 2000.

15. Quoted in McLeod, "Another Loss Draws Family Even Closer."

16. Quoted in Stephen Buckley, "Slow Change of Heart," *St. Petersburg Times*, 2 September 2001.

17. Tim W. McCann, "Framing the Antiques District," *Bradenton Herald*, 29 September 2002.

18. Quoted in Lori Rozsa, "Arcadia Welcomes Small-Town Honor," *Miami Herald*, 18 July 1993.

19. Ian Trontz, "Rules Blamed for Shortages in Migrant Housing," *Tampa Tribune*, 21 December 1995; Ian Trontz, "Shared Dwellings under Fire," *Tampa Tribune*, 16 May 1995; "Hispanic Population," chart, *Tallahassee Democrat*, 29 March 2001.

20. Brian Haas, "Migrant Victims Face New Obstacles," *Bradenton Herald*, 27 August 2004.

21. John Mulliken, "Citrus Belt Slipping a Notch to the South," *Fort Lauderdale News*, 24 March 1985.

22. Haas, "Migrant Victims Face New Obstacles."

23. Betsy Clayton, "Arcadia Takes Growth by the Horns," *Fort Myers News-Press*, 9 March 2002; "Revival," *Tampa Tribune*, 21 October 1995; Richard Dymond, "Law Varies in Manatee Prayer Issue," *Bradenton Herald*, 30 July 2003.

24. Curtis Krueger, "State Mental Hospital Shuts Down," *St. Petersburg Times*, 9 February 2002.

25. Curtis Krueger, "The Town That Lost Its Job," *St. Petersburg Times*, 27 February 2001.

26. Lisa Ramirez, "G. Pierce Wood Announces Stepped-Up Closing Date," *Fort Myers News-Press*, 29 January 2002.

27. Quoted in Krueger, "Town That Lost Its Job."

28. Liz Freeman, "Media, Patients Face Uncertain Future," *Naples Daily News*, 18 June 2000.

29. Quoted in Mary McLachlin, "Defense Lawyers Target Tests Used to Hold Molesters," *Palm Beach Post*, 6 December 2003.

30. Jason Grotto, "Predators among Us," series part 2, *Miami Herald*, 29 January 2006.
31. Jason Grotto, "Predators among Us," *Miami Herald*, 30 January 2006.
32. Jason Grotto, "Arcadia Facility 'a Powder Keg,'" *Bradenton Herald*, 30 January 2006; Abby Goodnough and Monica Davey, "Treatment Center for Cesspool," *Orlando Sentinel*, 5 March 2007.
33. Joel Anderson and Stephanie Garry, "Victim Relieved Rapist Caught," *St. Petersburg Times*, 11 February 2008.
34. Lori Rozsa, "Friend Charged in Slaying of Pair on Gulf Coast," *Miami Herald*, 19 April 1997; "Closing Arguments to Begin Today in Charlotte Murder Trial," *Naples Daily News*, 8 March 1999.
35. Christy Feinberg, "Ford Eyed in DeSoto Case," *Port Charlotte Sun*, 9 September 2012.
36. Anonymous comment on "Justices Let Stand Sentences of Death," *Florida Issues* (blog), 13 April 2007, https://florida-issues.blogspot.com/2007/04/justices-let-stand-sentence-of-death.html.
37. Bob Norman, "Murder Suspect Linked to DeSoto Case," *Fort Myers News-Press*, 19 April 1997.
38. Quoted in Don Moore, "'76 DeSoto Death Revisited," *Englewood Sun*, 26 May 1997.
39. Moore, "'76 DeSoto Death Revisited."
40. Paul Sullivan, phone interview with the author, 4 March 2024.
41. Lindsey Williams, "Series of Rancher Murder Ended Era of Open Ranges," *Englewood Sun*, 25 July 1999; "Former Deputy Shot While Riding Truck," *Fort Myers News-Press*, 10 March 1930.
42. "Woman Is Jailed on Perjury Charge in Cattle Feud Trials," *Tampa Morning Tribune*, 29 January 1937; "State Rests Case in Murder Trial," *Sarasota Herald*, 29 January 1937.
43. Sullivan, interview, 4 March 2024.
44. 2022 Census of Agriculture, National Agricultural Statistics Service, US Department of Agriculture, https://www.nass.usda.gov/Publications/AgCensus/2022/Online_Resources/County_Profiles/Florida/index.php.
45. Quoted in David Dorsey, "A Growing Concern: The Diminishing Base, Uncertain Future of Agriculture in SWFL," *Gulfshore Business*, 1 April 2022.
46. Allman, "Arcadia 'Won't Be the Same.'"
47. Quoted in Pittman, "Arcadia Harks Back to Days of Bone Mizell."
48. Adam Kovac, "Woman Charged in Bird Slaughter," *Fort Myers News-Press*, 16 October 2002.
49. Grant Boxleitner, "Bird Killings Net $5,000 Fine," *Fort Myers News-Press*, 27 November 2003.
50. Brian Haas, "17,000 Homeless—Storm Shelters Bulge," *Bradenton Herald*, 20 August 2004.
51. Quoted in Steve Newborn, "Arcadia Moves on 10 Years after Hurricane Charley," WUSF, 9 August 2014, https://www.wusf.org/culture/2014-08-09/arcadia-moves-on-10-years-after-hurricane-charley.
52. "Man Killed in Arcadia Is Identified," *Sarasota Herald-Tribune*, 17 August 2004.
53. Quoted in Erin Bryce and Tiffany Lankes, "Arcadia's Homes, Heart Torn by Storm," *Sarasota Herald-Tribune*, 15 August 2004.

54. John W. Allman, "DeSoto Suffers Devastating Blow," *Tampa Tribune,* 15 August 2004; Michael Braga, "For Ranchers, Storms Bring a Soggy Stampede of Troubles," *Sarasota Herald-Tribune,* 9 September 2004.

55. Robert Bowden, "DeSoto Is Reopen for Business," *Port Charlotte Sun,* 13 August 2006.

56. Quoted in Susan Salisbury, "A Blow to Citrus," *Palm Beach Post,* 20 August 2004.

57. Robert Bowden, "2005 Was Citrus Growers' Nightmare," *DeSoto Sun,* 31 December 2005.

58. Robert Bowden, "Citrus Trees Continue to Be Uprooted and Burned," *DeSoto Sun,* 7 June 2006.

59. James A. Jones Jr., "It's the 'Worst of Times' for Area Farmers," *Bradenton Herald,* 22 July 2009; Clinton Burton, "DeSoto Named Poorest County," *Port Charlotte Sun,* 13 July 2012.

60. Robert Eckhart, "A Safety Net, Spread Thin," *Sarasota Herald-Tribune,* 24 November 2011.

EPILOGUE

1. Quoted in Gregory Enns, "CBS Buys Exonerated Suspect's Life Story," *St. Petersburg Times,* 12 August 1995.

2. Novelda Sommers, "Ex-Death Row Inmate is Free, at Peace," *Tampa Tribune,* 9 June 2000.

3. Susan E. Hoffman, "State Denies James Richardson's Innocence," *Port Charlotte Sun,* 26 September 2008.

4. Quoted in Brittany Levine, "Ex-Prisoner's Move Will Test New Law," *Miami Herald,* 18 July 2009.

5. Quoted in John Kennedy, "Wrongful Conviction: State Considers Changing Law to Compensate Man after 24 Years," *Palm Beach Post,* 13 September 2013.

6. Quoted in Cheryl Waldrip, "Her Most Important Role," *Tampa Tribune,* 29 March 1993.

7. Quoted in Waldrip, "Her Most Important Role."

8. Tom Fiedler, "In Rural Florida, A Fear of Change," *Miami Herald,* 5 February 1995; Heather M. Iarusso, "Councilman Apologizes for Remarks," *Tampa Tribune,* 22 March 1995.

9. The Richardson documentary is *Time Simply Passes,* directed by Ty Flowers (Tanman Films, 2018).

10. Bob French, "Seminole Paper Brings Honors, News to Tribe," *Fort Lauderdale Sun-Sentinel,* 15 May 1990.

11. Quoted in Susan E. Hoffman, "Richardson Returns to Warm Welcome in Arcadia," *The Arcadian,* 31 October 2013.

12. Ian Cummings, "Frail and Aged, Man Returns to Arcadia and a Hurtful Past," *Sarasota Herald-Tribune,* 27 October 2013.

13. Quoted in Peter B. Gallagher, "James Richardson Seeks Relief from Florida Legislators," *Seminole Tribune,* 2 April 2013.

14. Quoted in Ian Cummings, "Payment on Way at Long Last," *Sarasota Herald-Tribune,* 21 June 2014.

15. Gallagher, "Poisoned Justice," *Freedom Magazine,* 38.

16. Quoted in "Delayed Justice for an Innocent Man," editorial, *Florida Times-Union,* 16 May 2019.

17. Quoted in Pittman, "Arcadia Harks Back to Days of Bone Mizell."

INDEX

Abiaki, 163
Adams, Bob, 119
Adams, Moody, 141–42
African Americans, 39, 62, 127, 211n40; Jim Crow laws in Florida and, 19–20; jury pools in Florida and, 75; Summer of Rage and, 40; use of convict labor in Florida turpentine industry and, 21. *See also* Arcadia; DeSoto County; the Quarters
AIDS. *See* HIV/AIDS
AIDS Medical Foundation, 133
Alabama, 62
Albany (NY), 81–82
Albritton, Arcadia, 11–12
Albritton, Ben, 11
Albritton, Maggie, 158–59
Alcoholics Anonymous, 193
Aledort, Louis, 114
Algeria, 153
All Children's Hospital, 109, 131, 179, 187–88, 191
Allen, J. Garrott, 108
All-Florida Rodeo, 23, 192–93, 212n7; founding of, 25–26; parades for, 26–27
Allman, John W., 9
Alpha Therapeutics, 109
Alva (FL), 74
American Academy of Pediatrics, 130, 139
American Agronomics Corporation, 28–29, 103. *See also* Citrus industry
American Bar Association, 67, 81
American Broadcasting Corporation, 184
American Indian Movement, 101
American Legion, 122
American Medical Association, 130

American Red Cross, 115, 139
American Spectator, 137
Anderson, Lonnie, 184
Anderson, Louis, 38, 58, 77
Andy Griffith Show, 92
Angola Penitentiary, 108
Arcadia (book), 7, 87; depiction of Arcadia in, 96–97; interviews in, 89–92; main argument of, 89; reviews of 87–89, 93; town response to, 92–94
Arcadia (CA), 4
Arcadia (FL), 1, 2, 49, 64, 69; Arcadia (IN) and, 148–49; African-American workers in city of, 32, 175; Baptist churches in, 124; cross burnings in, 93; discovery of phosphate near, 12–13; economic development of, 102–3; evolving racial views in, 31–34, 203; fire of 1905 and, 18; first black mayor and, 31–32; founding of, 12; Hispanic population in, 192; historic insularity of, 9, 197–98; honky-tonks in, 26, 195; Hurricane Charley and, 198–99; KKK in, 21–33, 33–34; naming of, 11–12; national views of, 4, 135, 149, 189–90; Orange Avenue and, 47, 175; poverty in, 12; profile by Richard Nellius and, 61–62; racial problems in, 9, 19–22, 26–27, 32–33, 66, 93–94, 96, 203, 211n40, 212n7; residents' response to media and, 4–5, 145; revitalization of downtown and, 192; rodeo parades in, 26–27; selected best small town in America, 192; violence in, 13–16, 26, 196–97; voter discrimination in, 175–76. *See also Arcadia* (book); DeSoto County; Quarters, the
Arcadia (IN), 148–49

Arcadia Champion, 22
Arcadia General Hospital, 31, 38. 54
Arcadian, 20, 60, 67, 92–93, 144, 150
Arcadia Police Department, 91, 160
Arizona Daily Star, 149
Armentrout, Steven A., 136–37
Armour Pharmaceutical Co., 109, 182–84
Aronowitz, Stanley, 81
Assembly of God, 144
Associated Press, 60, 118, 132
Atkins, Joel, 66, 68, 177
Atlanta (GA), 169
Auburndale (FL), 36
Aynesworth, Hugh, 83

Babcock Ranch, 26, 197
Bailey, F. Lee, 50; Carl Coppolino trial and, 50–53; oratorical skills of, 50–51
Baldwin, James, 86
Baltimore, 111
Barbosa, Jerry, 109–110, 123, 126, 128, 188; background of, 131; DeSoto County School Board and, 132; invitation to debate Moody Adams and, 141–42; testimony at federal hearing and, 136–37
Barnard, Richard, 91, 167–69; letter insisting Cline framed Richardson and, 168
Barr, Duncan, 183
Barrar, Robert, 202
Bartels, John R., 119
Bartow (FL), 37, 129
Bastanzio, Tony, 156
Baxter Pharmaceuticals, 108–9
Bayer Pharmaceutical, 109, 182
Bay Minette (AL), 126
Beechler, Billy, 148
Behrens, Dave, 60
Behringworke AG, 109
Belle Glade (FL), 122–23
Belleville (IL), 4
Bernard, Eileen, 74
Bernstein, Carl, 204
Bethesda (MD), 187
Bethune-Cookman College, 68

Beverly, Cheryl, 102
Big Cypress Seminole Reservation, 162, 164
Big Sur Inn, 84
Billie, James, 162–64
Birmingham (AL), 82, 92
Black, Evelyn, 166, 169–70
Black Panthers, 153
Blair, Harry, 128–30, 136–38
Blood on Their Hands, 114
Bolita, 46
Bond, Julian, 8
Booker Middle School, 185
Boom, John, 69, 71, 167; reputation of, 69–70
Boston Strangler, 50
Bowden, Hazel, 160–61, 163–64, 166
Bowden, Robert, 199
Bradenton, 31, 49, 53, 98, 172, 192; Tamiami Trail and, 23
Bradenton Herald, 8, 179, 192, 194
Bradford County (FL), 85
Broadway, 84
Brooklyn Law School, 81
Broward County (FL), 103, 165
Brown, Johnny C., 195–97
Browning Larry, 125, 131–32, 180–81, comparison of HIV to citrus canker and, 130
Brown v. Board of Education, 2, 130
Bryant, Leonard, 46
Buckley, Stephen, 180
Bugliosi, Vincent, 82
Burns, Hayden, 39
Burton, William, 94

California, 116, 136, 148–49, 153, 183
Caloosahatchee River, 13, 22
Calvary Baptist Church, 32
Cape Coral (FL), 49, 74–75, 97
Carlino, Joseph, 81–82
Carlstrom Field, 29–30
Carnal, Bob, 148
Carnestown (FL), 98

Carrol, Clay
Case, Chris, 131–32
Castor, Betty, 181
Castro, Fidel, 87, 163
Cattle industry, 1, 20, 25; fencing of ranchlands and, 18; Florida's Cracker cowboys and, 14–16; Florida scrub cows and, 16, 25; Hurricane Charley and, 199; introduction of Brahman breed and, 18; introduction of hardier grasses and, 18; laborers in, 26; lightning strikes and, 142; Ninety-Mile Prairie and, 15; number of cattle in, 18; origins in Florida of, 14; range wars and, 15–17, 196–97. *See also* King, Ziba
CBS Evening News, 53
Cecil Webb Wildlife Refuge, 21
Centers for Disease Control, 111–13, 116, 130, 139; AIDS taskforce guidelines and, 131, 137; attempts to warn hemophilia sufferers about HIV and, 114; emergency AIDS meeting of, 115
Central Intelligence Agency, 153
Central Missionary Baptist Church, 124
Charlotte County (FL), 4, 11, 26, 100, 194–95; agricultural industry in, 197; board of commissioners and, 100; Deer Run development and, 100–101; growth of, 97; household income in, 102; ranches in, 23–24; vacant lots in, 97, 100. *See also* Port Charlotte; Punta Gorda
Chicago (IL), 84, 186
Chicago Eyewitness, 84
Chicago Tribune, 117, 149
Christian Coalition, 190
Cicero (IN), 148
Citizens Against Aids in Schools, 1, 3, 149, 181; August 1987 rally by, 2, 140–141, 143; formation of, 139–40; Sarasota rally of, 150–51
Citizens Against Misinformation, 150–51
Citizen's Dissent, A, 84
Citrus industry, 19–20, 35, 37; African Americans in, 20; DeSoto County and, 16, 18, 31, 98, 192–93; Hurricane Charley and, 199–200; migrant laborers and, 27–29
City University of New York, 81
Civil Rights Act, 93
Cleaver, Eldridge, 153
Clement, David, 88
Cleveland (FL), 158
Clewiston (FL), 160–61, 163
Cline, Adrian, 193
Cline, Donna Jo, 42
Cline, Frank, 6–7, 38, 49, 54, 57, 86, 89, 139, 159, 163, 193, 198, 202; background of, 39–40; depiction by Lane of, 92; description of, 42; DNA testing of, 47, 169, 202; Earnell Washington and, 76; election of 1966 and, 40, 169; election of 1968 and, 92; false claims regarding Richardson and, 61, 78; FDLE investigations and 167–69; initial investigation of Richardson deaths and, 43–45, 47–48; interview of Reese by, 89–90; jailhouse treatment of Richardson by, 70; Lane accusations of, 166–67; *Official Detective* and, 91; polygraph test of Richardson and, 63; post-sheriff's career of, 155–56, 160; pretrial statements regarding Richardson and, 67–68, 73; rumors related to, 6, 41, 46–47, 160, 166–70; Spot Weaver and, 90; statement regarding African-American intelligence by, 27, 62; testimony at coroner's inquest and, 64–65; testimony at Richardson trial and, 78–79; views on policing African-Americans of, 40
Clinton, Bill, 188, 190
Coca-Cola, 157
Colby, Ronald, 122
Collier County (FL), 69, 97
Colorado, 113, 116
Comacho, Hector, 163
Concerned Citizens and Parents of Western Middle School, 120–21

Congressional Black Caucus, 174
Conner, Eugene, 92
Coppolino, Carl 49, 71; background of, 50; Florida trial of, 50–53; New Jersey trial of, 50
Coppolino, Carmela, 49–50, 52
Cosey, Beatrice, 76
Costa Mesa (CA), 108
Cotton, Hubert S., 169
Couch, Marvin, 190
Cracker, 13; embrace of moniker by white Florida natives and, 14; etymology of, 13
Crampton, Norman, 192
Cronkite, Walter, 53
Cuba, 16
Cumberland University School of Law, 67
Cunningham, James, 71–73, 80, 166, 168, 173
Cure AIDS Now, 137
Cutter Laboratories, 182–84

Dade County (FL), 36, 103, 175
Dade County School Board, 119; settlement with Haitian triplets and, 129
Dallas Morning News, 83
Darrow, Clarence, 164
Davidson, Vicky, 198
Daytona Beach, 25, 91, 152, 162, 164, 168
Daytona Beach Inter-Racial Advisory Board, 68
Daytona Beach Junior College, 68
Daytona Beach News-Journal, 93–94
David L. Wolper Productions, 204
Deer Run, 100–101
DeLand (FL), 49, 64
Delaware, 99, 118
Democratic National Convention, 84
Democratic Party, 67
Dennis, Virginia, 174
DePrince, Elaine, 107–8
DeSoto Correctional Institution, 33, 158, 198; conditions in, 104–5; establishment of, 30; importance to local economy of, 104; low wages of, 104–5
DeSoto County (FL), 4, 11, 27, 49, 87–88, 130, 152, 181, 189, 198; attempts to secure I-75 and, 98; cattle industry in, 14–18, 20, 25, 31, 196–197, 199; citrus industry in, 16, 18, 31, 98, 192–93, 199–200; comparison to neighboring counties of, 102; Deer Run development and, 100–101; division of 1925 and, 23; employment in, 25; Hispanic residents in, 28–29, 192; Hurricane Charley and, 198–99; jail of, 39, 65; lack of economic growth in, 97, 99, 102–3, 197–98; lynchings in, 22; migrant workers in, 192; original settler families in, 11; poverty in, 25, 200; range wars in, 15, 196–97; size of, 18; subprime mortgage crisis and, 199–200; support for George Wallace in, 62; voter suppression in, 8–9, 175–76. *See also* Arcadia
DeSoto County Board of Commissioners, 100–101, 133, 180
DeSoto County Chamber of Commerce, 103
DeSoto County Courthouse, 11, 64, 156, 158, 176
DeSoto County News, 21
DeSoto County School Board, 1, 127, 132, 179–80; African-American boycott of schools and, 96; AIDS-related boycott of schools and, 3, 143–144; banning of Ray children by, 125; bomb threats to schools and, 3, 145–46; discrimination against African-American students by, 20; insults of Rays by, 130; Kovachevich hearing and, 136–39; Rays' attorney and, 128–30; Rays' doctor and, 132; return of Rays to school and, 143–46; school graduation rates of, 102–3; school integration and, 2, 61, 94–96; segregation of Ray children and, 1, 129–30; settlement with Rays and, 151–52, 184. *See also* Smith-Brown School
DeSoto County Sheriff's Office, 91, 104, 139, 145, 160, 169, 211n40
DeSoto High School, 2, 31; hiring of first

African American football coach at, 32; historic insularity of, 99; integration of, 40–41, 95–96
DeSoto Middle School, 180
DeSoto National Bank, 94
Devil's Garden, 160, 163
DiMaggio, Joe, 197
Disneyland, 183
Donahue, 148, 150
Donahue, Phil, 3, 183
Dorr Field, 29–30
Doughtie, John, 167–70, 174, 176
Douglas, Kirk, 2
Dow, Marguerite, 104
Duggar, Leonard, 162
Dunbar, Peter, 166
Duval County Sheriff's Office, 65
Dymally, Marvin, 174

Earl, Bill, 128
Edison, Thomas, 73
Education for All Handicapped Children Act, 119
Edwards, Isadore, 74
Elgin (IL), 117
Elizabeth Baptist Church, 59
Ellenton (FL), 170
Eloise (FL), 27
Enemy Among Us, An, 188
Englewood (FL), 21
Environmental Land and Water Management Act, 100
Equal Employment Opportunity Commission, 175
Evening Express (ME), 4
Evening Independent (FL), 126
Everglades, 60, 98

Factor VIII, 1, 182; attempts to remove hepatitis from, 108; delay in making a virus-free version of, 109; invention of concentrate of, 106–7; lawsuits over, 182–184, 191; sourcing of plasma for, 107–8, 113

Fagan, L. T., 39, 42–43, 86, 166, 173, 177; insurance issue and, 72–73
Faison, James, 41
Faison, Ruby, 37–38, 41, 77, 88
Farber, Marjorie, 50
Farley, Rosemary, 99
Faulkner, William, 149
Federal Bureau of Investigation, 39, 41, 153
Felder, C. S., 59, 96
Fernandina Beach (FL), 128
Fife, Barney, 92
Florida Baptist College, 124
Florida Board of Regents, 135
Florida Bureau of Law Enforcement, 63
Florida Civil Commitment Center, 193–94, 198
Florida Department of Agriculture, 36
Florida Department of Education, 102, 119; HIV guidelines of, 181
Florida Department of Health and Rehabilitative (later Rehabilitation) Services, 103, 119, 181–82
Florida Department of Law Enforcement, 26, 41, 174; Frank Cline and, 167–69
Florida Division of Mental Health, 30
Florida Governor's Taskforce on AIDS, 136
Florida Highway Patrol, 39–40, 156, 160
Florida House Criminal Justice Subcommittee, 204
Florida House of Representatives, 190
Florida Legislative Black Caucus, 204
Florida Parole and Probation Commission, 152
Florida Sheriffs Association, 160
Florida Southern College, 67, 203
Florida State Attorney's Office, 189
Florida State Hospital at Chattahoochee, 29, 103
Florida State Prison at Raiford, 7, 85, 90, 104
Florida Supreme Court, 87, 101, 172, 176, 182
Floridian, 61–62

Flowers, Charles, 47, 70, 161; background of, 162; movie rights and, 204; "Poisoned Justice" article and, 173; Richardson case and, 166–68, 170–71, 203
Flowers, Ty, 203
Fonda, Jane, 101, 167
Ford, James Dennis, 194–197
Ford, Lawrence, 196
Fort Lauderdale (FL), 9
Fort Lauderdale News, 31, 149
Fort Lauderdale Sun-Sentinel, 162
Fort Meade (FL), 42
Fort Myers (FL), 22, 36, 39, 49, 169; cattle industry and, 13, 16; decline of agriculture in, 197; growth of, 73–74, 97; racial problems in, 74–75; Richardson trial in, 6, 74, 90, 93; Tamiami Trail and, 23. See also Lee County
Fort Myers News-Press, 33, 67, 75, 88, 145, 156
Fort Ogden (FL), 16
Fort Walton Beach (FL), 177
Foy, James, 54, 56
Fox, Michael J., 183
Francis, Donald, 115
Frankel, Louise, 181–82
Frizzell Ranch, 197
Freedom of Information Act, 152
Freedom Riders, 82
Frost, David, 173–74
Fuentes, Carl, 124–125
Fugate, John, 189
Fugitive, The, 50

Gaetz, Matt, 204
Gainesville (FL), 131
Galichia, Joseph P., 201
Gallagher, Peter B., 47, 70, background of, 162; movie rights and, 204; "Poisoned Justice" article and, 173; Richardson case and, 162–64, 166–68, 170–71, 203
Gamiotea, Raul, 124–25, 134
Gardner, James, 127
Garrison, Jim, 87
Garry, Charles, 153

Garza, Dorothy, 4
Gator Slough, 196
General Development Corporation, 103
Georgia, 69, 98, 169
Geraldo!, 183, 186–87
Glades Central High School, 123
Glades County (FL), 23, 49, 98, 155, 160; agriculture in, 26, 197
Glades Day School, 123
Glendale (AZ), 4
Gocio Elementary School, 150
Goldberg, Whoopi, 184
Good, Robert A., 136–37
Goodman, Sharon Thomas, 150, 204; background of, 203; Richardson funeral and, 58–59, 150
Good Morning America, 121
Goss, Porter, 190–91
Go Towards the Light, 188
Gottfried, Robert, 118
G. Pierce Wood Memorial Hospital, 103, 163, 198; closure of, 193; conditions in, 29–30, 103–4; establishment of, 29; importance to local economy of, 30, 103
Grace Lutheran Church, 189
Graham, Bob, 191
Gregory, Dick, 84, 177, 201
Griffin, Mark, 157
Griffin, Remus, 157, 163, 166, 195; background of, 157–58; Mark Lane and, 157, 161, meeting with James Richardson and, 177
Gross, Samuel, 136–37
Gulf Naval Stores, 29, 42, 89, 101
Gulf of Mexico, 12–13, 16, 23, 198
Guss, Mark, 127
Guyana, 152–54

Hackney, Bill, 60, 67, 92–93
Haiti, 107, 113
Halpin, Donald, 104
Hamlin, J. L., 65
Hardee County (FL), 4, 11, 23, 31, 97, 152, 154
Hardee County Farm Bureau, 97

Hardee Manor Nursing Home, 152
Harlem (NY), 7, 81–82
Harper's Magazine, 16
Harris, Bettinita, 126–27, 132
Harris, Doris Harris, 152
Harrison, Kay, 157–58
Hartley, Bernice, 79
Hays, Gordon, 39, 43–44, 56, 63, 77, 86, 88–89; background of, 64; coroner's inquest and, 63–65; death of, 73; use of previous testimony at Richardson trial and, 80
HBO, 167
Hefner, Hugh, 184
Heine, Robert W., 203
Helpern, Milton, 52
Hemo Caribbean, 113
Hemophilia, 1, 105; cause of, 106; first reports of HIV among patients of, 113; hepatitis and, 107–8. *See also* Factor VIII; National Hemophilia Foundation; Ray family; White, Ryan
Hendry County (FL), 26, 49, 98, 197
Hendry County Sheriff's Office, 160, 163
Hendry, E. A., 69
Hendry, James M., 12
Herndon, Grady, 21
Hickey, Michael, 148
Hicks, L. Wayne, 172–73
Hickson, Eugene, Sr., 58, 96, 159, 175, 206, 212n7; election of 1971 and, 31–32
High, Robert King, 68
Highlands County (FL), 14, 23, 26, 100–101, 152, 176
Highway 1 (CA), 84
Hill, Leroy, 78
Hillsborough County (FL), 104
HIV/AIDS, 109; CD4 T "helper" cells and, 111; defining illnesses of, 111; early names for, 112; first known American cases of, 113; first reports among hemophilia patients and, 113; Florida AIDS law of 1988 and, 181–82; groups most affected by, 114; irrational fear of, 116–18; Lyndon LaRouche and, 116; Miami school case and, 119; movies about, 188; quarantine initiatives and, 116; Ronald Reagan and, 133; Ryan White and, 120–122; school districts and, 118–123, 129; stages of, 111; origins of, 112–13; transmission of, 111–12
Hixson, Terry, 97
Hollywood (CA), 143, 167, 183, 201
Hollywood (FL), 162
Holt, Rinehart, and Winston, 87
Holton, Inez, 39–40
Holton, Lloyd, 39
Houghland, Calvin, 26
Hudson, Rock, 133
Humphrey, Hubert, 62
Hunter, Houston, 40
Hurricane Charley, 198–199
Hurricane Katrina, 113
Hyland Laboratories, 108

Illinois, 106, 185
Immokalee (FL), 49, 69–70, 98–99
Indianapolis (IN), 121, 148
Inside Edition, 8, 167, 173–74
Interstate 4 (I-4), 98
Interstate 75 (I-75), 98–99
In the Heat of the Night, 91
Izaak Walton League, 127

Jackson, Myrtice, 37, 77
Jacksonville (FL), 17, 65–66, 79, 201
Jaffe, Steve, 167, 201
Jennings, Peter, 133, 135
JFK, 87
Johnson, John E., 133, 181
Johnson, Roosevelt, 94–95
Jones, Claudia, 32
Jones, Jim, 101, 152–54
Jones, Sarah E., 79
Jonestown (Guyana), 101, 152–54
Joshua Grove, 29
Journal of the American Medical Association, 108

Judd, Robert, 190
Justice, John, 71, 73, 77–79, 87

Katz, Bob, 84, 88–89
Kavanaugh, Judith, 127, 129, 147–48; background of, 127–28; DeSoto County School Board and, 128, 132, 180; Kovachevich hearing and, 136–39; lawsuit against pharmaceutical companies and, 182–84; lawsuit against school board and, 184
Keen, Vernon, 195
Kelly, Clifton, 176–78
Kennedy, John F., 7, 82–84, 87, 101, 154. *See also* Lane, Mark
Kennedy, Stetson, 16
Kerner, Dave, 202–5
Key West (FL), 118
King, Larry, 3, 183
King, Martin Luther, Jr., 101, 175
King, T. B., 18
King, Ziba, 16–18, 26
Kinshasa (Congo), 112
Kirk, Claude, 66, 87
Kirkland, Mary, 169
Kissimmee River, 13
Knott's Berry Farm, 183
Kojak, 165
Kokomo (IN), 120–22, 125
Kokomo Tribune, 121
Koop, C. Everett, 130–31
Koppel, Ted, 183
Kovachevich, Elizabeth, 140, 179; Ray hearing and, 135–138
Krim, Mathilde, 133
Krop, Michael, 129
Krum, Kellie Jo, 195–97
Krum, Kelsi, 195–97
Ku Klux Klan, 21–22, 33–34, 156, 187
Kunkletown (PA), 4

LaBelle (FL), 22, 49, 98–99
Lake City (TN), 4
Lakeland (FL), 67, 101, 124, 167, 203

Lakeland Ledger, 204
Lake Okeechobee, 22, 39
Lane, George, Jr., 103
Lane, Mark, 7, 40; background of, 81–82; criticism of Arcadia by, 7, 96–97; description of, 81–81, 88–89; depiction of Cline and, 92; Ellis Rubin as co-counsel and, 164–65, 167–68, 172–73; "end-the-silence" meeting and, 8, 155–57; first meeting with Richardson and, 86; Free James Richardson Fund and, 167; Jim Jones and, 101, 152–54; Kennedy assassination and, 82–85, 154; legal career of, 101; *National Guardian* and, 82–83; op-ed in *Playboy* and, 87, 93; Remus Griffin and, 157, 161; Richardson hearing of 1989 and, 177; *Rush to Judgment* and, 83–84, 88; Schaub lawsuit against, 172–173; Steve Jaffe and, 167, 201; stolen Richardson files and, 164, 166–67. *See also Arcadia* (book)
Lanier, Jack, 195
LaRouche, Lyndon, 116, 137
Larry King Live, 186
Lattimore, Lyle, 41
Lebanon (TN), 67
LeBaron, Francis, 12–13
Lee, Robert E., 73–74, 80
Lee, Tom, 202
Lee County (FL), 11, 22, 26, 102; agricultural industry in, 197; discrimination in, 74–75; growth of, 97; integration of, 74; naming of, 73–74. *See also* Fort Myers
Lehigh Acres (FL), 97, 197
Lesbian and Gay Freedom Ride, 156
Lesotho, 107
Lexington (GA), 136
Liberty Behavioral Health, 194
Liberty City (FL), 175
Life, 53, 111
Lifton, David, 154
Limestone (FL), 31
Lindberg, Wenonah, 186–88

Lockman, Lawrence, 141
Long, Bobbie Joe, 165
Longboat Key (FL), 49–50
Look, 53
Los Angeles (CA), 84, 107, 112, 115, 183
Louganis, Greg, 121
Louisiana, 108
Lowell State Women's Prison, 45, 170
Lucky Lee Ranch, 197
Lykes Brothers Ranch, 26

MacDill Air Force Base, 36
MacDonald, John D., 50–51
Mack, Connie, Jr., 191
Mad Max, 163
Malnory, Greg, 194–95, 197
Malnory, Kim, 194–95, 197
Manatee County (FL), 17, 90, 127
Manatee County Bar Association, 172
Manatee County School Board, 132
Manson, Charles, 82
Mariel boatlift, 175
Marriott, Jimmy, 36
Martinez, Bob, 8–9, 166, 173, 181; Janet Reno and, 174–76
Marton, Mel, 187
Maryland, 116
McDuffie, Arthur, 175
McLain, Denny, 135
McPherson, Myra, 4
Medical College of Virginia, 131
Memorial Elementary School, 94, 144, 150
Mercer, Kaye, 198
Miami (FL), 40, 51, 119, 129, 165, 175; Tamiami Trail and, 23
Miami Beach (FL), 25, 164
Miami Herald, 58, 149, 192, 194, 203–4; reporting on Richardson case and, 8, 47, 60, 65, 161–62
Miami News, 67
Miami Vice, 175
Middle District of Florida, 135
Miller, Rod, 118
Minoughan, Joseph, 91

Mississippi Burning, 189
Mizell, Morgan Bonaparte, 17, 26
Mobile (AL), 126
Monmouth County (NJ), 50
Montura Ranch Estates (FL), 163
Morbidity and Mortality Weekly Report, 112–13
Morgan, Dave, 137–38
Mother Jones, 88, 152–53
Mount Zion African Methodist Episcopal Church, 203
MSN Money, 200
Mulock, Edwin, 173
Murphy, Jack, 102

Nader, Ralph, 88
Naples, 49, 98, 101; Carl Coppolino trial and, 51, 53; Tamiami Trail and, 23
Nassau County School Board, 129
National Association for the Advancement of Colored People (NAACP), 8, 27, 66, 74–5, 82, 94, 177; defense of Richardson and, 68; Helen Washington and, 176
National District Attorneys Association, 53
National Guardian, 82–83
National Hemophilia Foundation, 114; early inactivity regarding HIV/AIDS and, 115; Factor VIII manufacturers and, 114–15
National Enquirer, 153
National Indian Gaming Commission, 162
National Institutes of Health, 187
National Lawyers Guild, 81
Nebraska, 97
Negron, Joe, 202
Nellius, Richard, 60–63
New Jersey, 50, 120, 129
New Orleans, 87
Newsweek, 84
New York, 13, 53, 74, 81, 148, 183, 186
New York (magazine), 154
New York Assembly, 81–82

New York City, 84, 87, 113, 121, 136, 156
New York City Board of Education, 119
New York Department of Mental Hygiene, 81
New York Times, 53, 60, 83, 99, 154
Nightline, 148–49
Ninety-Mile Prairie, 15
Nixon, Richard M., 62, 173
Nocatee (FL), 42, 89, 95, 101, 146, 169
No Deadly Drug, 51
Nordheimer, Jon, 60–61, 65–66
North Carolina, 116
North Port (FL), 97, 103, 197
Norton, Milton, 196
Nowitzke, Charles, 172

100 Best Small Towns in America, The, 192
O'Neil, Ryan, 167
Oak Ridge Cemetery, 59, 195, 205
Ocala (FL), 45
Ocala Evening Star, 22
Official Detective, 91
Ohio, 106, 113, 116
Ohio Department of Health, 117
Okeechobee (FL), 146
Okeechobee County (FL), 4
One Flew Over the Cuckoo's Nest, 193
Oprah Winfrey Show, 186
Orange County (FL), 190
Orlando, 93, 98, 188
Orlando Sentinel, 30, 42, 103, 114, 131, 194
Oswald, Lee Harvey, 82–84, 87, 154
Oswald, Marguerite, 84

Padgett, Sharla, 139
Pahokee (FL), 36
Palestinian Liberation Organization, 155
Palm Beach County (FL), 39, 122
Palm Beach Post, 183
Palmdale (FL), 22
Panama City News, 67
Parathion, 43, 45; accidental deaths caused by, 35–36, 38; poisoning of Richardson children and, 6, 37–39, 43–45, 47–48, 61, 64–65, 79–80, 90, 155, 174, 202; uses in citrus industry and, 35
Parham, Harry, 171–72
Parker Brothers Ranch, 26
Parker, Cpt. John, 25
Parker, John, 36
Parker, Zeb, 196
Pasco County (FL), 204
Patton, Melody, 142–43, 149, 181
Peace and Freedom Party, 84
Peace River, 12–13, 23, 97; accidental dumping of parathion in, 35–37; discovery of phosphate in, 13; pollution in, 37, 42
Peeples, Vernon, 181
Pennsylvania, 106
People, 122
People's Temple Agricultural Project, 152
Petrow, Steven, 2, 143
Philadelphia Daily News, 149
Phosphate industry, 12–13, 17
Pinsdorf, Marion, 88
Pitney, Gene, 2
Pittman, Craig, 12
Playboy, 87, 93, 184
Plessy v. Ferguson, 20
Polk County (FL), 11, 15, 17, 33, 98, 168
Polk County Sheriff's Office, 167
Pope John Paul II, 147
Port-au-Prince (Haiti), 113
Port Charlotte (FL), 49, 62, 103, 144; building of, 25; 97, 197. *See also* Charlotte County
Port Manatee (FL), 127
Port St. Lucie (FL), 117
Powell, Clifford, 63
Price, Amber, 193
Puerto Rico, 72
Pulitzer Prize, 162, 204
Punta Gorda (FL), 9, 21, 100, 158, 194–95; growth of, 97; Tamiami Trail and, 23. *See also* Charlotte County
Punta Gorda Isles, Inc., 100–101
Punta Rassa (FL), 16

Purvis, Gerald, 6–7, 49, 73, 78, 89, 158, 177; attempts to sell Richardson a policy and, 44–45, 54–57; coroner's inquest and, 64–65; description of, 54; later interviews of, 170; polygraph and, 63; "receipt" and, 80

Quarters, The, 2, 6, 8, 38, 47, 95, 152, 206; establishment of citizens' patrol in, 40; lack of school bussing to, 96; policing in, 33, 211n40; poverty in, 60–61, 96–97; Richardson visit to, 178, 200, 202–4. *See also* Arcadia
Queens (NY), 120
Quiñones, John, 133–35

Rapaport, Emmanuel M., 108
Raphael, Sally Jessy, 183
Ray, Andy, 146–48, 189
Ray, Candy, 110, 125–26, 137
Ray, Clifford, 1, 3, 105, 110, 124–25, 130, 134, 137, 143, 146–47, 180; *Donahue* and, 150; media attention and, 183, 186; Ricky's death and, 188; Robert's death and, 191; school board settlement and, 184
Ray, James Earl, 101
Ray, Louise, 1, 110, 124–25, 130, 134, 137, 143, 146–48, 180, 184–188; media savviness of, 183; *Nightline* and, 150; on leaving Arcadia behind and, 190; political campaign of, 190; work in support of hemophilia sufferers, 190–91
Ray, Randy, 1, 105, 110, 134, 184; death of 205
Ray, Ricky, 1, 105, 110–11, 125, 134, 184, 189, 191; declining health of, 179, 187–88; girlfriend Wenonah Lindberg and, 186–88; Sarasota experiences of, 186
Ray, Robert, 1, 105, 110, 134, 184–85; declining health of, 179, 191; 187
Ray family, 1, 9, 11, 131–32, 192, 198, 203, 205–6; ABC's *World News Tonight* and, 2, 132–33; attempt to sell video tape and, 187; celebrity status of, 183–88; Central Missionary Baptist Church and, 124–125; death threats and, 3, 143, 186–87; description of, 127; Dr. Barbosa and, 109–10, 123, 126, 128, 131–132, 137, 188; emotional struggles of, 184–85; establishment of relief fund for, 148; failed movie deal and, 184; federal rulings and, 1, 135–139; fire at home of, 3–4, 8, 146–50; 189–90; hiring of attorney by, 128; Kovachevich hearing and, 136–39; move to Alabama and, 126; move to Orlando and, 188; move to Sarasota and, 147–48, 150–51, 179, 183–85; opposition to school board and, 125–26; residents' opinion of, 2–4, 125–26, 142–43; settlement with DeSoto County School Board and, 151–52, 184; settlement with pharmaceutical companies, 182–84; test for HIV and, 109–10; testimony before US Senate and, 148
Rayford, Robert Lee, 113
Reagan, Nancy, 133
Reagan, Ronald, 132–33
Reclaiming History, 82
Reedy Creek Improvement District, 101
Reef & Beef, 26, 146
Reese, Betsy, 6, 8, 38, 44, 55–56, 63–64, 72, 79, 86, 202; background of, 45–46; finds bag of parathion and, 47; interview with Barnard and, 91; interview with Lane and, 89–90; Lane accusations of, 166–67; relationship to Richardsons and, 46; nursing home statements of, 8, 151–2, 155–56; rumors related to, 45–47, 166–68
Reese, Eddie, 64
Rehabilitation Act of 1973, 128–29
Rembert, Johnny, 27–28
Remington, Frederic, 13–14, 16
Reno, Janet, 9; 176–78; appointment to Richardson case and, 175
Research, Testing, and Development Corporation, 136
Reynolds, Burt, 184

Reynolds, Gary, 169
Richardson, Alice, 37–38, 178
Richardson, Annie Laura, 65
Richardson, Annie Mae, 6, 38, 44, 55–56, 63, 66, 70, 76–77, 86, 167; children's funeral and, 58–59; defense of James at trial and, 79–80; hearing of 1989 and, 177; marriage to James and, 46, 201
Richardson, Betty Jean, 38, 73, 174, 178, 231n3
Richardson, Diane, 38, 46, 178
Richardson, Doreen, 38, 178
Richardson, James, 6, 11, 38, 76, 84, 87–89, 163, 192, 198; alleged beating by John Boom and, 70; attempts to compensate, 202–5; bail set for, 71; chooses Robinson as attorney, 68; conditions at Raiford and, 85, 102; Congressional Black Caucus and, 174; coroner's inquest and, 63–65; death of, 205; first meeting with Lane and, 86; Florida Supreme Court upholds conviction of, 101; Free James Richardson committee and, 157, 167, 173; hearing of April 1989 and, 176–178; *Inside Edition* and, 8, 167, 173–74; Janet Reno and, 9; 175–78; Lane's description of, 86; lawsuit against Schaub and, 201; life in Wichita and, 201; marriage to Annie Mae and, 46, 201; meeting with Remus Griffin and, 177; movie deal and, 167, 201; polygraph test of, 63; post-release visits to Arcadia and, 178, 200, 202–4; questions of insurance and, 43–45, 54–57, 72–73; reaction to death of children and, 39; release from prison of, 9, 176–78; selection of jury at trial of, 75–76; trial of, 77–80; Weaver perjury and, 167–68
Richardson, James, Jr., 38, 46, 59, 178
Richardson, Sampson Jehovah, 65
Richardson, Susie, 38, 59, 79, 178
Richardson, Teresa, 201
Richardson, Vanesa, 38, 46, 178
Richmond Times-Dispatch, 107

Ricky Ray Hemophilia Fund Act, 191
Riley, John, 149
Ringling Brothers and Barnum & Bailey Circus, 25
Rivera, Craig, 173
Rivera, Geraldo, 3. 273
Robert F. Kennedy Award for Excellence in Journalism, 204
Roberts, Burl, 34
Robertson, A.D.J., 136–37
Robertson, Pat, 190
Robinson, John Spencer, 67, 71, 73, 93, 155, 162, 202; agrees to defend Richardson, 68; background of, 67–68; closing arguments at Richardson trial of, 80; Bobby Woods and, 90; defense of Richardson at trial and, 77–80; filing of habeas corpus petition by, 68, 71; first meeting with Lane and, 85–86; Lane's opinion of, 164; motion for retrial and, 87; post-conviction work for Richardson and, 152; stolen Richardson files and, 159, 161–64
Rockefeller, Nelson, 82
Røed, Arne, 112–13
Romeo, Belinda, 152, 155–56
Roosevelt, Eleanor, 81
Roseburg (OR), 4
Ross, Jack, 168
Rozsa, Lori, 192
Rubin, Ellis, 8, 167–68, 177, 201–2; background of, 164–65; Schaub lawsuit against, 172–173
Rush to Judgment, 88
Russ, James, 53
Russia, 153
Russiaville (IN), 4, 120, 122, 148
Russiaville Home Study School, 122
Rutgers University, 118
Ryan, Leo, 153–54
Ryan White Story, The, 188

Sachs, Jeffrey, 112
Sacramento (CA), 84

Safety Hill, 74
San Juan (PR), 72
San Francisco (CA), 113, 153
Sanders, Bernie, 81
Sanders, Robert, 139
Sanibel, 190
Sarasota (FL), 2–3, 12, 44, 71, 98, 127, 160, 205–6; growth of, 97; Rays flee to, 147–48, 150–51, 183–85; Tamiami Trail and, 23
Sarasota County (FL), 97, 102; agricultural industry in, 197
Sarasota County Health Department, 179–80
Sarasota County School Board, 179, 181
Sarasota County Sheriff's Department, 187
Sarasota Herald-Tribune, 8, 93, 172, 186, 200, 204
Sarasota Marine Corps League, 53
Sarasota Sertoma Club, 53
Sass, Janet, 196
Schaub, Frank, 6, 8, 56–57, 69, 89, 127, 167, 202; background of, 49; career as judge and, 171–72; conviction rate of, 53–54; Coppolino trial and, 50–53; defeat of F. Lee Bailey by, 54; description of, 51; Gerald Purvis and, 170; indictment of Richardson and, 72–73; Lane accusations regarding, 166–67; lawsuit against Lane and, 172–73; Nowitzke trial and, 172; opening statement at Richardson trial of, 77; Richardson hearing of 1989 and, 177; resistance to charging Richardson and, 63; Richardson lawsuit against, 201; strategy at Richardson trial and, 77–80; withholding of exculpatory evidence by, 6–7, 72–73, 158, 166, 173
Schlossberg, Nat, 93–94
Schmierer, Elmer, 77
Scott, John, 173
Scott, Rick, 204
Seaboard Coast Line, 101
Sebring, 176
Seminole County (FL), 190

Seminole Tribe of Florida, 160, 162
Seminole Tribune, 8, 162
Shalimar (FL), 204
Shanbrom, Edward, 108–9
Shaw, Clay, 87
Shaw, Donna, 114
Sheppard, Sam, 50
Shields, Brooke, 121
Shoemaker, Veronica, 74
Silvertooth, Lynn, 52
Sisco, Peggy, 141
Skid Row, 107–8
Sloan, Frank, 42–43
Sloan-Kettering Institute for Cancer Research, 136
Smith, Charlie, 47–48, 63, 79, 89, 155
Smith, George, 142, 150
Smith, James O., 120
Smith, Nathan, 115
Smith, Sue-Ellen, 142
Smith-Brown School, 31, 37–38, 77, 94; arson of, 40–42; closing of, 94; "end-the-silence" meeting and, 8, 155–57; funeral of Richardson children and, 58–59; opening of, 20. *See also* DeSoto County School Board
Smithers, Jimmy, 146–48
Sonrise Christian Academy, 144
South Bay (FL), 39
South Daytona Beach (FL), 159
Southern Baptist Convention, 124
Southwest Florida, 1, 8, 11–12; development of, 23, 97, 99, 197–98; first African-American elected to office in, 31; subprime mortgage crisis and, 200
Soviet Union, 154
Speer, Paul P., 23, 25, 31–32, 37
Stancel, Robert, 90
Stanford University, 108
Star-Telegram (Fort Worth), 93
State Road 70 (FL), 97
State Road 72 (FL), 97
Staton, Beth, 141
Stepford Wives, 96

Stetson Law School, 49, 64
St. John's Missionary Baptist Church, 32, 178
St. Johns River, 12
St. Louis (MO), 113
Stone, Chuck 149
Stone, Oliver, 87
St. Paul's Catholic Church, 148
St. Petersburg, 94, 126; All Children's Hospital in, 109, 131, 179, 187–88, 191
St. Petersburg Times, 27, 42, 60–61, 161–62, 180, 204
Streisand, Barbra, 167
Sullivan, Paul, 195–96
Sun-Herald (Charlotte County, FL), 196
Sun Herald (Winter Park, FL), 92
Sunland Center, 30
Sunshine, 162
Sunshine Skyway Bridge, 98, 109
Sunshine Spiritual Church, 79
Sutton, Percy, 82

Tallahassee (FL), 36, 166–67, 181, 202, 204
Tamiami Trail, 23, 53, 98–99
Tampa (FL), 16–17, 35, 54, 85, 160, 170, 183, 201; I-75 and, 98; Kovachevich hearing in, 135–38; Richardson grand jury in, 73; Tamiami Trail and, 23
Tampa Bay, 109
Tampa Bay Buccaneers, 184
Tampa Magazine, 13
Tampa Times, 97
Tampa Tribune, 9, 22, 39, 62, 65, 98, 102, 128, 161, 186–87; breaking of Ray story and, 126–27; Ray editorials and, 138–39, 189; review of *Arcadia* in, 88
Tanay, Emmanuel, 172
Taylor, Elizabeth, 121
Tew, Danny, 139–40, 180–81, 198
Texas, 116, 127
There's Nothing to Be Afraid Of, 190
Thomas, Danny, 51
Thomas, Robert, 139, 160
Thompson, Flanders, 74–75

Thompson, Geraldine, 202–3
Tijuana, Mexico, 38
Time, 53, 136
Tinsley's IGA, 156
Today (show), 148
Tokyo (Japan), 190
Tomoka Correctional Institution, 162, 166, 173
Tonight Show Starring Johnny Carson, The, 84
Toothman, Mary, 187, 189
Toronto (Canada), 106
Town without Pity (film), 2
Trafficante, Henry, 90
Trafficante, Santo, Jr., 90
Treadwell, John H., III, 47–48, 56–57, 65, 72, 170; Lane accusations and, 166–67; resistance to charging Richardson and, 63; stolen Richardson files and, 158–60, 172
Tropic (magazine), 161–62, 173
Tropicana, 127
Trump, Donald, 132
Tucson (AZ), 60
Turner, Eugene, Jr., 26
Turpentine industry, 21. *See also* Gulf Naval Stores
Tuskegee Airmen, 149

Union County (FL), 85
Union Life Insurance Company, 44, 54
Universal Studios, 183
University of Alabama, 62
University of California at Irvine, 136
University of Florida, 131, 136
University of Madrid, 131
University of Miami, 142, 164
University of North Carolina, 92
University of South Florida, 85, 136
US Army Air Corps, 29
US Army Corps of Engineers, 12
US Department of Agriculture, 197
US Department of Health and Human Services, 116

US Department of Justice, 116
US Food and Drug Administration, 114–15
US Indoor Diving Championships, 121
US Justice Department, 75
US Public Health Service, 130
US Route 17, 97–98, 198
US State Department, 153–54
US Supreme Court, 75, 102, 128, 130, 193

Varnadore, Joe, 147, 155–56, 177
Victims of Wrongful Incarceration Compensation Act, 202
Vietnam War, 84, 101, 162
Villages of DeSoto, 103
Virginia, 107
Volusia County (FL), 190
Volusia County Big Brothers Association, 68
Voting Rights Act of 1965, 176

Wade, Henry, 82
Wallace, George, 62
Wallis, Marcille, 95
Walmart, 193
Walt Disney Company, 101
Warren County (NJ), 120
WAPG, 124
Washington (NC), 92, 118
Washington (State), 116
Washington, D.C., 133, 155, 183
Washington, Earnell, 73, 76, 90, 166, 173
Washington, Helen, 8, 176, 178, 198
Washington Post, 4, 53
Wassaic Hospital, 81
Watergate, 173
Wauchula (FL), 151, 155
Weatherford, Will, 204
Weaver, Charles, 95

Weaver, James, 73, 80, 90, 173; admissions of perjury and, 167–68
Weinberg, Eric, 114
Weissmuller, Johnny, 197
Welles, Orson, 66
Werner, Bob, 139, 149, 181
West Palm Beach (FL), 181, 193
Westberry, James, 130
Western Middle School, 120
Weston (FL), 9
Wheeler's Restaurant, 143
White, Jeanne, 120–21, 148
White, Ryan, 4, 133; celebrity status of, 121–22; high school in Arcadia (IN) and, 148; mistreatment of, 120–22; movie about, 188
Whitson, Richard, 77
Wichita (KS), 201, 205
Wildmon, Donald, 93
Williams, Alan, 204
Williams, Lindsey, 196
Williamson (WV), 117
Wills, Gary, 84
Winfrey, Oprah, 183–84
Winter Haven (FL), 66
Winter Park (FL), 92
Wisconsin, 99, 137–38
Women's World, 183
Woods, Bobby, 90–91
Woodward, Bob, 204
World News Tonight (ABC), 2, 133–35
World War II, 108
WTSP, 187

Yates, Don, 140
Yothers, Tina, 183
Young, Bruce Allen, 194

Zamora, Ronnie, 164–65
Zion Hill Baptist Church, 66

Originally from Punta Gorda, Florida, JASON VUIC is an award-winning author and historian whose books include *The Swamp Peddlers: How Lot Sellers, Land Scammers, and Retirees Built Modern Florida and Transformed the American Dream* and *The Yucks: Two Years in Tampa with the Losingest Team in NFL History.*